KANT'S THEORY OF A PRIORI KNOWLEDGE

KANT'S THEORY OF A PRIORI KNOWLEDGE

ROBERT GREENBERG

THE PENNSYLVANIA STATE UNIVERSITY PRESS
UNIVERSITY PARK, PENNSYLVANIA

Library of Congress Cataloging-in-Publication Data

Greenberg, Robert, 1934–

   Kant's theory of a priori knowledge / Robert Greenberg.
      p.   cm.
   Includes bibliographical references and index.
   ISBN 0-271-02083-0 (alk. paper)
   1. Kant, Immanuel, 1724–1804. Kritik der reinen Vernunft.
2. A priori—History—18th century. I. Title.

B2779.G74   2001
121—dc21   00–037453

It is the policy of The Pennsylvania State University Press to use acid-free paper for
the first printing of all clothbound books. Publications on uncoated stock satisfy
the minimum requirements of American National Standard for Information
Sciences—Permanence of Paper for Printed Library Materials, ANSI Z39.48–1992.

CONTENTS

To my wife, Maida,
And my children, Judith, David, and Jonathan,
Who have brought me love and friendship

PREFACE

The interpretation of Kant's *Critique of Pure Reason* that is presented in this book originally had a somewhat different form. It was first presented as an ordered series of closely interrelated yet self-contained papers on several important topics in Kant's theory of the possibility of a priori knowledge. As the chapters progressed, and with the help of transitional passages, they gradually built up a unified interpretation of that theory.

The content of the present offering does not differ from the content of the original in any fundamental way. But its form is now that of a regular book: its chapters are not self-contained; rather, later chapters depend on earlier ones for their comprehension.

The finished product is the result of many years of thought about the *Critique*. During this time I have given an ever changing course on the same material to my students and have also given papers on these topics at various conferences, here in the United States, in the United Kingdom, and in Germany. In addition, some of the material in the book has already appeared in proceedings of these conferences and in journals. Finally, the intended audience for the book comprises advanced undergraduates and graduate students in philosophy, philosophers generally, and, of course, Kant scholars.

The image that most often comes to mind when I think of my work is that of a mosaic, which seems apt, considering the etymology of the term. I consider four of its interlocking pieces, literally *theses,* as central to the total picture I am trying to convey. As each piece grew in significance, especially as it became intertwined with the other three, still other pieces fell into place, and the mosaic got filled out in greater and greater detail, until, at the end, the finished product appeared as a comprehensive unity. I then felt that I had put in their proper places most of the pieces that I had wanted to include.

The most important thesis consists in my view that the *Critique* is primarily concerned with the possibility, or relation to objects, of *a priori,* not empirical, knowledge, and that Kant's theory of that possibility is quite defensible. It can safely be said, I believe, that the prevalent Anglophone inter-pretations of the *Critique* definitely do not accept both aspects of this view of mine. This first major thesis is intertwined with the second. It is only a theory of the possibility of a priori knowledge, not a theory of the possibility of empirical knowledge, that is committed to an ontology of objects that is distinct from the conditions of the possibility of the knowledge in question, that is, the knowledge whose possibility the theory is supposed to explain. Accordingly, the second major thesis of the book consists in my view that Kant's transcendental ontology—the ontology of his theory of the possibil-ity of specifically a priori knowledge—must be distinct from the conditions of that possibility, a thesis undergirded by my interpretation of that ontol-ogy. This thesis in particular has important consequences for a new interpre-tation of Kant's transcendental idealism as well. Like the first, this thesis, too, is at odds with standard Anglophone commentary on the *Critique*.

Of perhaps lesser significance, the third main thesis is my view that the logic Kant calls *transcendental* includes his discussion surrounding the Table of Judgments and that, accordingly, his logical functions of judgment have *content;* that is, they make a contribution to the possibility of a priori knowledge, or its (a priori knowledge's) relation to objects. Again, one of my central theses is to be contrasted with a view that today is standard among Anglophone commentators on the *Critique*. Without exception, all such commentators hold that the discussion in question belongs to formal, or what Kant calls *general,* logic, and, accordingly, that the logical *functions* of judgment are none other than the logical *forms* of judgment, which be-long to formal logic and thus have no content whatsoever.

The fourth fundamental thesis, one that weaves in and out of the other three, is a methodological and terminological thesis. It is that Kant's distinc-tion *and* interrelation between two types of relation—certain *ordering* rela-tions (*Verhältnisse*) and certain *reference* relations (*Beziehungen*)—must be kept uppermost in mind at key junctures in our attempt to understand the *Critique*. The relative neglect of both the distinction and the interrelation between the relations in the Anglophone tradition of interpretation has, in my opinion, contributed to many shortcomings in our understanding of the *Critique*. So, once again, I am offering a view of the *Critique* that many in our tradition will find to be at odds with their own view. Together, these four theses, and the attendant propositions that are introduced in accor-dance with them, present a new way of looking at the *Critique* that may prove to be not only a challenge to the presently accepted approaches to the work but a way of making sense or harmony out of what have so far been considered its discordant themes.

*   *   *

A work whose composition has taken such a long time to bring to completion generally has been the recipient of a certain amount of customary beneficence. But I would like to take this opportunity to express my special gratitude to a Kant scholar who early in my attempt to get my work on Kant published expressed confidence in its eventual publication and serious reception among Kant scholars. He is Richard E. Aquila. His encouragement is especially noteworthy, given the many divergences between our respective points of view on the *Critique*. He is blessed with an intellectual tolerance that sometimes strikes me as being in rather short supply in our field of study. Other Kant scholars whom I would like to thank for their review of my writing and for their expressions of esteem for or agreement with at least certain aspects of my work include Robert Hanna, Eric Watkins, and Kenneth Westphal. I am also indebted to two of my professors, the late Manley Thompson and Sir Peter Strawson, for their instruction, both in person and through writing, not only in Kant's theory of knowledge but in logical theory as well. I would also like to express my gratitude to Sanford Thatcher, Director of Penn State Press, who, at the very start of my dealings with the Press and on the basis of his own reading of my manuscript, saw a place for my work on his list at the Press. In this connection, I would also like to thank the two external readers for the Press who gave me many very valuable suggestions for improvement of my manuscript and even saved me from some blunders. Of course, the proverbial author's acceptance of responsibility for any errors that remain is very much in order as well. In addition, I would like to acknowledge the Mazer Fund of Brandeis University for help in defraying expenses incurred in the preparation of the manuscript. Moreover, it should be noted that Chapter 1 contains material that has appeared in my article in the *Proceedings of the Twentieth World Congress of Philosophy: Metaphysics;* and Chapters 9 and 13 are revisions of two of my articles in the *History of Philosophy Quarterly.* I would like to thank the respective editors of these publications for their kind permission to include the material here. And finally, I would like to express a word of thanks to all those who have served as conscientious and fair-minded referees on papers that I have submitted either for publication or for delivery at conferences.

Newton, Massachusetts
September 2000
R.G.

PART 1

INTRODUCTION

THE PROBLEM

The Possibility of A Priori Knowledge

I

Among those who view Kant's *Critique of Pure Reason* as a theory of the possibility of knowledge, none in the recent English-speaking tradition has yet produced a book devoted primarily to his theory of the possibility of a priori knowledge, where "a priori" means "independent of all experience." On the contrary, following P. F. Strawson and Jonathan Bennett,[1] commentators in this tradition, almost without exception, have considered all the defensible features of the *Critique* to belong to Kant's theory of the possibility of empirical knowledge, or his theory of possible experience.[2] Accordingly, they have devoted the bulk of their analysis to that aspect of the work. When they see the *Critique* in a favorable light, it is concerned with showing how empirical knowledge, or experience, is related to objects of experience

1. P. F. Strawson, *The Bounds of Sense: An Essay on Kant's "Critique of Pure Reason"* (London: Methuen, 1966). Jonathan Bennett, *Kant's Analytic* (Cambridge: Cambridge University Press, 1966).
2. One such commentator is actually quite explicit about his belief in the ease of a transition from a theory of empirical knowledge of objects to a theory of a priori knowledge of objects. He thinks the considerations he brings to bear on the former can be extended to the latter without difficulty. See Robert Hanna, "The Trouble with Truth in Kant's Theory of Meaning," *History of Philosophy Quarterly* 10 (1993): 18 n. 3.

through certain general—and, for some, even a priori—representations or conditions.

In the first instance these representations or conditions are space, time, and our supposedly fundamental concepts of objects in general—Kant's categories. From these primary representations or conditions of possible experience and its objects there is supposed to "flow" (B 40) certain a priori knowledge, including (1) mathematics, comprising arithmetic (e.g., B 14ff.) and Euclidean geometry (e.g., B 16ff. and B 40); (2) the principles of the relations of time, and therewith (a) the possibility of experiences and of our "instruction" with respect to them (A 31/B 47) and (b) the possible comprehension of the "possibility of an alteration" and thus the possibility of "the general doctrine of motion" (B 49); and (3) the laws of nature in general (B 165).[3] It is all these supposedly a priori representations and cognitions that are said to be related to objects only insofar as they are conditions of the relation of *empirical* knowledge to objects. At least this is the view of those features of the *Critique* that current Anglophone commentary considers defensible.

The major contention of this book, however, is that this view of the *Critique* reflects a fundamental misunderstanding of the work. According to the view to be presented here—and this can be taken to be my interpretation of how Kant himself understood the problem of a priori knowledge—the work is instead concerned with showing how these same representations (space, time, and the categories), and consequently the a priori knowledge Kant claims they make possible, are themselves related to objects. Consequently, the interest that is of the first importance for Kant and that can also be given a sympathetic defense on his behalf is the possibility of *a priori* knowledge, as distinct from the possibility of *empirical* knowledge, or experience. And this remains the case even though the explanation of the former possibility, and hence the justification of our claims of a priori knowledge, actually depend on the latter possibility.

II

The now classic statement of the opposition between these two views of the *Critique* and of the rejection of Kant's theory of a priori knowledge in favor

3. All references to Kant's *Critique of Pure Reason* are to the standard first- and second-edition pagination, and all translations thereof are taken from the Norman Kemp Smith trans-

of his theory of experience belongs to Strawson. He was quite aware that Kant wanted to explain how space, time, and the categories, and the knowledge that can come from them, are themselves possible. But he found Kant's endeavors in this regard so misguided that he advised that we separate this regrettable aspect of the *Critique* from the other one, which is quite independent of it, namely, that which is concerned with the possibility of experience. We should then, Strawson advises, discard Kant's theory of the former and instead put our efforts into understanding and even defending at least parts of his theory of the latter.

Strawson's success in adopting this line on the *Critique* was at the time so complete among English-speaking philosophers quite generally, and not just among Kant scholars, that he clearly became the pivotal figure in the surge of interest in Kant's theory of knowledge. After I comment on Strawson's influence on us in this regard, I shall go on to discuss one of the major contentions of his work, namely, that Kant's only defensible contribution to epistemology in the *Critique* consists in his alleged theory that space, time, and the categories are related to objects only insofar as they are necessary conditions for experience to be related to objects. Again, this theory is to be distinguished from the other one Kant also wanted to put forward, a theory of how space, time, and the categories, and the a priori knowledge that comes from them, are themselves to be related to objects. And yet again, my contention is that the possibility of experience is not itself at issue for Kant; it only comes into play in his explanation of the possibility of a priori knowledge, and hence in the justification of the claims of a priori knowledge. But before I begin my exposition and defense of my contention, I shall, in order to place my discussion of the issues within the Anglophone tradition that has followed Strawson in this regard, first deal with Strawson himself.

Well before the publication of his essay on the *Critique,* Strawson had, of course, already taken positions on many philosophical issues. In the postpositivistic spirit of J. L. Austin and Ludwig Wittgenstein, he famously challenged the authority of Russell's Theory of Descriptions.[4] Logical theory, he

---

lation (London: Macmillan, 1929), except where otherwise noted. For the most detailed recent work on the knowledge in the exact sciences Kant took to be a priori, see Michael Friedman, *Kant and the Exact Sciences* (Cambridge, Mass.: Harvard University Press, 1992), esp. 34–37, 44ff., 167ff., 171, 174, and 203ff.

4. J. L. Austin, *Collected Papers,* ed. J. O. Urmson and G. J. Warnock (Oxford: Oxford University Press, 1961). Ludwig Wittgenstein, *Philosophical Investigations* (New York: Macmillan, 1953). P. F. Strawson, "On Referring," *Mind 59* (1950), reprinted in *Essays in Conceptual Analysis,* ed. A. G. N. Flew (London: Macmillan, 1956).

argued, should instruct us regarding the logic actually employed in everyday (ordinary) language, not that designed as an ideal for mathematics and science.[5]

Fidelity to ordinary language within a systematic approach to logic led Strawson to consider what he might find if he took a similar approach to metaphysics. This distinguished his investigation from earlier work that also hewed to ordinary language. This work had proceeded piecemeal, on the conviction that particular problems solved on the basis of material provided by ordinary language had to follow a method that is itself particularistic. Strawson's new approach to metaphysics, combining the descriptive features of ordinary-language philosophy with the systematic properties of logic, took the form of a systematic description of how we actually think of the world we live in, that is, the one we can know through experience.[6] His widely recognized success in this endeavor constituted an invitation to analytic philosophers to try their own hand at solving traditional problems in metaphysics in a systematic way, without worrying unduly about being labeled "obscurantists."

Strawson was walking a fine line. The thrust toward system ran the risk of elevating merely empirical propositions into a priori ones, because of their central, indeed apparently inescapable, role in our thought about the world. This was a danger Quine had clearly warned against.[7] Strawson's method had to be exercised with great caution. We might actually find ourselves practicing the sort of philosophy positivism was designed to eliminate, root and branch: mouthing the meaningless claims of metaphysics. Foremost among these were those Kant considered to be "synthetic a priori." For positivism, aside from formal logic and the analytic rules of language, if knowledge has foundations, they consist of empirical propositions alone. The principle of meaning governing significant discourse demands no less.

And postpositivism stayed true to this blanket rejection of nonanalytic a priori judgments.[8] So Strawson walked us to the edge of experience but, like Kant himself, warned us of the dangers of going over it. The central

5. P. F. Strawson, *Introduction to Logical Theory* (London: Methuen, 1952).

6. P. F. Strawson, *Individuals: An Essay in Descriptive Metaphysics* (London: Methuen, 1959).

7. W. V. O. Quine, "Two Dogmas of Empiricism," *Philosophical Review* (1951), reprinted in *From a Logical Point of View* (Cambridge, Mass.: Harvard University Press, 1953).

8. Quine, it should be mentioned, recommended dispensing with the analytic-synthetic distinction altogether (ibid.).

propositions of our thought of the world are inescapable, all right, but not quite a priori.[9]

Could Strawson see Kant himself in this light? Could he read the *Critique* as a precursor of his own work, only bedeviled by the insupportable belief that metaphysics has to be a priori? This takes us to the more specific question concerning Strawson's influence on Anglophone commentary on the *Critique,* namely, his role in shaping the current view that for Kant the relation of space, time, and the categories to objects consists only in their being necessary conditions for experience to be related to objects.

With the audacity befitting a commentator accomplished as a philosopher in his own right, Strawson set out this view of what he took to be the defensible arguments of Kant's work without so much as a single reference to previous commentary on the subject.[10] He divided the work into the strands that are acceptable to an analytic empiricist philosopher such as himself and those that go beyond the "bounds of sense," a priori metaphysical claims that have no possible application in experience. Just as Kant admonished his predecessors for failing to tie down their metaphysical speculations to possible experience, so Strawson takes Kant to task for doing the very same thing himself as he attempted to secure metaphysical foundations of our a priori knowledge of objects.[11] How was it that Kant was led into this misguided foray into nonsensical metaphysics?

First, says Strawson, Kant's original interest is to be heartily commended: laying out "the general structure of ideas and principles which is presupposed in all our empirical knowledge."[12] But instead of resting content with this wholly conceptual investigation, which stands in no need of any metaphysical underpinnings whatsoever, Kant inquired after the possibility of the investigation itself;[13] he wanted an explanation of our knowledge of the necessities that emerge from it, as though conceptual analysis could not, in terms of the methods that stand on their own in analytic philosophy and without any dependence on metaphysics, account for the necessary truths that emerge from it.[14] Not only is this very endeavor of Kant's completely misguided, but he compounded his troubles by adopting as a model for

---

9. Here, too, Quine demurred to Strawson, staying within the Peircean American pragmatic tradition of fallibilism and provisionalism.
10. Strawson, *The Bounds of Sense.*
11. Ibid., 15–16.
12. Ibid., 19.
13. Ibid.
14. Ibid., 43.

this unnecessary study the scientist's investigation of nature. As the scientist searches for the hidden powers and properties of things in the world of nature, so Kant went on to employ the "psychological idiom" belonging to an investigation of "the structure and workings of the cognitive capacities of beings such as ourselves."[15]

The scientific model of Kant's investigation into our cognitive capacities led him to an analogous view of the objects with which we are causally involved in our cognition. The model takes the objects that affect us through our senses as producing the appearances we have of them because of the combination of the constitution of our senses and the properties of the objects as they exist apart from us—as they are "in themselves"; so Kant looks to things as objects that affect us in the same way, that is, as things in themselves. But where the model can fall back on space and time to describe the affecting objects that are, along with our neurosensory makeup, responsible for their appearances in our experience of them, Kant cannot avail himself of these fundamental dimensions of things in order to describe the objects (the Kantian things in themselves), since space and time have already been co-opted by his descriptions of our cognitive capacities. As such, they are also essential and exclusive to his description of the appearances themselves, which, according to the model he has adopted, have to be distinguished from the affecting objects (the things in themselves) that produce the appearances. For the necessary truths our knowledge of which Kant's model is supposed to explain pertain, at least in part, to space and time themselves. He is therefore left with a conception of the affecting objects as nonspatial and nontemporal. And the same lack of recourse to space and time holds for his description of ourselves as beings that can have such knowledge, and therefore also for the affecting relation between ourselves and the objects. However, since Kant himself adopts the principle that the significance of all of our descriptive concepts depends on their applicability to possible experience and its objects, the exclusion of space and time from these Kantian conceptions of ourselves as cognitive subjects, of the objects that affect us in our cognitive involvement with them, and of the affecting relation between us and them, renders these conceptions illegitimate and the items that purportedly exemplify them—ourselves, the objects, and the relation between us and them—unintelligible. Consequently, Kant's model of how the mind can have a priori knowledge of objects must itself be pronounced not only unintelligible but incoherent as well.

15. Ibid., 19.

No doubt Strawson is correct in his observation that Kant tried to explain, in terms of our mental capacities, our knowledge of the necessities that govern possible experience. And he is also correct that that is what Kant's "Copernican Revolution" in philosophy amounts to (B xvi–xvii). The question then becomes whether Kant can be defended against the unwelcome consequences that arise from Strawson's interpretation of Kant's explanation of our knowledge of these necessities. Does Kant's talk about our mental capacities in this regard deserve all the opprobrium Strawson casts upon it? In section v below and in section iv of the next chapter, I contend that it does not.

Nevertheless, I can now sum up my discussion of Strawson so far with the observation that it was he who helped introduce many of us in the English-speaking tradition of commentary on the *Critique* to the need that Kant thought he perceived for an ontology that is distinctive to his epistemology. Though I do not agree with Strawson that the ontology is to be divided into two sets of objects—appearances and things in themselves—to the *exclusion* of a single set of objects, namely, *things simpliciter,* which only then are to be divided, somewhat as Strawson proposes, I, along with an entire generation of Kant commentators in this tradition, am indebted to him for having helped make us aware not only that Kant believed his epistemology must have an ontology of its own, but that special attention must be paid to the question of its intelligibility.

Besides his criticism of the ontology he attributed to Kant on the basis of Kant's allegedly mistaken belief that he had to explain the possibility of our knowledge of the necessary truths that delimit possible experience, Strawson also introduced into recent Anglophone commentary on Kant's theory of knowledge another, related concern. This is his concern about the precise status of the claims that make up Kant's arguments in his theory of knowledge. Though obviously officially a priori, are those claims themselves supposed by Kant to be related to objects of possible empirical intuition, perception, or experience as are the judgments the theory is supposed to explain or justify? If not, they are subject to the same criticism Strawson levels at the terms in which they are expressed, namely, terms for beings, such as ourselves, who are involved in the cognitions in question, the ontology of Kant's epistemology, and the affecting relation in which the latter acts on the former. This is the criticism that these terms, and now the claims in which the terms occur, plunge us into the unintelligibility that the principle of significance is supposed to guard against.

This is an issue that I address and by choice leave unresolved at the conclusion of the book, in Chapter 15, section v. For the present, however, I can at least remark that were Strawson's demand that the claims enjoy the same status as the judgments that Strawson can equably allow to satisfy the principle of significance and thereby earn a certain measure of legitimacy, then Kant's transcendental epistemology would rely on a *transcendental intuition* that would permit a *transcendental employment* of the transcendental concepts in question. Again, these are the concepts of cognitive beings such as ourselves, of the objects that affect us, and of the affecting relation in which the objects act on us. But such a transcendental employment of these concepts would violate Kant's principle of significance quite as much as Strawson contends the concepts themselves violate it. So the choice is between having a transcendental epistemology without such a transcendental employment of these concepts and having no transcendental epistemology at all.

In the concluding section of the book the question of such a choice is discussed a bit more fully. It is there reiterated that this is a choice—a choice of viewpoint—and no absolutely right or wrong answer is in the wings to support it, though this is not to suggest that the choice cannot be made on the basis of reasonable considerations. Philosophy seems replete with such choices.

III

The nearly unanimous view among Anglophone commentators that the defensible features of Kant's theory of knowledge belong to his theory of the possibility of experience cannot be due merely to the influence of Strawson. Nor can it be completely explained by simply adding that the commentators themselves begin their investigations into the *Critique* with an initial interest in the possibility of empirical knowledge (instead of a priori knowledge) that is part of their own philosophical predilections. And finally, a fully satisfying explanation of the near unanimity in question is not then provided with the further observation that the commentators' project in theory of empirical knowledge leads them to an ontological commitment to the objects of such knowledge—empirical objects. No, there has to be something in the fundamental propositions of the *Critique* itself that also lends credence to Strawson's views among such commentators and that prompts them to approach the *Critique* in the same terms they adopt in their investigations into epistemology in general. To find at least one factor that quite probably can explain a large part of this near unanimity of interpretation, we need look no further than the central principle of Kant's transcendental idealism, namely, that we can have a priori knowledge of objects only insofar as they are viewed as appearances, and not as things in themselves. Whether the a priori concept that specifically provides for our a priori knowledge of objects is the concept of space, time, or a category, the question of its necessary relation to an object is answered in the affirmative for Kant only if the object of the knowledge is empirical (A 93–94/B 125–27 *et passim*). It is particularly not surprising, therefore, that philosophers already ontologically committed to the empirical object through their own theory of the possibility of empirical knowledge and who are impressed with the success of Strawson's work will interpret this principle of Kant's as a precursor of their own commitment to the same object. In this manner, it is understandable how they might have come to propose an interpretation that is especially congenial to them as the correct way of understanding what they consider to be the particularly defensible features of Kant's theory of knowledge.

But, again, I claim that this has been an unfortunate development in recent Anglophone scholarship on the *Critique* and that this view of the work reflects a fundamental misunderstanding of it, despite all these factors that have thus far been given here in explanation of how this view has come to be so prevalent among us. To repeat, I view the work as concerned instead with showing how these same representations (space, time, and the categories), and consequently the a priori knowledge Kant claims they make possible, are themselves related to objects of experience. In support of my view I now begin by pointing out that Kant himself says the same thing about transcendental philosophy, and hence about the *Critique* itself, as I am saying:

> I entitle *transcendental* all knowledge which is occupied not so much with objects as with the mode of our knowledge [*Erkenntnisart*] of objects in so far as this mode of knowledge is to be possible *a priori*. (B 25)

> Not every kind of knowledge *a priori* should be called transcendental, but that only by which we know that—and how—certain representations (intuitions or concepts) can be employed or are possible purely *a priori*. The term 'transcendental', that is to say, signifies such knowledge as concerns the *a priori* possibility of knowledge, or its *a*

priori employment. Neither space nor any *a priori* geometrical determination of it is a transcendental representation; what can alone be entitled transcendental is the knowledge that these representations are not of empirical origin, and the possibility that they can yet relate [*beziehen könne*] a priori to objects of experience. (A 56/B 80–81)

If passages such as these are read according to the view being recommended in this book regarding Kant's own understanding of the problem of a priori knowledge, empirical knowledge only gives us the necessary objects (namely, appearances) to which these a priori representations and the a priori knowledge that arises from them must be related, if the representations and the knowledge are to be possible. Though empirical knowledge, or experience, and its possibility are necessary parts of the justification of the claims of a priori knowledge, its own justification, and hence a theory of its own possibility, are not themselves at issue. The *Critique* has no independent interest in it. I would therefore make the conjecture that any attempt to provide a unified, coherent interpretation of the *Critique* as a theory of the possibility of empirical knowledge, or experience, will inevitably end in distorting, if not actually discarding, much of what Kant considers to be essential to his work. That is why I am contending that we have not yet been presented with what is generally acknowledged to be a unified, coherent interpretation of Kant's theory of the possibility of knowledge.

These two passages from the *Critique,* and others like them, can add to our understanding of the nature of the opposition between the two views of the *Critique* that is central to this book. While it is agreed on all sides that for Kant the possibility of empirical knowledge does indeed partly consist in the representations of space, time, the categories, and the a priori knowledge that arises from them, it is, as I have said, the principal contention of this book that the problem with the bulk of present-day Anglophone accounts of Kant's theory of knowledge is that their defense of it does not extend beyond his theory of the possibility of empirical knowledge to reach his theory of the possibility of a priori knowledge. These Anglophone accounts thus read the passages quoted above, and others like them, along Strawsonian lines: merely as invitations by Kant to search for space, time, and the categories, as well as the a priori knowledge arising from them, in the "general structure" of experience—as immanent conditions of possible experience—as though it were enough for Kant to conclude that experience would be impossible were its objects not to be represented through these representations and knowledge. Though the passages surely commit Kant to the view that the representations and knowledge have to be a priori, these accounts continue, by themselves they do not also commit him to the view that the knowledge in question must be a priori. Empirical knowledge, or experience, can very well be substituted for knowledge *simpliciter* in the passages, and a quite plausible reading, surely more plausible than, say, the one recommended in this book, can ensue.

Unfortunately, as I read them, the passages in question do not sustain this view of Kant's understanding of the problem of a priori knowledge. As conditions of our empirical knowledge, space, time, and the categories are not themselves thereby possible a priori, which is what the passages require; rather, they are necessary with respect to possible experience; that is, they are necessary with respect to what is possible a posteriori. Nor as conditions of possible experience are they thereby "employed" a priori; clearly, their employment in experience must be empirical. It may be thought that what Kant is envisioning in these passages is that they can be employed in possible experience and that that employment is a priori. But this is really no different from my own reading of the passages. If we substitute "possible experience" for "knowledge" in the middle of the second passage, then the a priori possibility, or a priori employment, of the "knowledge" turns out to be the a priori possibility of possible experience, which is precisely the a priori possibility that I claim Kant's theory is supposed to explain. But this further possibility—the possibility of the possibility of experience—is not the one that the predominant Anglophone commentators are intent to defend. They hold that Kant is trying to explain the possibility of experience itself, and not that of its own possibility. So we must conclude that these Anglophone readings of what Kant means by "transcendental" in the passages in question, not to mention others as well, fall short of what Kant was getting at.

To sum up, a theory of the possibility of experience does not explain the possibility that is of interest to Kant, that is, the possibility of those very representations and the a priori knowledge they give rise to: how are they (not experience) related to objects of experience? It is these latter possibilities that Kant is truly interested in, as his characterizations of transcendental knowledge attest. Most of the present Anglophone interpretations of Kant do not even address this problem of the possibility of our a priori employment of these representations, especially their employment in the a priori knowledge that arises from them, at least not in a sympathetic manner, and those that do tend to consider it at some distance from the center of their own investigations into the *Critique*. This book is distinctive in that this particular problem stands at the center of its investigations.

IV

Returning now to the review of recent Anglophone commentary on the *Critique,* we can note that there was bound to be a reaction to Strawson's prohibitions. A subsequent generation of Kant commentators loosened Strawson's empiricist "principle of significance" just enough to allow important philosophical discourse about the nonetheless a priori conditions of possible experience.[16] We can thus get an a priori theory of the possibility of experience. This approach seemingly satisfies both Strawson and Kant. Apart from their application to possible experience, the claims have no significance; but they are nonetheless a priori in their independence from all particular experiences we as subjects actually enjoy. They are thus not characterized as extremely high-level generalizations from experience, to which Strawson restricted his theory.[17] As thus independent of experience, they are necessary and universal with respect to all possible experience—a claim Strawson felt we are in no position to make.

In addition to allowing Kantian claims of an a priori nature that could not obviously be reduced to analytic propositions about our concept of experience, Henry E. Allison, a leader in the English-speaking Kantian tradition, took issue with Strawson's *dualistic* interpretation of Kant's ontology—appearances and things in themselves, or the worlds of phenomena and noumena. Following Gerold Prauss in this matter,[18] Allison has argued for a *monistic* interpretation of Kant's ontology. Though I shall deal with this issue of monism versus dualism in some detail in Chapter 6, I might take this opportunity to distinguish myself from Allison, since mine, too, is a monistic interpretation of Kant's ontology.

In a word, according to the view advanced in this book, Allison latched onto the wrong object for his monism. It is not the empirical object, as Allison would have it (but see item 1 of the appendix to this chapter for a revision in Allison's position), but a quite distinct object, one on which the empirical object depends. As I see it, it was, among other things, Allison's failure to distance himself sufficiently from Strawson that probably led him to posit the empirical object as the denizen of Kant's ontology. That object will do quite well for this purpose, provided Strawson is right, that the only

16. Among the leaders in this group is Henry E. Allison, *Kant's Transcendental Idealism: An Interpretation and Defense* (New Haven: Yale University Press, 1983).

17. Strawson, *The Bounds of Sense,* 271–73.

18. *Kant und das Problem der Dinge an sich* (Bonn: Bouvier Verlag Herbert Grundmann, 1974), chap. 2.

defensible strand of the positive side of the *Critique* is its account of the possibility of experience. It is one of the main contentions of this book, however, that the same object cannot satisfy the demands of a theory of the possibility of a priori knowledge. Only an object thought distinctly, at least from sensibility, can perform that role. There are other major issues that separate Allison's views and mine, but they will have to wait until we direct our attention to the actual details of Allison's arguments, later in the book.

So went Kant scholarship in the Anglophone tradition, until Paul Guyer pointed out, admittedly in the manner of Strawson, that though this approach might accommodate some strictures of Strawson's, it could not do the same for Kant.[19] The basic flaw, as Strawson himself pointed out, is that it cannot philosophically motivate Kant's transcendental idealism—the theory that the only objects to which our knowledge is related are "mere representations" of the ordinary things we customarily take ourselves to know in everyday experience. This is the theory that we cannot know how these things are independently of our experience of them; that is, we have no knowledge of things in themselves. Again in the manner of Strawson, Guyer seems to have successfully argued that a theory of our possible experience of things, even an a priori theory, does not entail that we cannot know how things are independently of our possible experience of them. Strawson thus turns out to have been right all along at least in one respect: Kant's transcendental idealism, with its talk about how things are independently of our possible experience of them, cannot be construed as a theory of the possibility of experience. According to Guyer, it must be construed as a theory of our possible a priori knowledge of things. So Strawson is correct in his contention that Kant's notion of the possibility of our a priori knowledge of objects and his notion of the impossibility of our knowledge of things in themselves go hand in hand. Kant had no reason thus to restrict our knowledge of objects except for his interest in the possibility of a priori knowledge.

It has been customary in our tradition of commentary on Kant to give him his due, but only within what we take to be the strictures of defensible philosophy itself. Matters are no different with Guyer. Whereas he recognizes that it is only a theory of our a priori knowledge of objects that entails transcendental idealism, he cannot find any argument in Kant to support Kant's claim to the effect that we do indeed possess such knowledge. It is

---

19. Paul Guyer, *Kant and the Claims of Knowledge* (Cambridge: Cambridge University Press, 1987), 335.

rather a mere assumption of Kant's.[20] The claims for which he does adduce arguments, some of which are quite good indeed, are all claims on behalf of the possibility of experience. With work, the scholar can find in the *Critique* a powerful theory of the possibility of experience that is free of the trappings of transcendental idealism, as any good theory of possible experience should be. With that, the Kant scholar should be content.

Alas, such has not been the case. The meticulous work of Michael Friedman offers us a precise statement of the a priori knowledge of objects belonging to the exact sciences Kant may have intended in his attempt to demonstrate the very possibility of our a priori knowledge altogether.[21] Friedman's is a work that explores the details through which Kant can be said to have combined his transcendental epistemology with the mathematics and science, as well as the logic, of his day—a work that also compares that math, science, and logic with our own.

With Kant's interest in the possibility of our a priori knowledge thus rehabilitated, we are in a more secure position to proceed upon a more general inquiry into the structure and philosophical grounds of Kant's arguments in support of that possibility, that is, the possibility of a priori, not empirical, knowledge. Of necessity, since it is concerned only with Kant's interest in the possibility of a priori knowledge, such an inquiry will have none of the mathematical or scientific detail that is contained in Friedman's work. It will rather follow the general admonition—directly contrary to Guyer's advice, which, as I have said, in both its praise and its criticism of Kant belongs to the Strawson tradition of recent commentary on the *Critique*—that the Kant scholar should not rest with a Kantian theory of possible experience, even one that is a priori. On the contrary, Kant's overwhelming interest in the *Critique* is in a theory of the possibility of our a priori knowledge; experience, and hence its possibility, only enter the discussion as the knowledge without which a priori knowledge is not possible with respect to existing objects. The former is only the knowledge the latter must be related to if the latter is to be possible in that respect. But the question of its own possibility never arises; indeed, it cannot if the question of the possibility of a priori knowledge is to be resolved on its basis. Kant's predominant concern with proving the possibility of our a priori knowledge, moreover, effectively rebuts Guyer's allegation that Kant did no more than assume that we have such knowledge. Rather, his account of its possibility constitutes its proof.[22]

20. Ibid., 362ff.

21. Friedman, *Kant and the Exact Sciences*.

22. I would like to thank Dale W. Jorgenson for a line of provocative questions that suggested the structure for the first part of this chapter.

V

Though Strawson could get away without making a single reference to the literature on the subject, few others would be so audacious, especially today, when we have such an abundance of first-rate Kant commentary coming out of our tradition since Strawson and Bennett published their books. In fact, today, what the commentators have said is almost as important as what Kant himself said, since the commentary occupies so much of our research. After Strawson and Bennett, one ignores the commentary at the risk of rendering oneself irrelevant to ongoing concerns in the Kant literature.

So it is in keeping with the spirit of the times that we address Kant's theory in the context of the issues that have arisen in the literature on the theory. This suggests a method in which issue is taken, not with Kant himself, but with those in our tradition who have offered us important interpretations of his thought. As such, its negatively critical aspect relates more to those in the literature of our tradition who have interpreted the *Critique* for us than to the *Critique* itself. In pointing out the shortcomings of various interpretations of Kant, this book cannot help but be a defense of his work. This is the place, therefore, to state that, except for one very important part of Kant's work, namely, the first-edition Deduction of the categories of the understanding, this book does not go beyond its criticism of others to offer its own negative critique of Kant's theory, although it surely offers its own positive critique of that theory. I am solely concerned with trying to understand, from our present position, what Kant said. It is what we have so far made of Kant's thought that takes us back to the *Critique* itself, to see if we can determine to our own satisfaction the actual defensible content of that thought.

Here I adopt this method by dividing Kant's theory of the possibility of a priori knowledge into two parts, transcendental ontology and transcendental logic, where only the latter follows the actual course of the *Critique* itself and where the foundation of the former part—"Transcendental Ontology"—is actually laid in the very next chapter, which I have included here in the Introduction to enhance the clarity of the exposition of my interpretation. The two parts are then tied together in the book's concluding chapter, which proposes an integrated account of Kant's theory of our a priori knowledge of objects—*transcendental epistemology*.

The next chapter and Part One itself are based on a rejection of what most will agree is the current customary view of the ontology of Kant's only defensible theory of the possibility of our knowledge, leaving aside for the moment the question whether the knowledge is a priori or empirical. By "ontology" I mean, à la Quine, all the objects that must exist for all the affirmations of a theory to be true.[23] To bypass for the present the question whether Kant even has an ontology that would satisfy this Quinean style criterion, it should be noted that the customary interpretation, anyhow, presupposes that Kant does have one, since it is an interpretation of the objects that would have to exist for Kant's theoretical affirmations to be true. In this book, moreover, since Kant's theory is taken to be a theory of the possibility of a priori knowledge, I shall proceed on the assumption that his ontology consists of the objects he says we can intuit or know—both of which are terms that obviously belong to epistemology, even though there are some who would disagree with this epistemological approach to the *Critique*.

The customary view of Kant's ontology maintains that the ontology is not independent of the a priori representations (i.e., space, time, and the categories) or knowledge whose possibility the theory claims to demonstrate. That is, the objects in the ontology would not exist independently of the conditions represented by the a priori representations whose possibility the theory purports to explain (e.g., the things that exist in Euclidean space would not exist independently of that space). A consequence of the customary view is that since the ontology consists of the objects whose existence the theory is committed to, these a priori representations (again, space, time, and the categories) become necessary conditions of the existence of these objects. A further consequence is that the ontology of the theory is identical with the ontology of the very knowledge the theory claims to be possible.

Corresponding to this customary view of Kant's ontology is a customary interpretation of it. The interpretation maintains, first of all, that Kant generally refers to the objects in his ontology as appearances or, more particularly, as empirical objects. "Appearance" covers objects of empirical intuition, perception, possible perception, experience, and possible experience, whereas the less frequent "empirical object" seems to cover just objects of experience or objects of possible experience, both of which are

23. Lest there be any misunderstanding, I should emphasize that any such set of objects would be merely an ontology of a theory of knowledge and thus not an ontology *tout court*. It would therefore not contradict Allison's claim that Kant's transcendental idealism is methodological, not ontological. Allison is distinguishing between conditions of knowledge of objects and conditions of existence of objects. The ontology intended here, however, is the ontology of the theory of knowledge. To put it another way, we are only interested in the existential presuppositions of Kant's theory of knowledge, not those of his theory of being or existence *tout court*—something Kant himself calls "ontology."

nonetheless appearances. ("Appearance" would also cover the "special" case of the self, where the manifold of one's representations is given only through what Kant calls "inner intuition," by means of his so-called inner sense alone. Consequently, according to Kant, one knows oneself only as one appears to oneself, not as one is in oneself [B 158]).

If the ontology of Kant's theory of the possibility of our a priori representations, or conditions, or knowledge, were to be viewed in the customary way and interpreted accordingly as consisting of appearances or, more particularly, empirical objects, then it would be impossible for the theory to explain the possibility of the representations or knowledge. The following argument is offered in support of this assertion.

First, I shall formulate a general problem that would confront any theory of the possibility of a priori representations or knowledge that has an ontology. The criterion of the a priori for Kant consists of the conditions of universality and necessity (B 3–4). This entails that for something, say, a representation, to be a priori (e.g., Euclidean space), its possibility with respect to existing objects cannot be restricted to just the sorts of existing objects or to just the particular existing objects that have actually been observed (the universality condition), nor can it be possible with respect to objects whose existence in its terms is just a contingent fact (the necessity condition). For Kant, the possibility of the a priori with respect to existing objects cannot allow any possible exception to the a priori that would be due to an unobserved object (including any object that for us is unobservable)—an exception in the sense that the unobserved object does *not* exist in terms of the a priori (the universality condition, cf. A 27/B 43), nor can it allow that any existing object with respect to which the a priori is possible exists in terms of the a priori as just a matter of *contingent* fact (the necessity condition). Next, it is assumed that whatever exists, whether particular sorts of objects or the particular objects themselves, is particular and contingent. Consequently, if the a priori is to remain a priori and yet be possible with respect to existing objects, it cannot allow this existence to keep it from being universal and necessary, even though the existence is particular and contingent. (So, Euclidean space must somehow remain a priori even though the only objects with respect to which it is possible exist in it.) Since an ontology of any theory of a priori representations or knowledge would consist of particular and contingent existences, any such theory that has an ontology would confront this general problem, of keeping the representations or knowledge a priori while making its own commitment to existing objects.

Moreover, if the objects in the ontology would not exist independently of the conditions represented by the a priori (e.g., if the things that exist in Euclidean space would not exist independently of that space), then the a priori would be a condition of their existence (e.g., Euclidean space would be a condition of the existence of the things that exist in it). As a condition of their existence, however, its possibility with respect to existing objects would be restricted to *them* (e.g., the possibility of Euclidean space with respect to existing things would be restricted to the things that exist in it). But, then, any unobserved object (including any object that for us is unobservable) that does *not* exist in terms of the a priori *would* constitute an exception to the a priori, which is precisely what the universality condition is supposed to preclude. Nor would it be *necessary* that the a priori is possible with respect to existing objects, no matter which objects exist, since it is just a contingent fact that objects exist in terms of such an a priori as, for example, Euclidean space; that is, the a priori would now be possible only with respect to objects whose existence in its terms would be just a contingent fact. Consequently, the a priori condition in question (e.g., Euclidean space) would cease to be a priori. Thus, the general problem would not be solved under these conditions.

These would be the conditions that prevail according to the customary view of Kant's ontology, since the customary view takes the ontology *not* to be independent of the a priori representations or knowledge whose possibility the theory claims to demonstrate. Since it would not be independent, the a priori would be representations of conditions of the existence of the objects with respect to which the a priori is supposed to be possible. Consequently, the possibility of the a priori would be restricted to them in the manner described above. The universality and necessity that constitute the criterion of the a priori would thus be contradicted by the particular and the contingent existence of these objects once the a priori were rendered possible with respect to objects that exist, again in the manner described above. Consequently, the ontology of Kant's theory of the possibility of our a priori knowledge cannot be viewed in the customary way. That is one reason why we need a new view of the ontology of Kant's transcendental epistemology. Perhaps that is also a reason why those who adhere to the customary view defend only Kant's putative theory of the possibility of empirical knowledge and why they apparently believe he considers the possibility of space, time, and the categories to consist in their being conditions of that possibility. Finally, it may also be why they also place so little stock in his attempt to prove the possibility of a priori knowledge.

For Kant, appearances exist according to the a priori (e.g., physical things exist according to Euclidean geometry). Therefore, by the argument above, if the a priori's involvement with something that exists were restricted to appearances, as it is according to the customary interpretation of Kant's ontology, it would cease to be a priori. That is, the extension and determination of the a priori would now be restricted to objects that do not exist independently of its terms. But this would keep the conditions that might otherwise be universal and necessary from being so. Consequently, the ontology of Kant's theory of the possibility of our a priori knowledge cannot consist of appearances. That is another reason why we need a new interpretation, as well as a new view, of the ontology of Kant's transcendental epistemology.

We can now address the question whether Kant even has a Quinean-style ontology. Some who may consider their views of these matters sufficiently mainstream to qualify as "customary" would answer this question in the negative. Accordingly, they might be considered a variation of the customary interpretation. The variation would be that for Kant the a priori need not be involved with anything that exists.

According to one form of this variation, the a priori involves only possible objects. Accordingly, this form of the variation would maintain that a theory of the possibility of either our a priori or empirical knowledge would be about merely possible appearances, and these are the same objects to which the knowledge itself is related. Like the customary interpretation, it therefore maintains that a single set of objects—now merely possible appearances—are the objects of *both* the knowledge whose possibility is to be explained by the theory *and* the theory itself. But unlike the customary interpretation, it maintains that these are merely possible objects. Since the customary interpretation has just been rejected on the basis of its involvement with objects that exist, this variation of that interpretation escapes from the thrust of that rejection.

How might appearances be merely possible and thus not exist? Their possibility cannot consist of merely the same a priori elements that constitute the empirical or a priori knowledge, or the theory of either, since that would leave us without any object with respect to which the knowledge, whether a priori or empirical, is possible. There must be something other than the a priori elements themselves that counts for being a possible appearance.

Perhaps it is being the object of a merely possible empirical intuition. Since the a priori intuition was just found to be insufficient to count for something's being a possible object, it would also be found to be similarly insufficient with respect to something's being a possible empirical intuition.

Sensation cannot be added, since that would take us too far, by making the empirical intuition actual.

Finally, perhaps an appearance is possible if it is the object of merely an empirical concept, not an empirical intuition. The trouble with this idea is that concepts are without objects if we cannot intuit the objects by means of the senses, or empirically. So we would simply have no object that would be distinct from its concept, and thus would be without the possible object in question.

There is another form of the variation in question that recently has received a lot of attention and become quite popular among Kant commentators. According to this form, Kant is indeed talking about objects of empirical intuition, that is, appearances, rather than merely possible appearances. The difference is that Kant's statements about appearances do not presuppose any existence that is independent of an intention of a subject, something through which the subject's thought is "directed" to an object.[24] The existence would thus be phenomenalistic in nature, and the approach could be phenomenological as well as intentional. The universality and the necessity of the a priori could thus be preserved because it would be restricted to these merely intentional objects.[25]

24. See Richard E. Aquila, *Representational Mind* (Bloomington: Indiana University Press, 1983). Aquila makes a good case for interpreting Kant's transcendental idealism ontologically as distinguishing between two senses in which objects may be said to exist. He makes the case in his contention of the "methodological," or "epistemological," interpretation, which makes heavy use of Kant's employment of the notion that we "consider," or "view," an identical object according to its "two aspects" (88ff.). His contention in this book is explicitly directed against the position of Gerold Prauss, although it clearly can be applied to the position of Allison as well, who is aware of this and deals with it accordingly in "Transcendental Idealism: The Two Aspect View," *New Essays on Kant,* ed. Bernard den Ouden and Marcia Moen (New York: Peter Lang Publishing, 1987), 160–66. For further discussion of Aquila's position, see my reference to him in the Appendix that immediately follows this chapter, as well as elsewhere in the book, especially Chapter 12.

25. Apart from intentionalist and phenomenological interpretations of Kant's ontology, there is also a related division between otherwise phenomenalistic interpretations and realistic ones. This controversy was played out in a classic pairing in which two authors reviewed one another's books in one and the same issue of a journal, namely, the *Philosophical Review.* For the realist's critical review of the phenomenalist, see P. F. Strawson, "Bennett on Kant's Analytic," *Philosophical Review* 77 (1968): 332–39; and for the phenomenalist's at least partial concession, see Jonathan Bennett, "Strawson on Kant," ibid., 340–49.

Finally, Carl J. Posy, "Britannic and Kantian Objects," in *New Essays on Kant,* argues for a combined phenomenalist-realist approach, the former determining a Kantian semantics and theory of truth, the latter a Kantian "notion of reference," whereby the objects referred to are "this 'transcendental object' " (38) or "transcendental objects" (46 n.10). Aquila, by the way, compares his approach to Posy's, claiming for his own approach certain of the benefits of Posy's, though they differ in that Posy's external object is the transcendental object, which

But can it? The intentional object proposed by this form of the variation is subject to the same form of argument that was used above against the customary interpretation itself. All that needs to be done is to substitute "intentionally exist" for "exist" in the argument; existence will now be modified as "intentional" for the sake of accommodating the intentionalist interpretation. The argument will still go through, however; only now it will be in terms of the substitution just suggested. We can then conclude that the intentional object, too, will not work as the object of Kant's theory of the possibility of our a priori knowledge, and we can dispense with it as well.

Even as an intentional object, an appearance is something particular whose intentional existence is a contingent matter, as any existence is particular and contingent (where it is understood that anything particular and contingent is apprehended by us only through the senses). Consequently, if something a priori is to remain a priori and yet be involved with anything that intentionally exists, it cannot allow that involvement to keep it from being universal and necessary. If, however, any appearance with which the a priori is to be involved would not intentionally exist apart from the a priori (e.g., it would not intentionally exist except in Euclidean space), then the a priori would be a condition of something's intentional existence. In that case, however, the a priori's involvement with something that intentionally exists (an appearance) would be restricted to objects (appearances) that would not intentionally exist apart from the a priori (e.g., they would intentionally exist only in Euclidean space). But then, once the a priori got involved with intentional objects that exist, its holding for intentional objects would cease to be universal and necessary—it would hold only for objects that intentionally exist in its terms (e.g., physical things that intentionally exist in Euclidean space). Consequently, the a priori item in question (e.g., Euclidean geometry) would cease to be a priori, even though it is restricted to merely intentional objects. That is, it would no longer hold for all intentional objects, nor would it necessarily hold for them no matter which objects intentionally exist, since it would now hold only for objects that intentionally exist in its terms (e.g., physical things that intentionally exist in Euclidean space). So, the universality and necessity that constitute the criterion of the a priori would again be contradicted by the particular and the contingent, only this time the contradiction would be due to the

---

cannot be known, and Aquila's is the object of our knowledge that takes the form of a judgment; see Aquila's *Matter in Mind* (Bloomington: Indiana University Press, 1989), 214 n. 34.

involvement of the a priori with something that intentionally exists instead of something that exists *simpliciter.*

In addition to introducing the case against both the customary view and interpretation of Kant's ontology and two forms of one of its variations, I should introduce the case for the new view and its corresponding interpretation to be presented in this book. To guard against misunderstanding, I should first note that the new interpretation does not prescribe a substitution of a new object for the one that is customarily taken to be Kant's object of knowledge, whether the knowledge is a priori or empirical. According to the new interpretation, that object remains an appearance. What is new about the interpretation in this regard is rather the idea that appearances are not the objects of the *Critique* itself; that is, they are not the objects of Kant's *theory* of our a priori knowledge of objects. This interpretation is in accordance with the new view that the *Critique* has its own ontology, one that is independent of the a priori knowledge whose possibility it is supposed to explain. According to the new interpretation, the ontology consists of objects that are real—what Kant calls *things.* Since they are the objects to which he himself ascribes existence (their being the objects of his ontology), the *Critique* itself speaks of them as real existences. (Late in the *Critique* Kant specifically defines these objects as objects of transcendental affirmation [A 574–75/B 602–3].) Appearances, on the other hand, are only empirically real. Their existence and reality is derived from the real existence of things insofar as things are given to us through intuitions of the senses. Furthermore, empirically real existence in turn is only a modification of the real existence that is ascribed to things thought distinctly from the thought of their being given in experience, since that distinct existence *simpliciter* is never modified as "empirical."

Things are the objects that appear to us; to put it another way, in Kant's terms, they are what appearances represent. It is their existence that accounts for any existence attributed to appearances that is considered independent of all our intuitions of the senses. (*Mutatis mutandis,* a similar remark can be made about the self in regard to one's inner intuition of it by means of inner sense.) Their being independent of all such intuitions entails that things are independent of appearances as well. Consequently, they are also independent of the application of the categories to appearances and therefore are independent of any employment of the category of existence, including its empirical employment, that is, its employment in empirical knowledge, or in experience.

This preview of the interpretation of Kant's transcendental ontology that is to be developed in the next chapter and in subsequent chapters as well can conclude with a return to the discussion of Strawson's interpretation of the ontology. Strawson, we recall, understood that Kant adopted an ontology that would be distinctive to his theory of the possibility of knowledge. According to Strawson, Kant's metaphysics of transcendental idealism provided that ontology. But that idealism entails that we can have no knowledge, and a fortiori no a priori knowledge, of the objects that belong to that ontology—objects that are distinct from appearances. I am arguing, however, that for Kant we can have knowledge of these objects, for these objects are *things,* not things in themselves, and we can intuit things and not merely think them, a restriction that holds only for things in themselves. But since we can intuit them only through sensibility, we can know them only as appearances. Nonetheless, since we can have a priori knowledge of appearances with respect to their necessary form (and know them a priori only with respect to that form), we can have a priori knowledge of the things that appear to us, but only as appearances, and that is knowledge of the appearances only with respect to their necessary form. In sum, we can have a priori knowledge of things because we can know them as appearances, and we can have a priori knowledge of appearances only with respect to their form. So it is not just the empirical world we can have a priori knowledge of, since that world represents a real world of things, which can be conceived in wholly nonempirical terms. But it does not follow from this that such a conception cannot be distinguished from Kant's conception of things in themselves, as Strawson might perhaps argue. That that proposition *does not* follow is one of the claims I argue for in the next chapter and in Chapter 8.

Some of Strawson's criticisms of Kant can therefore be discarded. The ontology of a theory of *empirical* knowledge, considered apart from a theory of a priori knowledge, need not be thought in terms that are distinct from those that are constitutive of appearances. Such a distinct ontology is unnecessary. On this score Strawson is surely right. But two things definitely do *not* follow from this dictum of Strawson's. One is that an ontology of a theory of the possibility of *a priori* knowledge also need not consist of such distinct objects, that is, objects that are distinct from the constitutive conditions of Kant's empirical objects or his appearances. This reasoning can be attributed to Kant himself. First, he could have realized that a theory of empirical knowledge, again considered apart from a theory of a priori knowledge, does not need such a distinct ontology. A principle of charity therefore suggests that since Kant's theory of knowledge *does* have such a distinct ontology, the theory must be of a knowledge that is distinct from empirical knowledge. Presumably, this knowledge would be a priori knowledge. So, from the very distinctness of Kant's ontology from the conditions he considers constitutive of experience, we might fairly conclude that the knowledge whose possibility he is trying to explain is a priori knowledge, not empirical knowledge. This conclusion, it will be recalled, is none other than the original thesis that opened this book and that was there put forward as its major contention. The reasoning just concluded might therefore be considered an indirect argument in support of this thesis.

The other thing that does *not* follow from Strawson's dictum is that such a distinct ontology that belongs to a theory of *a priori* knowledge must also consist of objects that we *cannot* know empirically, and hence cannot know a priori with respect to the necessary forms of appearances. Indeed, I contend that for Kant we *can* know, and hence can intuit, these distinct objects. His "only" two caveats are that we can know them only as *appearances* and that it is only the *forms* of their appearances that we can thus know a priori.

To sum up this introduction: we should by now have an idea of this book's position with respect to its own view and interpretation of Kant's notion of "transcendental knowledge," or what is called here "transcendental epistemology," and its corresponding "transcendental ontology," as well as the customary view and interpretation of both the knowledge and the ontology. Further arguments in support of this new position and in opposition to those that have become customary are presented in the chapters that follow.

Appendix to Chapter 1: Annotated Selected Bibliography of the Customary Interpretations of Kant's Ontology

1. Henry E. Allison, *Kant's Transcendental Idealism: An Interpretation and Defense* (New Haven: Yale University Press, 1983), 8; "Transcendental Idealism: 'The Two Aspect View,' " in *New Essays on Kant,* ed. Bernard den Ouden and Marcia Moen (New York: Peter Lang Publishing, 1987), 155. In "Transcendental Idealism: A Retrospective," in *Idealism and Freedom* (Cambridge: Cambridge University Press, 1996), Allison both reasserts his commitment to the empirical object (p. 3) as the single constituent of

Kant's ontology and yet, surprisingly, also casts "the transcendental object = x" in the same role (p. 16). Unfortunately this gives his position at least the appearance of inconsistency. In this same piece, Allison emphasizes his use of the term "thing" for referring to this object (empirical or transcendental?). This emphasis may be due to the nature of the piece, which is largely responsive to his critics, including the present writer, dating back to correspondence of 1991–92 and continuing through a paper delivered to the North American Kant Society in 1995. This same 1995 paper argued that for Kant things are taken as appearances if and only if they are viewed from the standpoint of sensibility, and hence as subject to our a priori sensible intuition, even when it is combined with the categories of the understanding, which is the position Allison now adopts in his 1996 paper.

2. Karl Ameriks, "Recent Work on Kant's Theoretical Philosophy," *American Philosophical Quarterly* 19 (1982); *Kant's Theory of Mind* (Oxford: Oxford University Press, 1982); and "Kantian Idealism Today," *History of Philosophy Quarterly* 9 (1994): 219–32.

3. Richard E. Aquila, *Representational Mind* (Bloomington: Indiana University Press, 1983), who (*a*) distinguishes between "appearances" as "intentional objects" and "things in themselves," for example, on pages 27–28; (*b*) seems to restrict certain of the objects we can know to the former, for example, on pages 35 and 85, where he says Kant may be invalidly making claims regarding our a priori knowledge of "real space"; and (*c*) seems to take the reality that can be known (which at first seems to be distinct from intentional objects, but with which the intentional object can [nonetheless] be "identified") to be "a genuine physical reality"—an "empirical realit[y]" that "Kantian appearances" are appearances of, an "actuality" and not a mere "possibility" that is an intentional object (97 and 97 nn. 21 and 22). All of this implies that this distinct empirical reality is both not the reality of things in themselves and yet still not distinct from the a priori conditions of possible experience. See also, especially, 102ff., where actual reality (i.e., "empirical reality") is "roughly" defined "in terms of relations among the members of whole sets of the objects of perception, considered purely intentionally." Empirical reality thus loses its initial appearance of being distinct from intentional objects. See also his *Matter in Mind* (Bloomington: Indiana University Press, 1989), 25–29, including notes 33 and 34 (as well as chapter 6), where intentional objects, understood as "the correlates of one's immediate consciousness of them," are taken up into "objectively real objects," understood as objects of "a suitably

generalized possible consciousness" (p. 26), "a higher order of consciousness of a special sort" (p. 27), or a judgment (yet still not distinct from the
a priori conditions of possible experience).

4. Jonathan Bennett, *Kant's Analytic* (Cambridge: Cambridge University Press, 1966), 22–23, where, besides the objects Kant says "we can know
about by means of our senses," that is, "phenomena" or "appearances,"
Bennett only acknowledges Kant's recognition of "noumena."

5. Graham Bird, *Kant's Theory of Knowledge* (New York: Humanities
Press, 1973), 29: "on Kant's view, there is only one thing at which to look,
namely, appearance."

6. Gordon G. Brittan Jr., *Kant's Theory of Science* (Princeton: Princeton
University Press, 1978), and see also "The Reality of Reference: Comment's
on Carl Posy's 'Where Have All the Objects Gone," in *Spindel Conference
1986: The B-Deduction (Southern Journal of Philosophy* 25, supplement),
ed. Hoke Robinson (Memphis: Department of Philosophy, Memphis State
University, 1987), 37–44. (Since Brittan seems to take Kant to be thinking
the "mind-independent" object through the a priori conditions of possible
experience, I would call his interpretation "empiricist, internal realist," even
though the object is "mind-independent" with respect to our *actual* empirical knowledge.)

7. Lorne Falkenstein, *Kant's Intuitionism: A Commentary on the Transcendental Aesthetic* (Toronto: University of Toronto Press, 1995), esp.
chaps. 9–11. Although Falkenstein's principal interest lies outside questions
about Kant's ontology, his approach still falls under the rubric of "customary" as defined here.

8. Paul Guyer, *Kant and the Claims of Knowledge* (Cambridge: Cambridge University Press, 1987), esp. part v: "Transcendental Idealism,"
where Guyer distinguishes between appearances as objects we can experience or know, a priori as well as empirically, and things in themselves, as
objects we cannot know at all.

9. Patricia Kitcher, *Kant's Transcendental Psychology* (New York: Oxford University Press, 1990), esp. 140–41.

10. Charles Parsons, "The Transcendental Aesthetic," in *The Cambridge
Companion to Kant,* ed. Paul Guyer (Cambridge: Cambridge University
Press, 1992), 85–87, 89–90, where Parsons is explicitly committed to an
interpretation that allows for the distinction between "representation" and
"object"; see also 85 for the same commitment.

11. Hoke Robinson, "The Transcendental Deduction from A to B: Combination in the Threefold Synthesis and the Representation of the Whole,"

in *Spindel Conference 1986: The B-Deduction (Southern Journal of Philosophy* 25, supplement), ed. Hoke Robinson (Memphis: Department of Philosophy, Memphis State University, 1987); "Objects for Transcendental Arguments," in *Proceedings of the Sixth International Kant Congress,* ed. Gerhard Funke and Thomas M. Seebohm (Washington, D.C.: Center for Advanced Research in Phenomenology and University Press of America, 1989), 279–89; and "Two Perspectives on Kant's Appearances and Things in Themselves," *Journal of the History of Philosophy* 33 (July 1994): 411–41. Robinson interprets the knowable object to be "a particular intentional object existing in the world of objective appearance" ("Transcendental Deduction," 54) and, "at least in some sense, created (posited, constituted, presupposed) by the mental act that intends" it ("Objects," 283), which suggests that Robinson should in this connection be grouped with Aquila, as Robinson himself observes (282 n. 10).

12. Kenneth Rogerson, "Kantian Ontology," *Kant-Studien* 84 (1993): 19: "necessarily any legitimate object conforms to our epistemic conditions"; see also 20ff.

13. P. F. Strawson, *The Bounds of Sense: An Essay on Kant's "Critique of Pure Reason"* (London: Methuen, 1966), 24 *et passim.*

14. Ralph C. S. Walker, *Kant: The Argument of the Philosophers* (London: Routledge & Kegan Paul, 1978), 107–8 and 129, where Walker attributes a "quasi-phenomenalistic" position to Kant.

KANT'S EXTERNAL REALISM

I

My argument thus far has led to the conclusion that a satisfactory interpretation of Kant's ontology requires that it must be distinct from space and time and from the categories as well, insofar as the categories give rise to our a priori knowledge of objects. I will now argue that within Kant's *theory* of the possibility of that knowledge, the objects Kant typically refers to as *things* are the only objects that meet the requirements of being distinct from these three conditions, or forms, of knowledge and yet being what we can intuit and know. That is, things alone are distinct from these conditions of knowledge and yet stand in such a relation to the *theory* of a priori knowledge that within the theory Kant can claim that we can intuit and know them. Indeed, as is developed further in Chapter 7, Kant maintains that we can have no a priori knowledge of them except as we intuit them. As distinct from these conditions of knowledge, they cannot be objects to which our a priori knowledge is related: that knowledge can be related only to *appearances* of them. That is why it is only as *appearances* or, more particularly, as *empirical objects* that they can be objects of our a priori knowledge. But with regard to Kant's *theory* of a priori knowledge, it is a different matter: they *can* be objects of that theory. To put it another way, things are involved in the relation of our knowledge to objects only if we intuit and know them. As such objects, however, they are taken up into the forms of knowledge and become appearances. A consequence of this line of reasoning is that Kant's *theory* of our a priori knowledge contains no intuition of its own (A 722/B 750)—it is a wholly conceptual investigation. That is why transcendental "knowledge" requires scare-quotes. Genuine knowledge contains intuition.

To complete this analysis of Kant's concept of a thing, let us ask ourselves at what point in his laying out the elements of a priori knowledge he begins to talk of things, and not appearances, as that which we intuit or that of which we have an intuition or knowledge. Where does he begin to speak of the things that appear, or the things appearances "merely represent," instead of the appearances themselves? There are two distinct places where this occurs; one is in the Aesthetic and the other is in the B-Deduction of the categories.

In the Aesthetic, after introducing appearances into the discussion, Kant asks whether space and time "would belong to *things* even if they were not intuited" (A 23/B 37, emphasis added) or whether apart from "the subjective constitution [*Beschaffenheit*] of our mind . . . they could not be ascribed to any thing whatsoever" (A 23/B 38, amended trans.). This is the first instance in the body of the *Critique* where Kant interrupts his talk of appearances to speak of things. Why does that shift occur precisely here?

In the immediately preceding paragraph, he announces that he is about to "isolate sensibility," first by abstracting the concepts of the understanding and then by removing sensation, so that "nothing may remain save pure intuition and the mere form of appearances" (A 22/B 36). In this manner he announces his search for "the mere form of appearances."[1] Our question thus becomes, why does Kant not ask whether space and time can belong to *appearances* without their being objects of our intuition? But he does not ask that question; rather, he asks whether space and time "would belong to *things* even if they were not intuited," and whether they could be ascribed to any *thing* apart from "the subjective constitution of our mind" (A 23/B 37, 38, amended trans., emphasis added). The question, of course, turns out to be rhetorical: unless things were intuited, neither space nor time would belong to them. That is, their being intuited is a necessary condition for space and time to belong to them.

---

1. Patricia Kitcher calls this "discovering the forms of intuition," in her article of the same title, *Philosophical Review* 96 (1987): 205–48.

Turning our attention to Kant's first reference to things in the B-Deduction, he begins by pointing out that "if no intuition could be given, . . . no knowledge of any thing [*Ding*] would be possible by means of [a category]" (B 146, amended trans.). At this stage in the B-Deduction, therefore, Kant relies on intuition to distinguish knowledge of a thing from mere thought of an object in general through a category. He goes on to assert that "*a priori* knowledge of objects, as in mathematics," which arises from "pure intuition," is not the knowledge of objects he is interested in, since, he says, it deals with the mere "form . . . [of] appearances." He then asks "whether there can be *things* which must be intuited in this form" (B 147, emphasis added). We again inquire, however, why in this context Kant does not ask whether there can be *appearances* that must be intuited in this form. Again, our question, of course, turns out to be rhetorical: unless things were intuited "in this form," it would not be knowledge that is being distinguished from thought.

What is common to both sets of passages is that our intuition of things in a form of appearances is a necessary condition of either the ascription of space and time to things or our knowledge of them. It seems that "appearances" cannot be substituted for "things" in either case, because the proposition that appearances are objects of intuition only in a form of appearances is *itself* necessary, whereas the proposition that things are intuited in such a form is *not* itself necessary; it is necessary only as a condition of the ascription of space and time to things and of our knowledge of them.[2] The necessity that appearances are intuited in a form of appearances could not possibly express such a condition. Any condition it might express in this context would be vacuous. So, both sets of passages reinforce my earlier conclusion that the objects Kant speaks of here are distinct from the a priori cognitions of space, time, and the categories. Their distinctness is entailed by the nature of the necessity that things be intuited in a form of appearances: it is the necessity that belongs to a condition that can actually determine the ascription and the knowledge in question. This only assures us that should we find a passage in which Kant gives an explanation of what a thing is that satisfies the theoretical desiderata that have accumulated from the beginning of our investigations into Kant's ontology—especially its distinctness from space, time, and the categories—that is, an explanation that satisfies our *view* of Kant's ontology, thereby adding to our confidence in it, we should offer that explanation as our *interpretation* of the ontology.

2. They are what Guyer would correctly call "conditional necessities." They are contingent consequents of conditional propositions.

In a passage in the section of the *Critique* entitled "The Ideal of Pure Reason" Kant does explain what a thing is in terms that in fact do satisfy our view of his ontology. He says, "Transcendental affirmation is therefore entitled reality, because through it alone, and so far only as it reaches, are objects something (things), whereas its opposite, negation, signifies a mere want, and, so far as it alone is thought, represents the abrogation of all thinghood" (A 574–75/B 602–3). After that, he remarks that "that which constitutes the thing itself [is] the real in the appearance" (A 581/B 609). And in the Dialectic there is another passage that supports this take on Kant's conception of a thing: "For to allow that we posit a thing, a something, a real being, corresponding to the idea [of reason], is not to say that we profess to extend our knowledge of things by means of transcendental concepts" [A 674/B 702]. Now, if we can understand how transcendental affirmation gives an analysis of the ontology of Kant's transcendental epistemology, we will seem to have the complete analysis of the concept of the denizen of Kant's ontology that we have been looking for.

I have already explained the "transcendental" part of the analysis as signifying Kant's *theory* of the possibility of our a priori knowledge of objects, as distinct from the possibility of the knowledge or from the knowledge itself. That is, the affirmation we are interested in is the affirmation involved in distinctly transcendental epistemology. This leaves only Kant's notion of affirmation to be accounted for. For that, we must look to his notion of a logical function of judgment, since affirmation involves such a function.

So long as Kant's discussion of the affirmative logical function of judgment is taken to belong to what he calls "general logic" and what today we call "formal logic," it is difficult to see how we can make any further progress in understanding his analysis of his concept of a thing as something that is distinguished from all other objects through transcendental affirmation.[3]

---

3. Kant is just as explicit on the subject of general logic in the discussion surrounding the Table of Judgments. I argue in Chapter 9 that that discussion as well as the Table itself should rather be taken as belonging to transcendental logic. If the logical functions of judgment are taken as I suggest, having first been isolated by abstraction of "all content from a judgment [in general]" (A 70/B 95) but not of all content from "knowledge in general" (A 71/B 96), they themselves do "determine a concept in respect of its content" (A 574/B 602). And this is precisely how Kant speaks of transcendental content in the passage presently under discussion.

It is this possession of transcendental content that distinguishes Kant's use of affirmation from Quine's in the determination of ontological commitment. Since Quine's belongs to formal, or general, logic, it has no content and thus serves merely as a criterion for determining ontological commitment "from a [formally] logical point of view," without any implication, as far as we can tell, of any commitment to a specific ontology of its own. Kant's use of transcendental affirmation, on the other hand, does carry content and hence a relation of

Any principle belonging to general logic "abstracts from the entire content of knowledge and is concerned solely with its logical form" (A 571/B 599). It thus could not be through the affirmation that belongs to general logic that Kant could distinguish things from all other objects as he does in his analysis of the concept of a thing. General logic provides us with no functions for distinguishing among objects in the manner desired. Whereas "logical negation," which belongs to general logic, "does not enable us to declare that we are thereby representing in the object a mere not-being," "transcendental negation," which belongs to transcendental logic, does enable us to make that declaration. Accordingly, transcendental affirmation "is a something the very concept of which in itself expresses a being" (A 574/B 602). The concept of the affirmation that belongs to general logic, on the other hand, does not express a being.[4]

---

knowledge to an object (A 55/B 79). Consequently, it does carry a commitment to a specific ontology of its own, namely, an ontology of things. It thus cannot be used as a criterion for determining the ontological commitment of theories in general, as Quine, it appears, intended his.

In a challenging discussion, T. K. Seung, "Kant's Conception of the Categories," *Review of Metaphysics* 43, no. 1 (1989): 107–32, argues that one of Kant's two conceptions of the categories takes them to belong to the same general, or formal, logic that the logical functions of judgment are said to belong to. Thus, Seung might object to my interpretation of the functions on the grounds not only that the functions have no content—since for Seung, as for virtually all commentators on the *Critique*, they are logical forms of judgment—but that the categories, in their employment in the first step of the second-edition Deduction, have no content as well. This approach, of course, goes in exactly the opposite direction from the one mine takes. It might be said that Seung reconciles the categories in step one of the Deduction with the logical functions of judgment by *removing* the content from the *categories*, whereas I reconcile them by allowing the *functions* to *keep* their content, as I would like to put it.

One question I would pose to Seung is, where in the discussion following the Metaphysical Deduction of the categories does Kant remove from them the transcendental content that he says the understanding introduces into them (A 79/B 105)? On Seung's reading of the Transcendental Deduction, it seems that its first step actually belongs to general, and not to transcendental, logic. But this is hard to accept, since the first step asserts that the B-relation of representations to an object is constituted by the unity of consciousness and that it is transcendental logic, not general logic, that is concerned with "all [B-]relation of knowledge to the object" (A 55/B 79). Since knowledge belonging to the understanding "consists in the determinate relation of given representations to an object" (B 137), the involvement of the unity of consciousness in the relation of representations to an object implies the involvement of the same unity in the relation of knowledge to the object. Since concern with that relation belongs to transcendental logic, we would have to conclude that since the first step of the Deduction is concerned with that relation, it too must belong to transcendental logic.

4. It is noteworthy that the third logical function of judgment under the head that includes affirmation and negation, namely, transcendental infinity, goes unmentioned in the passage presently under discussion. We might want to keep in mind that Kant characterizes space and time as two "infinite . . . non-entities [unthings]" (A 39/B 56). It might be that the very infinity of these "unthings" derives from the *transcendental* infinity that goes unmentioned in our

Transcendental affirmation is connected to the transcendental consideration of all possible predicates of things. Just as transcendental logic is said to "contain solely the rules of the pure thought of an object, [and] would exclude only those [cognitions] which have empirical content" (A 55/B 80), so the transcendental consideration of all possible predicates of things is restricted to those predicates whose content "can be thought a priori." The actual connection resides in the concept of the being we represent through just "some" of "all possible [a priori] predicates" (A 574/B 602). That being is a thing expressed in the concept of transcendental affirmation. To sum up, it is through *transcendental* affirmation that we distinguish a thing from all other objects, and this is a being expressed in the concept of that affirmation, that is, the concept of reality, and represented through just some of all possible predicates that have *a priori* content.

What we have left to do is to distinguish between the concept of a thing as just analyzed (in terms of transcendental affirmation) and the concepts of space, time, and the categories. Transcendental affirmation would not be fully distinct from space and time if the affirmation were to involve any putative transcendental intuition of ours and hence consist in space or time. For if it were, then, first, an "empirical object in its general character" could have a transcendental relation to an object, which for Kant is impossible (A 45/B 63). And second, space (or time) would itself be "a transcendental representation," which Kant explicitly denies (A 56/B 81). Having distinguished the concept of transcendental affirmation, and hence that of a thing, from space and time, what we now need to do is distinguish the same concept from the category of reality, which is the category that "agrees" with the affirmative logical function of judgment.

The distinction will be assured if the affirmation in which the *category* of reality is employed is not transcendental and if we represent the corresponding real object through possible predicates that have *empirical* content. The two conditions are actually logically related to one another, since, according to the interpretation of "transcendental" I have been proposing, the affirmation would be transcendental only if the possible predicates of the object were exclusively a priori. But a category cannot have exclusively a priori employment if it is to have objective reality or validity. And, indeed, the

---

present context. That is, since the concept of transcendental affirmation expresses a being and that of transcendental negation a not-being, then the concept of transcendental infinity might express a nonbeing, or an "unthing." This would lead us to look for a connection between the theory of the infinity of space and of time and a transcendental infinity that derives from transcendental logic and belongs to the theory of our a priori knowledge of objects.

penultimate conclusion of the second-edition Transcendental Deduction of the categories is that they do have empirical employment (B 161); that is, the possible predicates through which we represent objects of the categories must have empirical content if the categories are to have objective validity. So, it appears we can distinguish between the concept of reality that is thought in transcendental affirmation and the category of reality. If we combine the former concept of reality, the one employed in Kant's *theory* of the possibility of a priori knowledge, with the idea that such a reality is distinct from the three specific modes of a priori knowledge—space, time, and the categories—we can characterize Kant's ontology as an "external realism."[5]

II

Besides providing Kant with the necessary concept of objects that we can intuit and know but that are distinct from appearances or, more particularly, from empirical objects, the concept of a *thing* also occurs in two larger concepts of his theory of a priori knowledge, namely, the concept of *things in general* and that of *things in themselves*. How are things further conceived through these two larger concepts?

Kant says we "speak of *things in general*" "if we abstract from the sensibility of our intuition" (A 34/B 51, Cf. B xxvii, A 35/B 52, A 247/B 303, A 271/B 327, A 281/B 337). But this is not enough to distinguish things in general from things in themselves (or, for that matter, from things *simpliciter*), since the latter, of course, also are distinct from sensibility. Indeed, occasionally Kant speaks of "all things in general" and things in themselves in the same breath in this regard (B xxvii, A 34–35/B 51–52). Yet we must not confuse them with each other (or with things *simpliciter*), for several reasons.

First, we can have "perception" (A 719/B 747) as well as "intuition" (A 35/B 52) of a thing in general (as well as of a thing *simpliciter*) but, of course, not of a thing in itself. So, on this score, things in general are like things *simpliciter* and are unlike things in themselves. Furthermore, there is an entire cluster of other, related features of the concept of a thing in general, all of which are absent from the concept of a thing in itself. Related to

---

5. This characterization was suggested to me antipodally by Hilary Putnam's use of "internal realism" to describe his preferred interpretation of Kant's ontology. See his *Many Faces of Realism* (La Salle, Ill.: Open Court, 1987), 43.

the fact that we can have a perception of a thing in general is the further feature that "from concepts alone" "the philosopher" can deal with "a transcendental synthesis" in which any perception of a thing in general "can belong to possible experience" (A 719/B 747). And this, in turn, is clearly related to the further feature that a thing in general is something of which we can have "*a priori* synthetic knowledge." And this feature, in its turn, is related to the additional feature that the concept of a thing in general is a concept that "represents *a priori* this empirical content of appearances [i.e., their matter]," which it does by "giv[ing] us nothing more than the mere rule of the synthesis of that which perception may give *a posteriori*." Finally, Kant claims that the concept of a thing in general is the "only" concept that can give us an a priori representation of the empirical content of appearances (A 720/B 748). None of these features, of course, belongs to the concept of things in themselves.

We might try to sort out the three concepts in question in the following way. Though things, being objects of transcendental affirmation, and hence objects of transcendental judgment and understanding, are thought independently of sensibility, they are not thereby thought as being such objects, and hence as being independent of sensibility. For that they must be so thought, and that is done by means of the understanding, since the understanding is the faculty by means of which we think of objects in general (A 51/B 75). The concept of a thing in general is thus the representation through which things are thought as being objects of transcendental affirmation, and hence as being objects of transcendental understanding, and hence as being independent of sensibility. The concept of their being so thought thus must contain the features that involve the unity of apperception that have been mentioned above, since this unity is the unity of the understanding (B 134 n).

Though things in general are thus independent of sensibility, they may still be intuited and perceived (just as "the thought of an object in general" can be determined by an intuition [B 158]). If they are, the things as intuited or perceived are objects of sensibility, and hence are no longer things in general; they are now rather things as appearances. It would be an oxymoron for Kant to speak of things in general as appearances. So things can be taken as appearances, but things in general cannot be so taken, even though they can be intuited and perceived. It is rather that, *as* intuited or perceived, things are related to sensibility, in which case they cease to be thought as things in general.

Finally, things in themselves alone cannot be determined, limited, or conditioned by sensibility. If things *simpliciter* or things in general are determined by the understanding *alone,* to the exclusion of sensibility, they are objects of concepts alone, and thereby are objects of *reason,* that is, things in themselves.

III

In Chapter 6, I critically explore in some detail the controversy, among proponents of what I have been calling the *customary* interpretation of Kant's ontology, over whether the ontology consists of a single set of objects—appearances or, more particularly, empirical objects—and thus constitutes a certain monism, or, on the other hand, consists two sets of objects—appearances and things in themselves—and thus can be considered a dualism. And I do so in terms of a leading exponent of each interpretation, namely, Allison and Guyer. Now, however, I would like to clarify further my own interpretation and at the same time show another of its advantages by applying it to the controversy between the customary monistic and dualistic interpretations. The advantage over the customary interpretation resides in its rather satisfying resolution of the dispute in question.

Since the ontology as here interpreted consists exclusively of things, it is clearly monistic in nature. However, the interpretation distinguishes things from "all other objects," which implies that things are not alone among objects. In regard to Kant's transcendental idealism in particular, I have explicitly distinguished things from appearances and things in themselves, which, of course, for their part, are distinct from one another. This interpretation, therefore, leads to a transcendentally idealistic dualism with respect to things, and in this sense Kant's ontology could be considered dualistic. But this dualism is perfectly coherent with the monism: one set of objects viewed or existing in two ways.[6] Each way provides us with objects that are distinct from one another; namely, the original, or basic, objects—the things—*viewed both ways.* Things thus constitute unqualified, basic reality; when viewed both ways, we get empirical reality and transcendental reality—the sensible world of appearances, that is, phenomena, and the intelligible world of things in themselves, that is, noumena. We get a world (of objects) and not mere objects themselves (things) if and only if the things

---

6. I am not suggesting that the monistic interpretations represented by Allison could not be defended as "perfectly coherent" in precisely the same sense.

are thought to be determined *either* according to "qualities" that belong to us or to the subject *or* according to properties or laws that are intrinsic to them. These are properties and laws that belong to things the conditions of whose possibility are thought independently of their being further thought through the conditions of *sensibility,* and hence independently of the *categories* insofar as the latter are conditions of the possibility of our a priori *knowledge* of objects, since they constitute such conditions only insofar as they "can be applied to empirical intuitions" (B 147) or only insofar as they "prescribe to appearances . . . *a priori* laws" (B 165).

Finally, this investigation of Kant's ontology gives us a way of understanding certain of Kant's own remarks as perhaps being somewhat responsible for the allegedly erroneous, customary interpretation of it. Kant asserts that our a priori knowledge is related only to appearances; yet I have argued that he also holds that the objects that we can thus know are things, which are distinct from appearances. How can the objects we can know a priori—things—be distinct from the objects to which the knowledge is related?

When Kant speaks of the objects to which our a priori knowledge is related, he is thinking of the representation through which the knowledge is related to the objects as the "mode" (*Art*) of the knowledge. Since geometry, for example, is to be related to outer appearances, things must be represented through space, as the mode of intuition, by means of outer sense. When things are viewed as appearances, they are thus taken to be represented through the mode of the knowledge in question. This is so even if the mode of knowledge belongs to the understanding, that is, the categories. For they are modes of knowledge, and not mere forms of thought, only if they can be applied to empirical intuitions (B 146–47). What I have tried to show so far is that though the relation of knowledge to objects depends on the modes of knowledge through which the objects are represented, the objects that are thus known are distinct from those modes of knowledge, and hence are *not* themselves related to the knowledge. Only their *appearances* are thus related. Otherwise, I have argued, Kant's realism would be "internal," and he would lose the concept of distinct objects that is required for the knowledge to be synthetic a priori and for his arguments to be transcendental.

So, if we in the analytic tradition are concerned with the plausibility and even the very significance of Kant's notions of synthetic a priori knowledge and of transcendental arguments, notions that have given rise to so much adverse reaction in the subsequent history of philosophy, we would do well, it seems, to address his theory of transcendental affirmation, and its objects, things, if we want either to support or to shake those notions at their actual foundations.

IV

In sections II and IV of the previous chapter, I introduced Strawson's general criticism of what he took to be the ontology of Kant's epistemology. In the same sections, I also answered much of that criticism, along the lines of the interpretation of Kant's ontology advanced in this book. Now it is time to address the details of Strawson's criticism that are contained in his chapter "The Metaphysics of Transcendental Idealism," from *The Bounds of Sense*.

Many of these details support Strawson's general criticism that Kant's idealism violates the principle of significance that Strawson believes Kant himself adopts in his explanation of the possibility of knowledge, whether the knowledge is a priori or empirical. Strawson's statement of the first ("[1]") *"doctrine"* belonging to the idealism reveals what I have been arguing is a misreading of Kant's theory. Strawson says that Kant thinks of the affecting objects as "things as they are in themselves."[7] First, we have the difficulty this presents for a consistent reading of Strawson himself. He says that for Kant "we perceive the things which, by affecting us, cause our outer perception" (250). There are two concepts that are employed here and that need to be distinguished. Since the things in question "cause our outer perception" (concept 1) "by affecting us" (concept 2), Strawson ought to have distinguished between these two concepts. For it is absurd to say that a thing *does* something *by doing* that very same thing. So there must be a ground for distinguishing between the respective objects of (1) and (2). Yet Strawson's interpretation of Kant's ontology does not allow for two such objects. His dualistic interpretation of the ontology leaves no room to *interpose* things between appearances and things in themselves and thereby provide for the second object in question.

My interpretation of the ontology, on the other hand, provides precisely for that second object. It posits *things* as the affecting objects (2) and *things in themselves* as the causes of our outer perceptions (1). On my interpretation, things in themselves have the power to produce appearances in us and

---

7. P. F. Strawson, *The Bounds of Sense: An Essay on Kant's "Critique of Pure Reason"* (London: Methuen, 1966), 236. Henceforth page references to Strawson's *Bounds of Sense* are cited in the body of the text.

thus qualify as the causes of appearances. As the objects of transcendental affirmation or of the *transcendental* concept of reality, *things,* on the other hand, can be said to affect us, and thus exemplify concept (2). Furthermore, if, in turn, things are viewed as capable of producing appearances in us, the objects that then come into view are the same *things* but now as they are *in themselves.* Now things are also thought through the a priori conditions of the understanding alone. (Further discussion of this distinction between things and things in themselves is given in Chapter 8.)

A second detail of Strawson's criticism pertains to the title Strawson gives to the first doctrine just discussed. As a statement of Kant's considered views in the *Critique,* especially the second edition, the statement is quite misleading. Strawson has Kant speaking of "Appearances of things as they are in themselves" (238). But this is incoherent, even though at least once Kant himself seems to speak this way, in the appendix to the *Prolegomena.* If there could be such objects as these appearances, we *could* intuit things in themselves and thus *could* have knowledge of them, since we can always *think* them. (But, still, they could be known only as appearances.) Obviously, this would confound Kant's thesis that we *cannot* have knowledge of things in themselves. The reason we cannot is that we cannot intuit them (see Chapter 7 for the development of this idea). That is the deeper explanation of why Strawson's statement of the first "doctrine" is incoherent.

So, any charge of meaninglessness that Strawson, based on his own interpretation, levels against Kant's idealism in this regard is vitiated by the misguided nature of that interpretation. The same defense of Kant can be applied to Strawson's interpretation of Kant's idealistic distinction between a subject of representation or knowledge and the same subject "as it is in itself." Strawson makes no room for an identical subject *simpliciter,* the "I" of the thought "I am," which can be *interposed* between the appearance of the self and the self as it is in itself and hence can be viewed both ways (cf. B 157ff.). So, Kant can be defended against the charge of meaninglessness on this score as well.

The lack of provision for any such identical object of reference that can be interposed between an appearance (or phenomena) and a thing in itself (or noumena) in Strawson's account of Kant's idealism is ironically a criticism Strawson himself makes against Kant. This particular criticism is for Strawson another count against Kant's alleged failure to make his doctrines intelligible to us (250–52). Strawson maintains that for us an intelligible contrast between appearance and reality requires an identical object that can be viewed from two contrasting standpoints—an uncorrected view and a corrected view (252). Although the two Kantian standpoints do not yield uncorrected and corrected views, it is nonetheless Strawson's own interpretation of Kant that is responsible for the particular absence of the identical object itself from the theory. Not that Allison's monism will do the job either, as I point out in section II of Chapter 6. Rather, I am proposing that Kant employs the concept of a thing for this purpose.

The general criticism of meaninglessness is specified under yet another head—the fourth. The unintelligibility of the noumenal world for Strawson is due to the unintelligibility of what Strawson believes is the only faculty on which Kant relies to explain that world, namely, intellectual intuition (254 and 264–65). Whether such an intuition is intelligible or not, we can agree that it provides for Kant only a discredited sense of things in themselves and a noumenal world in which they exist. Kant's preferred way of describing such a world, however, is in terms of things considered as objects of the understanding alone, quite apart from intuition, including intellectual intuition (cf. B 306 et passim, and see Chapter 8, section v). The preferred way consists in what Kant calls a "negative sense" of noumena (i.e., as a limiting condition on sensibility), in contrast to a discredited "positive sense" that involves intellectual intuition (B 306–7, and again see Chapter 8, section v). So, it seems Kant should not be blamed for a certain unintelligibility that he himself recognizes and from which he therefore tries to distance himself.

Strawson includes under the head of meaninglessness yet a fifth criticism of Kant's idealism. At several places in the chapter under discussion, Strawson asserts that according to Kant's "critical standard" there really exist only two sets of objects within the two worlds that constitute Strawson's interpretation of Kant's supposedly dualistic ontology (260). The present charge of meaninglessness, then, of Kant's denial that "things in space and time are things in themselves" consists in the claim that "[a]part from perceptions, they [i.e., bodies in space] are really nothing at all" (237, and cf. 238, 242, and 257). However, this criticism would have no basis if Strawson were to adopt the interpretation of Kant's ontology offered here. The existence that is involved in appearances remains quite intact even if perceptions have been abstracted from them. This existence consists in the existence of the things that appear. While the spatial and temporal qualities of bodies do indeed disappear, the very existence involved in these appearances does not disappear along with those qualities. Therefore, if we adopt my interpretation of Kant's ontology, we should reject Strawson's assertion that for Kant there is no existence in appearances that is distinct from the dimensions of space and time. Consequently, the Strawson charge of meaninglessness that is based on this assertion should also be rejected.

Before closing the present discussion, I should mention once again that the concept of a thing advanced in this book as the preferred interpretation of Kant's ontology violates Strawson's stricture that the only terms Kant can legitimately be allowed are those whose contents can be applied in experience. Indeed, Strawson speaks out against the very "extraneous" viewpoint on possible experience that I attribute to Kant (262, 271). But I must leave my defense of Kant on this score to what I have already said about it in section II of the previous chapter and in section v of Chapter 15.

Of course, besides Strawson's general criticism that Kant's idealism is unintelligible, there is his equally important contention that it is unnecessary. I have already agreed that on this score Strawson is quite right, provided that the knowledge whose possibility is in question is empirical knowledge. And I have argued that since a priori knowledge is distinct from empirical knowledge, it does not follow that Kant's idealism is also unnecessary with respect to the possibility of the former knowledge. But an understanding of Kant requires something much stronger than that, namely, an interpretation of Kant's theory of a priori knowledge that shows how for him the possibility of that knowledge requires his transcendental idealism.

In summary, having provided in this chapter an account of the necessary concept of objects that we can intuit and know but that are distinct from the a priori conditions or representations of space, time, and the categories and hence are distinct from appearances or, more particularly, from empirical objects, and, in addition, having employed that account in reconciling monistic and dualistic interpretations of Kant's ontology, I can, in Chapters 7 and 8, turn to my account of the transcendental idealism that both interpretations have sought to explain. What motivated Kant to adopt this idealism? In the course of answering this question, I shall have occasion to distinguish things from appearances on the additional ground that they, but not appearances, have properties and laws that are *intrinsic* to them, and thus do not depend on the involvement of an extrinsic faculty of sensibility or "any understanding that knows them" (B 164). This is what makes it possible to take things, but not appearances, as they are *in themselves.*

With the account of Kant's concept of a thing given so far, however, we can consider much of the groundwork for our future work to have been laid. The need for an object that is thought distinctly from the representations of space, time, and the categories, and the nature of that object, have now been put forward. It is time to consider the plan for the rest of these investigations (the next chapter) and the central technical device I employ for carrying out these investigations (the following chapter). These two chapters complete the Introduction to this book. With that in hand, we can return to the question of the nature of Kant's ontology and bring our understanding of it to a conclusion (Part One). Following that, we will go on to investigate those aspects of his transcendental logic that complete his theory of the possibility of a priori knowledge (Part Two).

A SYNOPSIS OF THE SOLUTION
TO THE PROBLEM OF A PRIORI
KNOWLEDGE

I

It might be useful to get an overall picture of the rest of the new interpretation of Kant's theory of knowledge I am about to offer. I begin with a synopsis of the rest of my interpretation of Kant's solution to the problem of the possibility of a priori knowledge, which was formulated in Chapter 1.

In the next chapter I present a singularly methodological discussion that for purposes of possible reference introduces a model of what I take to be the structure of Kant's theory of representation. This model is at least implicit in virtually my entire account of Kant's transcendental epistemology. It is thus the subject of Chapter 4, which is eponymously entitled "A Model of Kant's Theory of Representation." Actually, its use begins in Chapter 4 itself, immediately following its own introduction into the book. In that chapter it is applied to the very opposition between the customary view and interpretation of Kant's ontology and the new view and interpretation presented here. Generally, the structure of the model is triadic. It is based on a distinction between Kant's generally distinct uses of two different German words, which Kemp Smith infelicitously translates with the single English word "relation." The two concepts of "relation" that Kant employs throughout the *Critique*, with only occasional exceptions, play a large role in the account of his theory offered here.

II

Part Two opens with the book's fifth chapter, entitled "Interpretation of Text; Theory and View," and it continues the detailed investigation of Kant's ontology begun in Chapter 2. I argue there that the customary *interpretation* does not provide an adequate reading of certain selected passages from the *text*. In several of these passages Kant actually uses the term "thing" to signify the objects he is talking about. I shall argue that we cannot make sense of these passages if we take Kant to be employing the concept of *appearance* or, more particularly, *empirical object* to refer to the objects he is talking about. We thus need another interpretation of his terms for these objects.

I further argue that the customary *view* of the ontology is beset with *theoretical* difficulties. Besides difficulties inherent in the customary view in general, there are specific difficulties in two distinct *versions of the interpretation* that go along with the *view*. These versions, as already indicated in section III of the previous chapter, divide over the issue of monism versus dualism of Kant's ontology. Before considering the two versions, we should keep in mind that the general interpretation common to both is that the object Kant says we can intuit or know is the appearance or, more particularly, the empirical object. It is this customary approach—view plus interpretation—that is the subject of this chapter.

The two versions of the customary interpretation are subsequently examined in Chapter 6, "Monism or Dualism?" One version of this interpretation, represented for us, as already indicated, by Allison, holds that Kant instructs us to take this very object (for Allison, the empirical object in particular) in a twofold manner when he is touting the benefits of his transcendental idealism. This has accordingly been dubbed the "two-aspect" interpretation of Kant's idealism. I also describe it as a "monistic" interpretation of the idealism. The other version of the customary interpretation, represented for us by Guyer, holds that Kant's ontology consists of two distinct sets of objects—representations of things, or appearances (which we can intuit or know), and things in themselves (which we cannot intuit or know). This can therefore be described as a "dualistic" interpretation of

Kant's ontology. Both versions are *dispensed with* in this chapter as part of its argument that we should adopt a *new* interpretation of Kant's ontology altogether, one that accords with a new view of it, according to which, as already indicated, its objects are independent of the possibility of the a priori knowledge Kant's theory is supposed to explain. This new approach to the ontology of Kant's transcendental epistemology is, I believe, to be found nowhere else in the literature.

The new *interpretation* of the ontology that is offered here has already been presented in the previous chapter. To review for the sake of this synopsis, the definition of the objects of the ontology is taken from a passage late in the *Critique* where Kant defines *things* as objects of *transcendental affirmation*. In reaching the definition of this concept of a thing this book uses, for the first time, substantial material from the Transcendental Dialectic, in particular, the section entitled "The Transcendental Ideal," and from "The Discipline of Pure Reason." This definition has, I believe, the twin virtues of allowing a coherent, defensible understanding of Kant's position and avoiding the misinterpretations of the text that are charged against the customary interpretation as well as the theoretical difficulties that are said to beset the customary view of the ontology.

Chapters 1, 2, 5, and 6 thus carry us through the arguments for an ontology that is distinct from our a priori knowledge of objects, and hence distinct from the objects of such knowledge, that is, an ontology that is distinct from *appearances*. They also carry us through the arguments for an interpretation of the ontology that meets that demand of distinctness, that is, an ontology of *things*. But I also argue that though things must be distinct from both of our sources of a priori knowledge—sensibility and the understanding—if the knowledge is to be possible, only *one* source, *sensibility,* is responsible for the objects of our knowledge being *appearances*. This thesis allows, however, that the objects of the *combination* of sensibility and the understanding are still *appearances*. It only maintains that their status as appearances is due to sensibility alone. Such is the concern of the arguments of the next and seventh chapter of the book, "The Necessity of Kant's Idealism." The eighth chapter, the final chapter dealing with Kant's ontology, provides additional arguments for the further proposition that, viewed as standing in relation to *the understanding alone,* things are what they are *in themselves*. This allows us to understand the twofold view of things recommended by transcendental idealism as a view divided according to the respective standpoints of sensibility, whether combined with the understanding or not, and the understanding alone, quite apart from sensibility. Accordingly, the title of this chapter is "Sensibility and the Understanding, Appearances and Things in Themselves."

III

Part Three is just as concerned as Part Two to view the *Critique* as a theory of the possibility of a priori, not empirical, knowledge. This change in perspective makes all the difference in my treatment of Kant's transcendental logic. This is a logic concerned solely with the relation of a priori knowledge to objects. A logic that does not distinguish a priori cognitions from empirical ones cannot be concerned with the relation of cognitions to objects at all and, a fortiori, cannot be concerned with the relation of a priori cognitions to objects. Such is the logic we today call *formal logic* and Kant calls *general logic*. In Part Two this distinction between the two types of theory—that of the possibility of a priori knowledge and that of the possibility of empirical knowledge—plays a crucial role in each chapter's account of a particular part of Kant's theory.

The first chapter of Part Three and the book's ninth chapter, "The Content of Kant's Logical Functions of Judgment," on the basis of this shift from the customary perspective on the *Critique* to the one recommended here, argues that the logical functions of judgment cannot be part of the relation of a priori knowledge to objects unless the functions have content, since content is what such a relation consists in. This thesis entails that the discussion surrounding Kant's Table of Judgments be located in transcendental logic, not formal, or general, logic, which is precisely where those who adopt the customary perspective on the *Critique* must place it. For those who take this customary perspective, Kant's logical functions of judgment should be treated as logical forms of judgment, which belong to formal, not transcendental, logic. On the basis of the shift to a new perspective on the *Critique* as a whole, this book adopts exactly the opposite interpretation of the functions.

Assigning content to these functions also supports Part One. In the first instance, the concept of a thing could not have been argued for as the object of transcendental affirmation unless the logical function of judgment called "affirmation" were taken to have content. For if things are to constitute the ontology, or reality, of Kant's transcendental epistemology, the term in which they specifically are explained, "affirmation," cannot be a term of merely formal logic, which abstracts from all content of knowledge.

The customary view of the logical functions of judgment, moreover, has a decided tendency toward a wholly unfavorable interpretation of Kant's Transcendental Deduction of the categories—for Kant, our fundamental concepts of objects. Since Kant attempts to ground the categories in the logical functions of judgment—indeed, to identify the categories with them—and since the categories are supposed to have "transcendental content," and, furthermore, since general logic with its forms of judgment abstracts from all content of knowledge, concepts that have content would be grounded in or identified with forms without content if these logical functions of judgment were logical forms of judgment,. And that would put Kant in an impossible position to defend, which is where virtually all commentators on this question actually put him.

The first chapter of Part Three of the book thus attempts to do two things at once: support the thesis of Part Two, that things alone constitute Kant's ontology, and improve Kant's chances for a coherent Transcendental Deduction of the categories.

Since the logical functions of judgment contain the original synthetic unity of apperception (B 131, B 142–43), the account of how the manifold of representations must be determined in respect of these functions, and thus must be subject to the categories, could not proceed apart from an explanation of how the same manifold must be subject to the original consciousness that is thought in the functions.

This latter explanation constitutes the high point of the Deduction. But a reconstruction of the Deduction cannot go forward until a decision is made regarding a highly disputed issue in the literature. This is the question whether—and, if so, how far—the Deduction can proceed in its account of the necessity of this high point (self-consciousness) and of its relation to the necessity of the categorization of objects without reference to the imagination and hence to sensibility. Kant came to think that he could—indeed, that he must—first argue for the necessity of the categories and of the unity of self-consciousness quite independently of the imagination and only later bring in imagination. Otherwise, the Deduction would contain what he calls an "obscurity." On that basis he completely rewrote the Deduction for the second edition of the *Critique* (the B-Deduction). But the most famous of his sometime students, Fichte, and those in the history of philosophy who have followed Fichte's lead in this matter, most notably among recent commentators, Heidegger, thought otherwise. Today, however, the prevalent view seems to side with the Kant of the second edition.

Those who hold the prevalent view, however, are involved in a certain incoherence, which should be corrected. Since possible experience depends on the imagination, and since the prevalent view requires that a Transcendental Deduction begin independently of the imagination, it must also require that such a Deduction begin independently of possible experience. However, those who hold the prevalent view also hold that the categories and the unity of self-consciousness are argued by Kant to be *necessary* precisely on the grounds that they are requirements of the possibility of *experience*. Consequently, those who hold the prevalent view are of two minds in regard to the first-, or "A-," edition Deduction of the categories. On the one hand, they maintain that it introduces the imagination too early into the Deduction, and, on the other, they also hold that Kant argues for the necessity of the categories and of the unity of self-consciousness on the grounds of their respective roles in determining the possibility of experience.

Chapter 10, "Kant's Categories Reconsidered," corrects for this incoherence. It agrees that the Deduction must begin independently of the imagination, but it then proceeds consistently by having Kant argue for the necessity of the categories and of the unity of self-consciousness quite independently of the demands of possible experience. Indeed, the "obscurity" Kant adduces as the reason for his completely rewriting the Deduction is, as explained in Chapter 10, precisely the role played by possible experience in the A-Deduction. In this manner the chapter lays the groundwork for a more favorable assessment of the second-, or "B-," edition Deduction.

It is now customary among those who adopt the prevalent view (against Fichte et al.) to consign Kant's discussion of the purely intellectual, that is, nonimaginative, role of the categories in our knowledge of objects to what Dieter Henrich has identified as the "first step" of the B-Deduction.[1] Three issues whose resolution is central to this book's positive reconstruction of step one have been prominent in the negative assessment of step one that is so common today. All three are addressed and resolved in the Chapter 11, "Three Issues in Step One of the B-Deduction." The negative assessment in each case is at bottom due to the customary view of the *Critique* as a theory of the possibility of empirical knowledge, or experience. The first issue, rep-

---

1. Dieter Henrich, "The Proof-Structure of Kant's Transcendental Deduction," *Review of Metaphysics* 22 (1969): 640–59.

resented by Patricia Kitcher,[2] who follows Bennett in this matter, concerns the already mentioned attempt by Kant to ground the categories in, and even identify them with, the logical functions of judgment. The originality of my discussion of the issue is based on the thesis of Chapter 9, namely, that for Kant the logical functions of judgment have content. The second issue, discussed in the version of it put forward by Allison, is whether an adequate defense can be provided for Kant's distinction between the subjective and the objective unity of consciousness—a distinction that is crucial to the concluding stages of step one. In attempting to provide such a defense, Chapter 11 responds to Allison's criticism of the distinction. And with respect to the third issue, resolved in response to Guyer's allegation that Kant begs the question when he relies on the concept of an object of knowledge in specifying the conditions of the unity of self-consciousness, the chapter argues that although for Kant there is a definite relation between the concept of self-consciousness and that of an object of knowledge, it is not of a question-begging variety.

The twelfth chapter, "Judgment, Consciousness, and the Categories," consists of a reconstruction of step one that, in keeping with the shift in perspective on Kant's epistemology recommended here, is free of any reference to possible experience. One of its more original features is its emphasis on a neglected ground of a thesis of Kant's that some have found in need of support, namely, that the same consciousness is involved in all acts of the understanding. In defense of Kant, the chapter draws attention to his assertion that all the acts of the understanding are themselves the same. A connection is then made between the identity of the consciousness of the acts and that of the acts themselves. Ultimately, the success of step one hinges on Kant's theory of the unity of a judgment (which continues to be a topic of controversy in philosophical logic).

An interpretation of the second-edition Deduction would, of course, be incomplete without a reconstruction of the second step of the Deduction. This is duly attended to in the thirteenth chapter of the book, "Perception and the Categories." This chapter deals with the issue, as presented in two versions, one by Kitcher, the other by Allison, of the success of the Deduction in demonstrating that all our possible perceptions must be subject to the categories. Whereas both Kitcher and Allison, among a host of others,

2. Patricia Kitcher, *Kant's Transcendental Psychology* (New York: Oxford University Press, 1990): 88–89.

deny that it is successful, this chapter reconstructs the argument as going all the way through to its desired conclusion—a proposition that actually extends beyond Kant's thesis that the connection of perceptions in experience is necessarily subject to the categories. This is the proposition belonging to Kant's so-called Copernican Revolution, namely, that the understanding is responsible for nature's necessary conformity to law, which instead belongs to Kant's theory of the possibility of a priori, and not merely empirical, knowledge. It is here that we can understand Kant's claim that we can have a priori knowledge of the laws of nature in general.

If there is a single issue that more than any other demands a systematic interpretation of the entirety of Kant's positive theory of knowledge, it is the question of "the transcendental character of the Second Analogy," which is the subject as well as the title of the fourteenth and penultimate chapter of the book. This is the Analogy in which Kant is concerned to prove that we can apply the concept of cause and effect specifically to all occurrences of alterations. At the minimum, this proof calls upon relatively well developed, systematically interrelated interpretive positions regarding virtually all of the issues covered in the book thus far. And yet it also depends on one's interpretation of the Analogy itself. It is thus a fitting issue with which to close our exegetical work on the *Critique*. In the resolution of this issue the various strands of the entire interpretation advanced here all converge.

It is also to be expected, therefore, with regard to this issue, that the shift in perspective on the *Critique* advanced here would distinguish itself from the customary perspective on the now familiar ground that Kant is primarily interested in establishing the possibility of a priori, not empirical, knowledge. It is on the basis of this reorientation of our entire approach to the work that we can try to dispense with many allegations that have been made against the proof, mostly by those inclined to see it as part of a theory of empirical knowledge.

There is, *inter alia,* Strawson's charge that the proof may work for our perceptions of events but not for the events themselves. We can also deal with James Van Cleve's and Lewis White Beck's claim that the proof depends on a cause-effect relation between "the perception of an objective item [an appearance] . . . and the existence of that item," a claim that creates problems for an interpretation and defense of the proof on what I consider the only proper transcendentally idealistic grounds.[3] I also rebut Guyer's

---

3. James Van Cleve, "Four Recent Interpretations of Kant's Second Analogy," *Kant-Studien* 64 (1973): 71–87 (quote from 81). Lewis White Beck, "Six Short Pieces on the Second Analogy," in *Essays on Kant and Hume* (New Haven: Yale University Press, 1978).

allegation that, despite what Kant himself says about the matter, the proof makes hardly any use of his transcendental idealism. Schopenhauer's charge that Kant committed a fallacy in postulating a causal connection wherever there is a change in objective states of affairs,[4] like Guyer's allegation, also misses what is fundamental to Kant's entire approach to the matter. Van Cleve's counterexamples to Kant's claim that mere irreversibility of objective states of a substance entails the involvement of causality are clarified in terms that are favorable to Kant. And finally, the chapter answers A. C. Ewing's objection,[5] shared by Van Cleve, that Kant's proof actually turns the principle that purportedly gets proved into an analytic judgment, whereas Kant wanted to prove a synthetic one.

Admittedly, this is an ambitious agenda for a single chapter of the book; but it nonetheless does get covered, largely because the chapter is the culmination of so much of a developed interpretation of Kant's transcendental epistemology. In other words, befitting its penultimate position in the book, it is packed with interpretation.

Finally, the book concludes with Part Four and Chapter 15, "Transcendental Epistemology." By way of review, carried out at an admittedly very high level of abstraction, it gives a unified account of Kant's theory of our a priori knowledge of objects.

Finally, a word is in order concerning the limited scope of this book. The text that it primarily deals with is the second edition of Kant's *Critique of Pure Reason* (1787), not the first (1781). There are several reasons for this limitation. Perhaps the most important is that, as the preceding synopsis of Chapter 10 suggests, the first edition of the main argument of the *Critique,* namely, the Transcendental Deduction of the categories, creates an egregious "obscurity" by introducing possible experience too early into the larger argument proving the possibility of our a priori knowledge of objects. It may very well have been his obliviousness to this error that kept Kant from realizing that many of his readers would see him as a latter-day Berkeleian. On the other hand, his emphasis on the importance of what in the previous chapter is called his "external realism"—his explicit ontological commitment to things—may have had a decided role in keeping him, whether intentionally or not, from repeating the "obscurity" he was worried about. Restricting commentary to the second edition also saves us from

---

4. Arthur Schopenhauer, *The Fourfold Root of the Principle of Sufficient Reason,* trans. E. F. J. Payne (La Salle, Ill.: Open Court, 1974).

5. A. C. Ewing, *Kant's Treatment of Causality* (London: Kegan Paul, 1924).

having to try to reconcile with the second edition first-edition ideas Kant himself did not deem worthy enough to retain in the text. It is enough to try to get clear about an author's commitments at the time of publication. Why complicate matters by trying to reconcile them with ideas to which he evidently is no longer sufficiently committed to include them in the publication at hand? And finally, a similar remark pertains to his earlier and later works. While we are not quite capturing a momentary object by confining the investigation to the second edition, we are keeping the length of time in Kant's intellectual history to a minimum. It is the least we can do.

Last, for reasons of time alone, with one important exception mentioned in the synopsis of Chapter 2, the book does not include material beyond the Transcendental Analytic of the *Critique*. The discussion, therefore, does not extend to the claims of metaphysics that are considered in the Transcendental Dialectic.

A MODEL OF KANT'S THEORY
OF REPRESENTATION

I

Before continuing with substantive concerns with the *Critique*, I should introduce a part of my interpretation that is more methodological in nature. Throughout this book I work with a structural model of what I take to be Kant's theory of representation. Indeed, immediately following its explanation, it will be applied to the opposition between the customary view and interpretation of Kant's ontology and the new view and interpretation offered here. The model is based on Kant's generally distinct uses of two different German words that, unfortunately, Kemp Smith translates with the single English word "relation." The German words are *Beziehung* and *Verhältnis*. For ease of reference I call the former relation the *B*-relation and the latter the *V*-relation.[1]

1. It should be noted that at the December 1996 meeting of the APA's Eastern Division in Atlanta, announcement was made (with a kind acknowledgment to me from the dais) that the distinction between *Verhältnis* and *Beziehung* had been adopted by Paul Guyer and Allen Wood in their then forthcoming Cambridge University Press translation of the *Critique*, which has since (1998) been published. They do not quite understand the distinction as I do, however. In a footnote at A 20/B 34 Guyer and Wood assert that Kant "reserve[s] the word *Beziehung* to denote the relation between objects and the cognitive subject (in which sense it is used only four times, to be noted below, in the final section of the 'Transcendental Aesthetic'). Since

I shall discuss B-relations first. If we call them *reference* relations, we will not only be following one of the accepted English translations of *Beziehung* (as "reference") but also reflecting a use of the term "reference" in recent logical theory,[2] a use that itself reflects Kant's use of *Beziehung*. Reference theory thus gives us a body of literature to fall back on to get an idea of what I take B-relations to consist in for Kant.

But we must be careful in adapting Kant to the thought and language of others. Kant himself speaks of a B-relation that a manifold of given cognitions has to the original apperception (B 142) *before* he speaks of the dependence of the categories on "*our* sensible and empirical intuition" for "body and meaning [*Sinn und Bedeutung*]" (B 149). So, for Kant, *Bedeutung*, a term also employed extensively by Frege and often translated from Frege as "reference," as well as "meaning," by contemporary philosophers of language, is not entailed by Kant's *Beziehung*. Therefore, if we do think of the B-relation as reference, we must distinguish it from both Kant's and Frege's *Bedeutung*. We can, moreover, readily distinguish Kant's use of *Beziehung* from Frege's *Bedeutung* by noting that Kant's term generally denotes the *relation* that, say, a representation has to something, say, an object, whereas Frege's term denotes the reference (meaning) to which a word is related. The term Frege tends to use for such a *relation* as is denoted by Kant's *Beziehung* is *Bezeichnung*, which is often translated as "designation" but

---

'relation' or its plural will thus almost always be translating *Verhältnis* or its plural, further notes of the occurrence of this term in the 'Transcendental Aesthetic' will be omitted." See Immanuel Kant, *Critique of Pure Reason*, trans. and ed. Paul Guyer and Allen W. Wood (Cambridge, Mass.: Cambridge University Press, 1998), 156. Among other things, this note of theirs unfortunately omits immediately preceding occurrences of *Beziehung* that signify a relation of a *cognition*, instead of the *cognitive subject*, to objects (A 19–20/B 33–34). The narrow senses that Guyer and Wood attribute to Kant also do not conform to his uses of the terms in the following passages from the "Transcendental Aesthetic": A 36/B 53, A 40/B 51, B 67, B 69 n.

Since many of the main theses of my book are stated in terms of the relation (*Beziehung*) of a representation, a cognition, or a manifold thereof to objects, I must take issue with the narrow use of *Beziehung* that Guyer and Wood attribute to Kant in this regard. Consequently, users of the new translation might question the accuracy of the translation of these two terms.

The importance of the distinction itself and of its consequences for the proper translation of the *Critique* into English was introduced at least into the Anglophone literature on the *Critique* by two papers of mine: "The Content of Kant's Logical Functions of Judgment," *History of Philosophy Quarterly* 11, no. 4 (1994): 375–92, and "Perception and Kant's Categories," *History of Philosophy Quarterly* 13, no. 3 (1996): 345–61. Earlier, the same distinction was also prominent in unpublished papers of mine that were then circulating among Kant scholars and were also mentioned in the first of the two published papers.

2. See, for example, P. F. Strawson, "On Referring," *Mind* 59 (1950), reprinted in *Essays in Conceptual Analysis*, ed. A. G. N. Flew (London: Macmillan, 1956).

which Russell, in his criticism of Frege's article "Ueber Sinn und Bedeutung" evidently translated as "denoting" when he spoke of that particular relation to objects which belongs to his "descriptions."[3]

Generally, Kant takes a term that can be said to (be) B-relate(d), or (be) refer(red), to something to be one of the following epistemological items: (a) a representation, (b) a cognition, (c) a manifold of (a) or (b), (d) a subject of (a) or (b), or (e) a mental faculty of (a) or (b). A term to which one or more of these items can (be) B-relate(d), or refer(ed), can for Kant generally include not just what he calls an object (by his use of either *Gegenstand* or *Objekt*) but also certain of the same items that themselves, in a different context, of course, can do the referring, namely, a representation, a cognition, or a subject or a faculty of either. That is, representations, cognitions, and subjects and faculties thereof can be taken by Kant as either referring to something or as themselves being referred to, but the context usually allows us to determine which. In addition, it should be noted that Kant sometimes speaks of something referred to as standing in a B-relation to what is referring to it, even though he generally speaks of the relation as going in the other direction. Moreover, he also sometimes speaks of a B-relation as a relation that two items have to one another (cf. A 92/B 124).

Kant's use of the B-relation can be illustrated with just a few examples that have been taken from its quite pervasive employment in the *Critique*:

> a cognition may [B-]relate to objects (A 19/B 33, amended translation)
> all thought must . . . [B-]relate ultimately to intuitions (A 19/B 33)
> if the object (the triangle) were something in itself, apart from any [B-]relation to you, the subject (A 48/B 65)
> the concept of the divisible [B-]relates to various other concepts (A 68/B 93, amended translation)
> all intuition in its [B-]relation to sensibility (B 136, cf. A 45/B 62)
> the necessary [B-] relation of the manifold of the intuition to the one 'I think' (B 140)

So far I have introduced the B-relation only by calling it a reference relation and counting on recent reference theory to provide a background for understanding the term. To get a deeper understanding of the B-relation, we

3. Bertrand Russell, "On Denoting," *Mind* (1905), reprinted in Robert C. Marsh, ed., *Bertrand Russell: Logic and Knowledge* (New York: Macmillan, 1956).

must ask for the conditions that determine it. For these we must turn to Kant's *V*-relation.

Generally, for Kant, *V*-relations are those in which various epistemological items can be *ordered*. The ordering can be carried out at one of the three levels (types) of representation or knowledge that in previous chapters I have already argued must be distinguished from one another in any comprehensive, unified, and coherent account of Kant's positive theory of knowledge. These are the transcendental (which is also a priori, of course), the nontranscendental a priori (whose possibility the transcendental is supposed to explain), and the empirical. We will begin with the transcendental.

The place at which Kant explicitly discusses such transcendental *V*-relations and not just actually employs them in his theory of knowledge is the appendix to the Transcendental Analytic, "The Amphiboly of the Concepts of Reflection." His point throughout the appendix is to show the difference his distinction between sensibility and the understanding makes in regard to several Leibnizian propositions or principles. These propositions or principles assume quite a different character from Leibniz's when they are interpreted according to Kant's distinction between these two faculties of the mind. Kant's central thesis here is that Leibnizian, overly "intellectualist" (A 267/B 323) interpretations of these propositions and principles leave out of account the essential contribution that *sensibility* makes to our a priori knowledge of objects. Kant tries to correct for that.

He does so by assigning concepts and, more generally, representations to their proper source, or faculty of the mind: sensibility and the understanding (A 261/B 317). Actually, such assignment extends to objects of either faculty, as can be seen in the paragraph immediately below, and presumably this is done through the assignment of their representations to the relevant faculty. This assignment—an ordering of the representations or objects, and thus a *V*-relating of them to one another, according to either of the two faculties—is made in what Kant calls "transcendental reflection" (A 262/B 319). He recognizes four types of such transcendental *V*-relations, the last of which, matter and form, he claims, "underlie[s] all employment of the understanding" (A 266/B 323). (The other three are identity and difference, agreement and opposition, and the inner and the outer.) The same *V*-relation is also said by Kant to be a relation between "the determinable in general" and "its determination" (A 263–65/B 319–21). Kant mentions here as an instance of such a relation the *V*-relation that obtains between the form of an empirical intuition ("as a subjective property of sensibility")[4] and the matter (sensations). In general, Kant maintains, the form determines the matter, and not the converse, which is something he says Leibniz "could not endure to think" (A 267/B 323). So, the transcendental V-relation of both an empirical intuition and its object, appearance, to the identical faculty of the mind, sensibility, tells us that its form, space or time, is prior to its matter, that is, the sensations that are contained in it.

Kant employs the four transcendental V-relations that are listed in the Amphiboly, especially the V-relation between matter and form, throughout his theory of the possibility of a priori knowledge. In the Aesthetic, for example, he speaks critically of philosophers who bypass space and time "if they seek to judge of objects, not as appearances but merely in their [transcendental] [V-]relation to the *understanding*," that is, as they are in themselves (A 40/B 58, emphasis added). Also in the Aesthetic, he says that "sense can contain in its representation only the [transcendental] [V-]relation of an object to the subject, and not the inner properties of the object in itself" (B 67). My last example of a transcendental V-relation from the Aesthetic can be found in the note to B 69, in which Kant speaks of "the determinate [transcendental] [V-]relation of these objects to the subject." In the Transcendental Logic, in fact in the Amphiboly itself, Kant, in speaking of the transcendental V-relation, says "things can have a twofold [transcendental] [V-]relation to our faculty of knowledge" (A 262/B 318). In summary, not only does Kant use the term *Verhältnis* to express his explicit employment of the concept of the transcendental V-relation itself, but throughout his theory of knowledge he uses other terms to express his employment of concepts of the four *sorts* of transcendental V-relations that are listed in the Amphiboly.

The next task is to look to the text of the *Critique* to support the claim that for Kant these transcendental V–(ordering) relations determine certain a priori, but nontranscendental, V–(ordering) relations (which, henceforth, will simply be called "a priori V-relations"), and in particular the a priori V-relations of space, time, and the categories. After that, as already indicated, we will turn to the empirical level of V–(ordering) relations. Only then can we deal with the ultimate task of showing how certain V-relations determine certain B-relations.

4. This use of "subjective" by Kant is not to be construed in the same sense that attaches to his use of "subjective" in "subjective constitution of a mode of sensibility," which figures prominently in the discussion below.

The task at hand is explicitly addressed in the Amphiboly: "it is the place [i.e., the faculty of knowledge, cf. A 268/B 324ff.] to which they [i.e., things] belong in this regard that determines the mode in which they belong to one another. For this reason the inter[V-]relations of given representations can be determined only through transcendental reflection, that is, through . . . their [transcendental] [V-]relation to one or other of the two kinds [i.e., modes] of knowledge [*Erkenntnisart*]" (A 262/B 318).

Moreover, Kant also expresses this same view in the Aesthetic, for example, in the passages cited above (A 40/B 58, B 67, B 69), as well as in further passages, some of which are discussed in detail below (A 19/B 33, A 20/B 34, A 28/B 44). Returning to the Logic, in a key passage we find Kant speaking of the "manifold of *a priori* sensibility, presented by transcendental aesthetic, as *material* for the concepts of pure understanding" (A 76–77/B 102, emphasis added). We have already seen that this implies that Kant is here employing the one transcendental V-relation that he considers to underlie all employment of the understanding (matter and form). Therefore, Kant's ensuing claims that the representations belonging to a manifold of an intuition can be a priori V-related to one another, not just spatially or temporally but also according to the categories, presuppose this earlier claim that employs the *transcendental* V-relation of matter and form.

We can now turn to *empirical* V-relations. Certain empirical V-relations among representations also depend on the particular empirical V-relation that these representations have to a particular faculty of the mind. But since these V-relations are not relations to the two original, a priori sources of our representations—sensibility and the understanding—but rather involve empirical faculties that might be characterized as "derived" from the original faculties, on the basis of "circumstances or empirical conditions" (B 139),[5] they do not, strictly speaking, come within the purview of "transcendental reflection." But if we keep this caveat in mind, we can, in this qualified manner, apply to them the form of analysis provided by our transcendental reflection on the proper cognitive a priori V-relations.

Perhaps most prominent among these empirical V-relations in Kant's theory of knowledge, especially in his contesting the views of Hume, is the empirical V-relation of "association" (B 140, B 142). In such a V-relation, which has "only subjective validity," the representations are said to be merely "conjoined" in one's "perceptions" (B 142).[6] Kant calls the faculty

---

5. For a fuller discussion of this concept of "derived," see Chapter 11, section III.
6. For a fuller discussion, see Chapter 12, section II.

of the mind that determines these representations so that they stand to one another in their merely *associative* V-relations "the reproductive imagination" (B 141, B 150), which, he goes on to say, "contributes nothing to the explanation of the possibility of *a priori* knowledge" (B 152). In contrast to these (empirical) associative V-relations stand the objective, a priori V-relations among representations in a judgment that belongs to the understanding (B 141), the faculty of the mind to which the representations must therefore be transcendentally V-related.[7]

Another prominent empirical V-relation in Kant's theory of knowledge is that in which representations stand to one another in a "subjective" temporal succession, in an "apprehension of the manifold of appearance," or in a "sequence that may occur solely in the imagination" (B 234). Again, as is evident from the last quotation, Kant explains such an empirical V-relation in terms of the empirical V-relation that the representations have to the imagination. This stands in contrast to the transcendental V-relation that the same representations can have to the understanding, which alone can provide the rule (causality) that can make the otherwise merely subjective succession objective (B 234ff.).[8]

We can now turn to the ultimate task—understanding how V-relations determine B-relations and, more precisely, how the former determine the B-relations of our representations or knowledge, especially those that are a priori, to objects. We can start with the very first sentence of the body of the *Critique*. Kant there says that it is through intuition that a cognition may immediately B-relate to objects (A 19/B 33). A partial reconstruction of this sentence according to the analysis offered here can be found in the summary statement of his overall theory that Kant gives at the beginning of the Transcendental Logic. He there cites sensibility as one of "the two fundamental sources" of our knowledge. He immediately goes on to say that intuition is one of the two "elements of all our knowledge" (A 50/B 74). The summary continues by further characterizing intuition as "contain-[ing] . . . the mode [*Art*] in which we are affected by objects" (A 51/B 75). And in the subsequent "Clue to the Discovery" of the categories (the *Leitfaden*), we find that intuition is characterized as actually *being* one of the two "modes" of knowledge and not merely "containing" such a mode (A 68/B 92). As a mode of knowledge, however, intuition is a determinant of knowl-

---

7. The first, or A, edition of the Deduction of the categories apparently did not heed this prohibition. For an extended discussion of this point, see Chapter 10.

8. For an extended discussion of this last point, see Chapter 14.

edge. It thus qualifies as a determinant of a cognition. This allows us to view the relation of intuition to the cognition as a transcendental *V*-relation, since, as I have already noted, the determining-determinable relation is recognized by Kant as a transcendental *V*-relation. This analysis of the relation between intuition and the cognition as a transcendental *V*-relation, therefore, can be offered as a seemingly plausible reconstruction of at least part of the first sentence of the body of the *Critique* as based on things Kant says later in the text.

On the basis of this analysis an equally seemingly plausible reconstruction of the rest of the sentence can be offered, and in so doing we can understand how this transcendental *V*-relation of intuition to the cognition *determines* the *B*-relation of the cognition to objects. This determination, we should recall, is the question presently before us. According to the analysis offered here, the proposition expressed by the sentence entails that the cognition *B*-relates only to objects that are a priori *V*-related to one another in intuition (which we have seen entails that they are transcendentally *V*-related to sensibility). That is, intuition *determines* the *B*-relation of the cognition to objects (specifically, its *immediate* *B*-relation to them) in the sense that the cognition *B*-relates only to objects that are a priori *V*-related to one another in intuition. Moreover, intuition is such a determination of the cognition's *B*-relation to objects only if it is transcendentally *V*-related to the cognition. So, precisely insofar as it is transcendentally *V*-related to the cognition, intuition determines the cognition's *B*-relation to objects; and conversely, precisely insofar as it determines the cognition's *B*-relation to objects, intuition is transcendentally *V*-related to the cognition. We can conclude, therefore, that intuition is transcendentally *V*-related to the cognition if and only if it determines the *B*-relation of the cognition to objects, and this entails that the objects are a priori *V*-related to one another in intuition, which in turn entails that they are transcendentally *V*-related to sensibility.

We might pause here for a moment to abstract from this reconstruction a quite general analysis of certain important epistemological terms that can be said to figure in it. We might say that a representation or condition belongs to the *content* of a cognition in the sense that it is *V*-related to the cognition, which entails that the content determines a certain *V*-relation among the only objects to which the cognition may be *B*-related. This is actually just another way of making the now familiar point that the *V*-relation of the representation or condition to the cognition *determines* the *B*-relation of the cognition to objects in the sense of determining a *V*-relation among the objects. In other words, it is the *content* that determines the

V-relation among the objects to which the cognition may be *B*-related, and in that sense it may be said that the content is what the *B*-relation consists in. Again, it is in terms of its content that a cognition refers to objects, or, yet again, the reference of a cognition to objects consists in its content.[9]

Another example of how a *V*-relation can determine a *B*-relation can be found in Kant's treatment of space and the so-called argument from geometry found in the "transcendental exposition of the concept of space" (B 40ff.). The transcendental *V*-relation between sensibility (the source or *mode* of our intuition of space) and outer sense (the *means* by which "we represent to ourselves objects as outside us" [A 22/B 37]), on the one hand, and our intuition of space, on the other, determines the *B*-relation of the intuition to objects. Since the concept of space is derived from its intuition, that same transcendental *V*-relation between sensibility and outer sense, on the one hand, and our intuition of space, on the other, determines the *B*-relation of our concept of space to objects (i.e., through our intuition of space). Sensibility and outer sense determine this *B*-relation of our intuition and concept of space to objects in the sense that they determine the a priori *V*-relations among the only objects to which the intuition and the concept of space may be *B*-related (B 41). This determination in turn depends on the transcendental *V*-relation of the objects to sensibility and outer sense. This transcendental *V*-relation would consist in at least the transcendental *V*-relation between matter and form, the determinable and the determining. It is therefore through the corresponding transcendental *V*-relations that space and spatial objects have to one and the same faculty of the mind, sensibility, that space and these objects can now be said to have, with respect to each other, that particular *possibility* which consists in the *B-relation* that obtains between them.

The particular concept of possibility involved here can be found at least in Kant's explicit connection between such a concept and the *B*-relation between a representation and an object, as stated in the following passage: "There are only two possible ways in which synthetic representations and their objects can establish connection, obtain necessary [*B*-]relation to one another, and, as it were, meet one another. Either the object alone must make the representation possible, or the representation alone must make the object possible" (A 92/B 124). Kant goes on to say that if the object

---

9. This is reminiscent of Frege's theory that a term designates its reference, or meaning (*Bedeutung*), in terms of its sense (*Sinn*) and that it is its sense that constitutes its content (*Inhalt*). It is thus its sense, or content, that provides for the term's designation of its reference, or meaning.

makes the representation possible, the "[B-]relation is only empirical, and the representation is never possible *a priori*." On the other hand, if the representation makes the object possible, "the representation is *a priori* determinant of the object, if it be the case that only through the representation is it possible to *know* anything *as an object*" (A 92/B 125). This is what today we might call an "epistemic possibility" (pertaining to something's being possible with respect to our knowledge of it) to distinguish it from an "ontological possibility," which in the same passage is indicated by Kant's remark about the *"existence"* of the object concerned.

If now we put these last remarks about the particular possibility that is connected to the *B*-relation together with the remarks about *content* that were made in the previous paragraph, we get the further proposition that the *possibility* that the intuition or concept of space and spatial objects have with respect to each other consists in the *content* of the intuition or of the concept. This proposition can be extended to cover, *mutatis mutandis,* the other a priori representations as well, that is, time and the categories.[10]

The category of causality provides another example of how *V*-relations determine *B*-relations. A manifold consisting of a temporal succession of representations can be *B*-related to an object (an appearance)—that is, the succession can be objective—only if the object is a priori *V*-related to an object that is thought as its cause. That is, a temporal succession of representations is an (objective) alteration of a substance, and not a passage of merely mental representations, only if the succession (the alteration) is a priori *V*-related to an object that is taken as its cause. But this a priori *V*-relation between an effect and its cause in turn entails that the manifold is transcendentally *V*-related to the concept of causality as material for the concept. The concept in turn must be transcendentally *V*-related to the understanding, which is the source of the concept, and to the understanding's transcendental unity of apperception, which is the means by which the manifold is united in the concept. Therefore, both the manifold of representations and the concept must stand in their respective transcendental *V*-relations, the former to the concept and, through the concept, to the understanding and its transcendental unity, and the latter, that is, the concept itself, to the same understanding and its transcendental unity, if the manifold is to be *B*-related to an object. Consequently, the manifold is *B*-related

10. We shall make use of these connections shortly, when we connect the present discussion with our underlying interest in the question of the defensible primary objective of Kant's theory of knowledge.

to an object (i.e., the succession is objective) only if it is transcendentally V-related through the concept to the same faculty of the mind to which the concept is also transcendentally V-related.[11]

The same form of analysis can be applied to the B-relation an empirical intuition has to an appearance. Such an intuition can be B-related only to an appearance whose manifold is determined according to the same spatial or temporal a priori V-relations that determine the intuition. But this entails that the manifold is transcendentally V-related to the mode of sensibility in which the manifold is given (space or time). And since the intuition must also be transcendentally V-related to the same mode of sensibility if it is to be an intuition of the appearance whose manifold is V-related in its terms, the intuition can therefore be B-related to the appearance.

This analysis entails something about the matter (sensations) of the empirical intuition, to which "corresponds," says Kant, the matter of the appearance, thereby indicating a distinction between the two "matters" (e.g., A 20/B 34). For their part, the sensations must also be V-related to the same mode of sensibility to which the appearance is V-related. But here Kant explicitly makes a distinction that has already been noted in regard to *empirical* V-relations. This is the distinction between two "constitutions" of one and the same mode of sensibility: the "objective a priori" (A 28/B 44) and the "subjective" empirical (B 44), the latter of which varies from observer to observer (A 30/B 45) "and is valid . . . only in [B-]relation to a particular standpoint or to a peculiarity of structure of this or that sense" (A 45/B 62). It is only the subjective constitution of the mode that is the source of the sensations. Nevertheless, even though the mode of sensibility itself (in its objective constitution) is not the source of sensations, unless sensations were V-related to it, they would *not* be "posited and ordered" in the form of the appearance in question (A 20/B 34). Rather, they would be V-related *only* to the senses; that is, they would not be V-related to "sensibility in general" and thus would not be "valid . . . in B-relation to sensibility in general." Kant initially expresses this point about the appearance's being subject to a form (of an object) by saying that "the form [of the appearance] must lie ready for the sensations a priori in the mind" (A 45/B 62). So, the sensations in the intuition are V-related to the same mode of sensibility to which the manifold of the appearance is transcendentally V-related. It is therefore this identical mode of sensibility to which both are V-related that accounts for the fact that sensations can be representations

11. For a fuller discussion of this issue, see Chapter 14, section II.

through which an empirical intuition is *B*-related to an appearance (A 19–20/B 34). Apart from intuition, however, and if accompanied by consciousness, sensations would instead be "[*B*-]related solely to the subject as the modification of its state" (A 320/B 376).

II

In the discussion of space above, I indicated that we can understand the particular Kantian concept of *possibility* that I have been concerned with in terms of the *B-relation* that obtains between an a priori representation or cognition and an object. In the same discussion I connected both a priori representation and object to the Kantian sense of *content* that I had just introduced with regard to the *V*-relation of intuition to a cognition. Now that we have examined the three levels (types) of *V*-relations and how *V*-relations determine *B*-relations, we can bring these two matters together. That is, we can now connect the results of our examination of Kant's *V*- and *B*-relations with the proposal, made in the course of that examination, that we understand a particular concept of *possibility* in terms of the *B-relation* of a representation or cognition to an object. The purpose of bringing them together now is to bring up to the present point in our investigations the issue with which the book began and to show how they jointly affect that issue. This is the issue of the proper identification of the defensible positive theory of knowledge that is contained in the *Critique*. Is it, following Strawson, only Kant's theory of the possibility of experience or, as I maintain, his more abstract theory of the possibility of our a priori knowledge of objects?

It has actually been in terms of this particular concept of possibility that I have been arguing from the beginning of the book that Kant is primarily concerned with the possibility of our a priori knowledge of objects, and not our empirical knowledge of objects. That is, it has been my contention that the primary theory of the *Critique* concerns the *B*-relation of our a priori knowledge to objects, and not the *B*-relation of experience to objects.

Those of us on *both* sides of the question recognize, I am presuming, that the critical question for Kant is both *whether* and *how* our knowledge of objects is possible, in the sense now specified in terms of the *B-relation* of knowledge to objects. Though we disagree about the nature of the knowledge whose possibility is primarily in question—they opting for our empirical knowledge, I for our a priori knowledge—I presume that we nonetheless both take Kant's main concern to be the necessary conditions of the possibility of the one type of knowledge or the other. And their view is that the respective possibilities of space, time, and the categories, and the a priori knowledge Kant claims can be derived from them, consist in their being at least necessary conditions of the possibility of experience: they are not themselves B-related to objects, but are B-related to them only insofar as they are necessary conditions for experience to be B-related to them. It is only as they constitute such conditions of possible experience that they themselves are possible, the customary view maintains. My view, on the other hand, takes issue with their view and holds that Kant is instead primarily interested in the B-relation these a priori representations and cognitions themselves have to objects, and hence that his concern is with the necessary conditions for that B-relation to obtain.

In either case, whether it is the customary view or my own, the question arises concerning the way in which anything can be (at least) a necessary condition of the possibility (in the now specified sense) of a representation or of a cognition (or of any other epistemological item designated above as (a)–(e)) with respect to objects. What is it for something to be such a condition of such a possibility? That is, how is such a condition so related to the item in question that the item is possible with respect to an object? If such conditions to a large extent consist of representations of objects, as I have from the start of these investigations indicated they are, then this question can be narrowed to how a representation can be so related to such items that they are thereby rendered possible with respect to objects. As the just concluded examination of how V-relations can determine B-relations should have demonstrated, the question can be answered in terms of these same V-relations. This brings the earlier results concerning Kant's theory of the possibility of knowledge up to where we presently stand in our interpretation of that theory.

III

We might now try to sketch a diagram that could serve as a template for the application of these explanations of B- and V-relations to my account of Kant's theory of knowledge, including both what has already been put forward and what will be offered in subsequent discussion.

```
R is ............................ V-related ............................ to S

   r                                                                      i
    e                                                                     s
     p
      r                                                                   B-
       e                                                                  r
        s                                                                 e
         e                                                                l
          n                                                               a
           t                                                              t
            s                                                             e
                                                                          d

                                                                          t
                                                                          o

                                                                          O
```

In the diagram above, I designate as "S" (to suggest its being in some sense a subject) such terms as (*a*) a representation, (*b*) a cognition, (*c*) a manifold of (*a*) or (*b*), (*d*) a subject of (*a*) or (*b*), or (*e*) a mental faculty of (*a*) or (*b*). These are the same terms, of course, with which we began this discussion. And to reiterate another point with which we started this discussion, a term to which an S can (be) *B*-relate(d), or refer(red), generally for Kant can include not just what he calls an object (by his use of either *Gegenstand* or *Objekt*) but also certain items that in a *different* context can also be designated as an S, namely, a representation, a cognition, or a subject or a faculty of either. Accordingly, in the above diagram I designate such a term when it occurs in the appropriate context as "O" (to suggest its being in some sense an object). That is, representations, cognitions, and subjects and faculties thereof can be taken by Kant as either subjects or as objects; but this should not present any great difficulty, since the context usually allows us to determine just which one it is. Finally, I designate as "R" a representation or, more generally, a condition, which can be *V*-related to a subject, S, as a determination of the *B*-relation that the subject can have to an object, O. In that capacity, representation can be said to *represent* the object to which a subject is *B-related,* and the object, in turn, can be said to be the object of the representation, in the sense that it is that which is represent*ed* through the representation. We can thus distinguish something's being an object of a representation that represents it from its being an object of some subject that is B-related to it.

IV

This model can be used to explain further the opposition between the customary view and interpretation of Kant's ontology and the view and interpretation that is presented here. The customary view, in taking the objects of the theory of the possibility of empirical knowledge to be identical with the objects of the knowledge itself, takes the *theory* (S) to be B-related to the same objects (O) to which the *empirical knowledge* (the S to be explained by the theory) is B-related. In both instances, the representations of space, time, or the categories (R) represent the objects (O) and are a priori V-related to the theory or to the knowledge. It is through these a priori V-relations of the representations to the knowledge that the knowledge is B-related to the objects. The customary interpretation, of course, is that these objects are appearances or, more particularly, empirical objects.

As I have already argued in Chapter 1, section v, in restricting the ontology of Kant's theory to things that exist in space and/or time, the customary view restricts space and time to just certain things that exist, that is, those that exist in space and time, and it lays down this restriction as soon as the theory tries to demonstrate that space and time are involved with things that exist. If existing things were not to exist in space and time, then the demonstration would fail, or at least would be merely conditional upon their existence. But that is just the sort of dependence on existence that Kant wants to avoid with his use of the a priori. The representations of space and time would thus lose their a priori properties of universality and necessity. In this manner the model of representation we are attributing to Kant can delineate a serious weakness in the customary view of his ontology.

The new *view*, on the other hand, in taking the objects of the theory of the possibility of a priori knowledge to be distinct from the objects of the knowledge itself takes the theory (S) to be B-related to objects (O) different from those to which the a priori knowledge (a different S, the one to be explained by the theory) is B-related (O). In the first place, space, time, and the categories neither represent these distinct objects nor are transcendentally V-related to the theory. The concept (R) that actually represents them and is transcendentally V-related to theory, and hence is that representation through which the theory is B-related to them, is the concept that is grounded in *transcendental affirmation,* namely, the concept of *reality,* or *being.* With respect to the objects to which the a priori knowledge is *B*-related, however, the representations of space, time, and the categories *do* represent them, and through their transcendental *V*-relation to that knowledge, the knowledge itself is *B*-related to them. The new *interpretation* of the ontology, as introduced in Chapter 2, is that the objects to which the *theory* is *B*-related are *things,* whereas the objects to which the *a priori knowledge* is *B*-related are *appearances* or, more particularly, *empirical objects.* This allows the a priori representations of space, time, and the categories and the a priori knowledge to which they give rise a certain independence from the things that exist, even after the representations get involved with things in the demonstration of their own possibility, and thus allows them (i.e., space, time, and the categories) to have the properties of universality and necessity.

The significance of the opposition between the customary view and interpretation and my own lies in something that has just been said but has not yet been sufficiently remarked upon in connection with the present discussion. According to the customary view and interpretation, the knowledge that is to be *B*-related to appearances or, more particularly, to empirical objects is *empirical knowledge,* and the representations or conditions that are to provide for that *B*-relation through their own *V*-relations to the empirical knowledge are, *inter alia,* the a priori representations of space, time, and the categories. According to the new view and interpretation, however, what is distinctive about *transcendental* "knowledge" is that it is only interested in the *B*-relation that these representations of space, time, and the categories themselves and the a priori knowledge to which they give rise (S) have, ultimately, to *empirical intuitions* (O). Since such intuitions are contained in experience, and since their objects are appearances, and since the objects of experience are empirical objects, transcendental "knowledge" also deals with the *B*-relations that these same a priori representations and their corresponding a priori knowledge have to *experience,* as well as to the objects of empirical intuitions, appearances, and, more particularly, to the objects of possible experience, that is, empirical objects. And the *B*-relations these a priori representations and knowledge have to empirical intuitions, experience, and so forth depend on the *transcendental V*-relations that *further* conditions have to these representations and knowledge. These further conditions consist of the two fundamental sources of representation or knowledge, sensibility and the understanding, and their respective means of representation or knowledge, outer and inner sense, on the one hand, and the transcendental unity of apperception, on the other.

So the difference between the customary and the new approaches to the *Critique* can be summed up as a difference in the node at which experience or, ultimately, empirical intuition is placed by each approach. The customary approach places it at the subject node (S), takes experience or empirical intuition to be merely *possible* by placing space and time and the categories at the representation node (R) (the two former, but not the latter, conditions are placed at that node if it is the possibility of empirical intuition alone that is in question), and finally places appearances and empirical objects at the object node (O). For *actual* experience or empirical intuition, the customary approach places *sensation* as well as these a priori representations at the representation node (R).

The new approach, however, ultimately places these a priori representations of space, time, and the categories—the *modes* of knowledge—along with the a priori knowledge to which they give rise, at the *subject* node (S) and relegates empirical intuitions and experience to the *object* node (O) to stand beside appearances and empirical objects at that node.

The customary approach allows appearances and empirical objects to stand on their own in Kant's ontology because it does not place space, time, and the categories and the apriori knowledge to which they give rise at the subject node, from which they or their corresponding knowledge are to be B-related to objects by *means* of outer and inner sense and the transcendental unity of apperception as well as through the originating conditions or *modes* of sensibility and the understanding, all of which are transcendentally V-related to them. The customary approach might be said to confine these a priori representations—these a priori *modes* of knowledge—to the same node (representation) to which the *new* approach assigns not just sensibility and the understanding but also their respective *means,* outer and inner sense and the transcendental unity of apperception.

To sum up the difference between the two approaches: The customary approach takes it to be *sufficient* for Kant's purposes that space, time, and the categories remain at the representation node as they stand in a priori V-relation to empirical knowledge, or experience, which stands at the subject node. This approach can thus be said to employ a concept of possibility *distinct* from that explained above in terms of the B-relation. Experience would now be *possible* in the distinct sense that space, time, and the categories would have an a priori V-relation to it. The possibility that experience would have with respect to *objects* (in terms of the B-relation) would now be determined by this distinct possibility. Consequently, when the customary view states that the possibility of these representations and their corresponding knowledge with respect to objects, that is, in terms of their *B*-relation to objects, consists in their being necessary conditions of the possibility, that is, *B*-relation, of *experience* to objects, they are actually thinking of the a priori *V*-relation that these representations and their knowledge have to *experience*. So, at bottom, what they mean by the possibility of these representations and their knowledge is that they are a priori *V*-related to experience as necessary conditions of the possibility of experience, where only the latter possibility is to be understood in terms of the *B*-relation to objects.

The new approach, however, takes it to be *necessary* for Kant's purposes that these representations and their knowledge be located at the *subject* node and that experience be relegated to the *object* node. According to the new approach, their possibility can thus be understood in terms of their *B*-relation, and not just their transcendental *V*-relation, to experience. To rephrase the point, experience itself can be said to be *possible* in terms of the *B*-relation that obtains between it and these representations and their knowledge, where experience is the *object* of this *B*-relation, and not just in terms of the distinct concept of possibility, namely that which is understood in terms of the a priori *V*-relation that experience has to these representations and their knowledge.

Perhaps the difference can be given in a word: the customary approach just does not sufficiently recognize the distinction between the two types of relation—the *V*-relation and the *B*-relation—at least not in the way that I understand it, and hence has no use for the model of the theory of representation attributed to Kant in this book. To put it another way, the customary approach does not adequately distinguish between a representation's *representing* an object and its being *B-related to* it. Keeping the distinction between the two types of relation as sharp as possible can thus be seen as one way of keeping the corresponding distinction between representing an object and being *B*-related to an object alive in the theory.

PART 2

TRANSCENDENTAL
ONTOLOGY

INTERPRETATION OF TEXT; THEORY AND VIEW

I

This examination of the relative merits of the customary and the new ap-proaches to Kant's transcendental epistemology can now continue in a more substantive vein. Nonetheless, we will continue to follow the model, laid out in the last chapter, of what I consider to be Kant's theory of representa-tion. In this return to a substantive interest in Kant's theory, we will first be confining our attention to his transcendental ontology. After that, we will deal with his transcendental logic.

With regard to his ontology, we will in this chapter first examine several passages that seem not to allow substitution of the terms preferred by the customary approach, namely "appearance" or, more particularly, "empiri-cal object," for the terms Kant actually employs, at least in these passages, if not in others as well, for certain objects he says we can intuit or know. In any case, neither "appearance" nor "empirical object" (nor, for that matter, "thing in itself") is substitutable for the term or terms he does use in the passages in question. So Kant, at least in these passages, is clearly referring to objects that cannot be designated as appearances or as empirical objects (or as things in themselves). Such objects seem to demand a place in Kant's ontology whose importance or centrality is commensurate with that of the passages in question.

In addition, this chapter concludes with some further theoretical consideration in support of the view that Kant's ontology must be distinct from the a priori conditions of possible experience.

II

Kant's own, presumably legitimate talk of things in themselves suggests an initial problem for the appearance or the empirical object. This problem concerns the distinction between the inherence of something in an object that is *independent* of us or of the subject and the inherence of something else that is only *in* us or only *in* the subject.[1] First, many passages make it clear that the "qualities" (*Beschaffenheiten*) Kant says *belong* to the appearance or the empirical object are, according to his transcendental idealism, actually inherent only in us or in the subject (e.g., A 26/B 42 [b], A 32/B 49 [a], B 164–65, *et passim*).[2] In two places, at least, though Kant explicitly

---

1. This way of putting the question automatically rules out the so-called neglected alternative, namely, that the "something" might be inherent in both the object and in us or the subject. The problem of the "neglected alternative" is considered further below, in connection with criticisms of the views of Allison and Guyer (see Chapter 6).

2. I use the term "quality" for Kant's *Beschaffenheit,* instead of "property," which Kemp Smith tends to use but which I think should be reserved for Kant's *Eigenschaft,* which seems to connote for Kant something intrinsic to that which is said to have it (see Chapter 7). Thus, since space, time, and the categories are not intrinsic to the appearance or the empirical object, but are rather in us or in the subject, they are "qualities" of the object (e.g., B 45, B 69, B 70). On the other hand, Kant speaks of "properties" of things in themselves (A 26/B 42, A 36/B 52), of space (B 40), and of the mind (A 22/B 37). Hilary Putnam discusses this distinction between extrinsic "qualities" and intrinsic "properties," to use my terms for the distinction, in order to cast doubt on the view that we are ever in a position to ascribe the latter to objects. That, he says, would be the view, in Kantian terms, that we can ascribe "properties" to things in themselves. See his *Many Faces of Realism* (La Salle, Ill.: Open Court, 1987), 8–9 *et passim.*

It should be noted, however, that Kant uses the same term, *Gesetzmäßigkeit,* "conformity to law," with respect to both things in themselves and all appearances in space and time (B 164–65). Perhaps the connection is that the latter is identified with "a nature in general," which signifies "[the] categories as the original ground of its [i.e., the nature's] necessary conformity to law," which in turn must signify independence from sensibility (B 144), since that is how the categories are introduced into the first step of the second-edition Transcendental Deduction. Since independence from sensibility is also the distinctive feature of things in themselves, conformity to law obtains in both cases under one and the same condition, namely, independence from sensibility. That he uses the same term in both cases may very well signify that it is the identical condition in both cases.

says of "the form of the intuition" that, "nevertheless, it belongs really and necessarily to the appearance" (A 38/B 55) or that it "must of necessity belong to the [object] itself" (A 48/B 65), he still considers it inherent only in us. In still other passages, in connection with this difference between extrinsic qualities and intrinsic properties, Kant cannot be referring to the appearance or the empirical object when he says such things as

(1) things are viewed from this twofold standpoint (B xix n);
(2) our representation of things, as they are given to us, does not conform to these things as they are in themselves (B xx);
(3) This predicate [space] can be ascribed to things only in so far as they appear to us (A 27/B 43);
(4) [Time] has objective validity only in respect of appearances, these being things which we take as *objects of our senses* (A 34–35/B 51);
(5) the categories, as yielding knowledge of *things,* have no kind of application, save only in regard to things which may be objects of possible experience (B 148).

To make the point explicitly: (1) there is no legitimate twofold standpoint with respect to the appearance or the empirical object—it is only legitimately viewed from the standpoint at which the "qualities" (*Beschaffenheiten*) in question are said to be inherent in us or in the subject; (2) there is no legitimate way to speak of the appearance or the empirical object as it is in itself; (3) there is no significance in *explicitly restricting* the ascription of space to the appearance or the empirical object "in so far as [it] appear[s] to us," since appearing to us belongs to the very concept of the appearance or the empirical object; (4) there is no sense in *explicitly restricting* the objective validity of time to appearances or empirical objects "which we take as objects of our senses," since, again, it is part of the very concept of the appearance (of things other than oneself) or the empirical object that it is an object of our senses; and (5) there is no sense in *explicitly restricting* the categories to our knowledge of the appearance or the empirical object, since, again, it is part of the concept of the appearance or the empirical object (in this context) that it is an object of experience. To sum up this first round of exegetical argumentation: I should add that it makes just as much sense to take Kant to be referring to things in themselves in such passages as (1)–(5) as it does to maintain that he is talking about the appearance or the empirical object. Therefore, we need a concept of an object that is distinct from both the concept of an appearance (and the empirical object) and that of the thing in itself if we are to make sense of such passages.

The same problem regarding the distinction between extrinsic qualities and intrinsic properties applies to the following putative substitution:

> (6) [space] must be regarded as the condition of the possibility of appearances (A 24/B 39),

but,

> (7) [s]ince we cannot treat the special conditions of sensibility as conditions of the possibility of things, but only of their appearances (A 27/B 43),

we can conclude that "appearances" cannot be substituted for "things" in (7).

Kant's further talk about this distinction between the extrinsic and the intrinsic presents additional difficulties for the appearance or the empirical object. He says:

> (8) Are they [i.e., space and time] only determinations or relations of things, yet such as would belong to things even if they were not intuited? (A 23/B 37)

To make the point explicitly: how can Kant significantly ask about the possibility of space and time belonging to the empirical object "even if [it] were not intuited"? It is a fundamental tenet of his idealism that space and time belong to the empirical object only if it is an object of our intuition (e.g., A 26/B 42, A 27/B 43, A 33/B 49, *et passim*). So we cannot substitute "the empirical object" for "things" in (8).

III

Shifting to another problem encountered by the appearance or the empirical object, we can ask, how does either object fare when Kant speaks of our *removing* sensations from our concept of an object? In a second-edition substitution in the introduction to the *Critique* Kant does speak of removing sensations "from our *empirical* concept of a body":

> (9) If we remove from [it], one by one, every feature in it which is empirical, the color, the hardness or softness, the weight, even the impenetrability, there still remains the space which the body (now entirely vanished) occupied, and this cannot be removed. (B 5)

He immediately goes on to say,

> (10) [I]f we remove from our empirical concept of any object, corporeal or incorporeal, all properties which experience has taught us, we cannot take away that property through which the object is thought as substance or as inhering in a substance.[3] (B 6)

If it is the appearance or the empirical object in (9) and (10), the removal of sensation from its *empirical* concept leaves no object at all for *transcendental* consideration, and hence no object for a corresponding *transcendental* concept; instead, only space and a category remain.[4] In the Aesthetic, Kant makes the same point with respect to just the concepts of space and of time. He there says that abstracting from "a particular standpoint or . . . a peculiarity of structure in this or that sense," which is to abstract the *empirical* content from a concept, leaves only "sensibility in general," and thus the a priori concepts of space and of time, without any "transcendental" rela-

---

3. It might be noticed that Kant here speaks of "properties" (*Eigenschaften*), which I noted just above he pointedly refrains from ascribing to the appearance or the empirical object. The contention still stands, however. There is an important difference between his discussion of objects here and the discussion addressed above, which occurs elsewhere in the *Critique*. Here, it is the empirical concept of an object Kant is talking about; but in the previous passages, it was the transcendental concept of an object that was under discussion, whether the object was referred to as a thing or as an appearance. Only with respect to the object under the transcendental concept would I maintain that Kant refrains from using "properties" (*Eigenschaften*) and uses instead what has been translated here as "qualities," namely, *Beschaffenheiten*. It is my contention that it is only with respect to the transcendental concept of the object that Kant wants to distinguish between us or the subject and the object. As far as the empirical concept of the object is concerned, it need only be said that he is not interested in such a distinction, since the distinction there is between appearances and reality in the empirical senses of those terms (cf. B 45, A 45–46/B 62–63).

4. See section vi below for further understanding of what I take to be the sense in which Kant employs the distinction between an empirical and a transcendental concept of an object.

tion to any object (A 45–46/B 62–63). Similarly, if the "subjective constitution [*Beschaffenheit*] of the senses in general [were] removed" from our concept of "the things which we intuit," he says,

(11) the whole constitution [*Beschaffenheit*] and all the relations of objects in space and time, nay, space and time themselves, would vanish. As appearances, they cannot exist in themselves, but only in us. What objects may be in themselves . . . remains completely unknown to us. (A 42/B 59)

So the absence of content from the *appearance*, considered in the Aesthetic under *both* its empirical *and* its transcendental concepts, leaves Kant with no object at all to speak of.

However, the absence of all *empirical* content from his *transcendental* concept of a *thing* does not keep him from speaking of *things*—they do not just "vanish." For example, when referring to the part of metaphysics that needs no special defense, namely, the analytic part, he speaks of concepts that we make for ourselves a priori of things (B 18). And when he is drawing a contrast between the empirical and "the transcendental concept of appearances," he says that "space is not a form which belongs as a property to things; but that objects are quite unknown to us in themselves" (A 30/B 45, Meiklejohn trans.).[5] Since all sensation has been removed from these a priori concepts, and since Kant continues to speak of certain objects, what remain after the removal of all sensation are not just the a priori concepts but those objects as well—the *things*. And if the a priori concepts of space and of time are removed as well, Kant still speaks of these objects.

IV

The same points are repeated when Kant removes the categories from our concept of things (as distinct from the concept of things in themselves):

(12) [A]ppearances are only representations of things which are unknown as regards what they may be in themselves. As mere

5. Immanuel Kant, *Critique of Pure Reason*, trans. J. M. D. Meiklejohn (New York: Willey Book Co., 1943; originally published 1855), 28.

> representations, they are subject to no law of connection save
> that which the connecting faculty prescribes. (B 164)

Here there is still talk of things, even apart from the "connecting faculty."
And though there can be talk of the appearance or the empirical object apart
from that faculty, that is, apart from the understanding, it definitely cannot
be appearances or empirical objects to which Kant is referring as "things"
here in (12). Appearances cannot be "only representations" of appearances:
appearances *are* appearances, and similarly with respect to empirical objects. Finally, it also makes no sense, of course, to substitute "things in themselves" for "things" in (12), since appearances cannot represent things in
themselves. If they could, we could have knowledge of things in themselves—as appearances. But we cannot have any knowledge of things in
themselves.

To sum up, when all sensation is removed from the *empirical* concept of
an object, what remain are only the a priori conditions of space, time, and
the categories, but not the objects of such conditions, and therefore no object of a *transcendental* concept. Moreover, when all reference to sensation
is removed from the *transcendental* concept of an object, not only do these
a priori conditions remain, but so do the objects themselves, that is, things;
we just cannot know what they are in themselves. Finally, when these a
priori conditions themselves are removed from the *transcendental* concept
of a thing, all that remains is the thing itself. But so far, the question regarding *its* properties or the conditions of its own possibility has not yet arisen.
If it does, it ceases to be designated a thing *simpliciter* and is rather called *a
thing in itself*. This object cannot be known at all.

V

In this investigation of the difficulties presented by the appearance or the
empirical object as the interpretation of Kant's ontology, we have yet to
recognize a quite simple, yet fundamental difficulty it poses in the passages
in which Kant speaks of empirical objects as "mere appearances" or "mere
representations" of objects. What are the objects that these are appearances
or representations of? What are the objects that appear? Furthermore, what
are the objects that are also to be viewed, let us remember, as things in
themselves as well as appearances?

If in answer to the first two questions those who adopt the customary interpretation say "the appearances or the empirical objects themselves," and if the answer to the last question is simply that they are not to be viewed as things in themselves at all, then the simple, yet fundamental question arises, why does Kant call appearances or empirical objects "appearances" and "mere representations"? Why then does he pronounce their a priori conditions "subjective," "in us," or "in the subject" and tell us to view certain objects and not others as "things in themselves"? In light of such further fundamental questions, these answers make *wholly* perplexing most of what Kant actually says about his transcendental idealism that is of significance and that has made his views both so controversial and difficult to understand.

VI

To conclude the objections to appearances or empirical objects as the objects in Kant's ontology, we can refer to a notorious group of passages dealing with Kant's theory of affection (e.g., A 19–20/B 33–34, B 41, A 26/B 42, B 129). These are supposed to cause insuperable problems for Kant, eventuating for many commentators in a so-called theory of "double affection."[6] With respect to these passages, the problems of interpretation

6. Moltke S. Gram makes much of the difficulties involved in such a theory, in his "Myth of the Double Affection," in *Reflections on Kant's Philosophy*, ed. W. H. Werkmeister (Gainsville: University Presses of Florida, 1975), 29–69. Charles Parsons, too, alerts us to its pitfalls, since they may be implicit in any theory, including Kant's, that takes space and time to be entirely subjective, and thus to be forms we impose on things, and therefore a theory that is "causal" in character; "The Transcendental Aesthetic," in *The Cambridge Companion to Kant*, ed. Paul Guyer (Cambridge: Cambridge University Press, 1992), 89 and 100 n. 63. In "Things in Themselves," *Proceedings and Addresses of the American Philosophical Association 57*, no. 1, (1983): 42, the late Manley Thompson, while dissociating himself from certain unpalatable views he finds in Kant, posts the following warning: "I want to present what I regard as the best face of Kant's epistemology." Thompson, also, seems to be avoiding attributing to the "good face" of Kant a "causal theory" of knowledge, one reason for which, he once told me in correspondence, is his concern about possible entanglements in a theory of "double affection."
   Allison, for one, claims to avoid the pitfalls of the theory by means of his interpretation of Kant's idealism as "methodological" idealism, " 'critical' agnosticism," or "purely logical" idealism; *Kant's Transcendental Idealism: An Interpretation and Defense* (New Haven: Yale University Press, 1983), 250 and 254. Since on this interpretation Kant makes no ontological commitment to things in themselves, there is no implication regarding the objective reality or existence of such a set of "entities" whose effects on us would have to be distinguished from those of empirical objects. It is also clear that Allison's interpretation does not address the

arise, not from trying to substitute "appearances" or "empirical objects" for "things," but from having to keep *separate* two distinct objects, both of which affect us or affect the subject: the appearance or the empirical object and the thing in itself. This "double affection" results in double effects upon us or upon the subject, and the problems that ensue concern the sorting out of these effects into a coherent, intelligible, and plausible theory.

The solution to these problems provided by the interpretation of Kant's ontology offered here is that a strict distinction should be kept between the transcendental and the empirical concepts of objects. With respect to transcendental concepts, it is only things and things in themselves that affect us or affect the subject, not empirical objects or appearances. The latter are "mere representations," which can have no effect on us or the subject. Accordingly, we or the subject can know only the things that affect us or the subject. That is, the objects of our empirical cognition, again under the transcendental concept of such objects' being "mere representations," cannot be said to affect us or the subject whatsoever. So there is no "double affection" here. With respect to the empirical concepts of objects, the situation is quite different. For example, we are affected by things, not their appearances; and it is things that we know, not their appearances. So far, the situation is just like the transcendental context. But in the empirical context, the objects of knowledge *can* be said to be the things that affect us, since now they are not "mere representations," and, on the other hand, the appearances can*not* be said to be the objects of knowledge, for they are subjective in an empirical sense (A 28–30/B 45, B 69–70, B 69 n). Nor do they have any effect on us, since they are the effect on us of things conceived in the empirical sense of the term. So again, now with respect to our empirical concepts of objects, there is no "double affection." Therefore, Kant can speak in distinct contexts, transcendental and empirical, of our being affected, respectively, by things thought transcendentally and by things thought empirically, that is, material things. There is no danger of his being ensnared in a theory of "double affection" when engaging in either type of thought, transcendental or empirical, provided he keeps the two types of thought separate.

In conclusion, appearances or empirical objects seem unlikely candidates for the objects to which Kant refers in the passages selected above. And, of course, the thing in itself would not do at all. Things, on the other hand,

---

specific objects that affect us, which are being proposed here as the constituents of Kant's ontology, namely, things *simpliciter* in contrast to things in themselves.

seem a much neater fit. This conclusion supports both the negative and positive claims of this book regarding the proper interpretation of Kant's ontology.[7]

VII

In Chapter 1, I argued that our representations that are a priori, whether intuitions (space and time) or concepts (the categories), have two properties in common. They are a priori only if they represent objects regardless of (1) which ones in fact exist and (2) which ones specifically and in particular are given and thereby provide the material that can be said to "realize" the representations. In this concluding section, however, I examine an opposition between the two sets of representations, with a view toward the implications it has for Kant's ontology.

Whereas our a priori intuitions do *not* extend over objects of intuition in general, the categories do have such an extension. Space and time do not extend over objects of (*a*) the understanding alone or (*b*) a sensible intuition in general, whether like ours or not, in which case the extension would *not* depend on the subject's being affected by the object for the object to be given to the subject (A 19/B 33). The categories, on the other hand, *do* extend over objects of intuition in general (A 79/B 105), and hence over objects of (*b*) above. Whether that generality extends as far as objects of the understanding alone, (*a*), is arguable, and a note to B 166 and remarks in the Amphiboly support the idea that they do extend that far.[8]

This opposition between space and time and the categories suggests that they have opposite implications for Kant's ontology. Since space and time are restricted to sensible intuitions that are at least like, if not actually identical to, ours in the relevant respect just mentioned and the categories are not so restricted, we have grounds for taking space and time as extrinsic conditions on objects that are distinct from them, and hence objects that are distinct from us as subjects of such intuitions. It is this distinctness of objects from our a priori intuition that, *inter alia*, entails that Kant's ontology must consist of objects that are distinct from space and time.

The categories get a very different treatment. As representations or cognitions that are themselves *B*-related to objects through intuitions, or as ele-

---

7. See, in Chapter 7, further considerations dividing the two sets of representations.
8. That they do so extend is argued in Chapter 8.

ments of our knowledge of objects, they determine the objects only through our intuitions of the objects. Since we have just concluded that the objects of Kant's ontology must be distinct from our intuitions, the same objects must also be distinct from the categories insofar as the latter depend on our intuitions.[9]

But as elements of our *transcendental* "knowledge" of the possibility of our a priori knowledge, they *can* determine objects apart from our intuitions. As the objects of such categorial determinations, things are objects of transcendental propositions. The concept of these objects is the subject-concept of such propositions, and the categories are the predicate-concepts. Since this subject-concept does not contain the predicate-concepts, it can be said to be distinct from these predicate-concepts, and the propositions of transcendental "knowledge" can be said to be "synthetic." Consequently, the objects of such propositions are, in the sense in question, distinct from the categories. The concept of the objects that can be thus determined, how-ever, is the *same* concept that is distinct, in the sense already explained, from our *intuitions* as well. That is, the same objects can be determined by the categories through our intuitions or apart from them. Consequently, the objects must be distinct from both our intuitions and the categories, in the respective senses in question.

This concludes all the theoretical considerations in support of the view that Kant's ontology must be distinct, in the respective senses in question, from the a priori conditions of possible experience—space, time, and the categories. It provides grounds not only for criticism of the customary view in general but for acceptance of the new view offered in Chapters 1, 2, and 4. But the new view challenges not just the customary view in general. It challenges also, and more specifically, the two particular mutually contra-dictory versions of the customary view—the monistic and the dualistic ver-sions mentioned in Chapter 2, section III. One reason to adopt the new view, I argued, is that it has an advantage that the two versions of the cus-tomary view cannot possibly enjoy, namely, the capacity to resolve the issue that divides them. It is now time to turn attention to that issue in order to see just what, in detail, I am recommending we put aside in favor of the view propounded here.

---

9. See Chapter 8, section II, for further discussion of this point.

MONISM OR DUALISM?

I

For quite different reasons both versions of the customary approach would contend that the customary view is quite adequate to deal with the propositions I have been contending entail that for Kant the objects we can intuit or know must be distinct from the three fundamental modes of possible experience—space, time, and the categories. The difference between the two versions stems from their opposite interpretations of Kant's transcendental idealism.

II

The first version, represented by Allison,[1] contends that our arguments for the distinctness of Kant's ontology from the modes of possible experience draws an erroneous ontological conclusion from merely epistemological premises. All that the distinctness of things from our modes of knowledge— which Allison calls "epistemic conditions"—amounts to is Kant's *method-*

---

1. Allison receives further extended critical discussion in Chapters 7, 11, and 13.

ological admonition not to consider appearances or empirical objects apart from the modes of our knowledge of them, that is, not to take them as things in themselves.[2] After all, Kant elsewhere does admonish us not to ask whether the empirical object represents a thing in itself (A 45–46/B 62–63)[3] and also not to take it as a thing in itself (e.g., A 490–91/B 518–19).[4] Kant's ontology indeed consists of a single set of entities that he calls "things," as I am proposing here, but according to Allison they are not distinct from our modes of empirical knowledge, but rather are identical with the objects of experience or possible experience. They are empirical objects.[5] Thus, like the approach advocated here, this version of the customary view holds that Kant's ontology consists of a single set of objects and that Kant calls them "things." But unlike my view of Kant's ontology, yet quite in keeping with the customary view of it, this view holds that things are not distinct from the modes of our empirical knowledge of them and thus are to be interpreted as empirical objects.

The differences between this monistic version of the customary view of Kant's ontology and that presented here can be illustrated by their contrasting interpretations of the following two passages from the *Critique*.

(1) The transcendental concept of appearances in space ... is a critical reminder that nothing intuited in space is a thing in itself. (A 30/B 45)

(2) [T]he things which we intuit are not in themselves what we intuit them as being. (A 42/B 59)

In neither of these passages can we who adopt the new interpretation proposed here let "the empirical object" or "the appearance" be the gram-

---

2. Strawson may have been the first to dub this as an "anodyne" interpretation of Kant's idealism. *Bounds of Sense*, 38. It was later picked up by Guyer, *Kant and the Claims of Knowledge* (Cambridge: Cambridge University Press, 1987), 338. It is immediately apparent that the very framework of Allison's entire interpretation of Kant's transcendental idealism makes it impossible for him to account for Kant's theory of the possibility of our a priori knowledge of *distinct* objects. It is a fundamental proposition of Allison's framework that the objects we can know must be thought through his "epistemic conditions." Consequently, he makes it impossible to provide a coherent account of Kant's theory of the possibility of our a priori knowledge of objects that are thought separately from those conditions.

3. On my view of things, it only represents a thing.

4. Allison is among those who call our attention to such admonitions; *Kant's Transcendental Idealism: An Interpretation and Defense* (New Haven: Yale University Press, 1983), 15–16.

5. But see the Annotated Bibliography above for Allison's more recent, but unfortunately more confusing, interpretation of "thing," according to which it—the identical object—*is both* an empirical object and the transcendental object, which is clearly impossible.

matical object of the verb or of the participle, but those who adopt this anodyne version of the customary view can. In (1) the new interpretation cannot substitute "no appearance" for "nothing," but the "anodyne" interpretation of Kant's idealism can. With respect to (2), according to my interpretation of Kant's ontology, it makes no sense for Kant to say that the empirical object is not in itself what we intuit it as being, but, again, the "anodyne" interpretation can give such a reading of the passage.

Allison's version of the customary view contains certain difficulties that are distinct from its divergence from the particular view of Kant's ontology urged here. The merely "methodological" distinction of Allison's has been criticized by, among others, Aquila, Guyer, and Walker for failing to explain why such conditions as space, time, and the categories cannot be conditions of both our knowledge of objects and the objects themselves.[6] It is thus alleged that Allison has not said enough to exclude this well-known "neglected alternative" to Kant's transcendental idealism.

However well grounded this criticism of Allison's position seems to be, it apparently has not yet taken into any detailed account the fact that Allison has explicitly rejected the "neglected alternative." So it is incumbent on those of us who are his critics to provide a response to the considerations Allison put forward as the basis of his conclusion.

His rejection of the alternative is based on a later distinction of his between "a property that only pertains to things in virtue of their being represented in a particular way and one that pertains to things as they are independently of being represented at all" (113).[7] Earlier, he made a related distinction between "forms of intuition." They either involve "an explicit reference to mind" or do not involve it (106–7). The question for Allison to answer now is how his earlier distinction between "epistemic conditions" and conditions belonging to objects themselves can be understood in terms of this later distinction between dependence on a particular way of repre-

6. Richard E. Aquila, *Representational Mind* (Bloomington: Indiana University Press, 1983), 84–86, 88–93, and 106–7, where Aquila apparently anticipates Guyer's objection to Allison concerning Kant's actual argument(s) for transcendental idealism. In a note to page 86 Aquila mentions Allison by name, and the interpretation of Kant's transcendental idealism that he is criticizing he calls the "double aspect" interpretation, which is the name commonly given to the interpretation Allison subscribes to. Guyer, *Kant and the Claims of Knowledge*, 336–42. Ralph C. S. Walker, review of Allison's *Kant's Transcendental Idealism, Philosophical Quarterly*, April 1988, 258.

7. Parenthetical page references included in the body of this section of the chapter are references to Allison's book, *Kant's Transcendental Idealism*. These are to be distinguished, of course, from my continuing references in the body of the chapter to the *Critique* itself.

senting objects and independence of representation altogether? That is, why should any particular way of representing objects be a condition of our knowledge of objects but not of the objects themselves? A similar question pertaining to the related distinction mentioned just above is, why should conditions of knowledge involve an explicit reference to mind but not an explicit reference to the objects that are known, considered independently of the mind? Allison seems in no better position to answer these questions than he was to answer the earlier questions.

Besides these questions, there are internal difficulties in Allison's actual formulation of his position. When he first introduces his concept of an epistemic condition, he characterizes it as "necessary for the representation of an object or an objective state of affairs" (10). (His later rejection of the "neglected alternative" thus actually amounts to a partial converse of this initial characterization of the distinction he is looking for. That is, the later distinction is based on the idea that a particular way of representing objects is necessary for something to be an "epistemic condition," whereas the initial idea is that an "epistemic condition" is necessary for representing objects.) He cannot leave his initial characterization at that, however, since concepts of objects as things in themselves, which are concepts of reason, are also necessary for representing objects (A 320/B 376), and indeed are necessary for representing objects "in a particular way," to use Allison's own expression for the later characterization of the distinction. Actually, since these concepts of reason represent objects "as they are independently of their being represented at all" (again, Allison's own terminology), we lose the difference on which Allison depends in his rejection of the "neglected alternative." That is, these concepts of reason are concepts that represent objects as independent of being represented altogether, which is a particular way of representing objects after all!

Allison initially tried to protect himself against objections to his concept of epistemic conditions by speaking of them as conditions that provide "that our representations" possess "objective reality" or "relate to objects" (10). Objections remain, however. First, Allison's reliance on Kant's use of "objective reality" cannot bear the weight of the argument, since the categories in particular, which for Allison are epistemic conditions, do not by themselves provide representations with "objective reality." For example, the so-called first step of the second edition of the Transcendental Deduction of the categories asserts that they are necessary for the unity of a sensible intuition in general, but it definitely does not assert that any unitary intuition thereby has "objective reality" (B 143). Sensibility is required for that, and it is not introduced into the Deduction until B 150.

With respect to providing our representations with their *B*-relation to objects, Allison's reference to such a relation is still not enough to distinguish between the epistemic conditions he has in mind—space, time, and the categories (10)—and what he calls "ontological conditions," by which he means "conditions of the possibility of the being of things," where "the being of things is here contrasted with their being known" (11). For Kant sometimes speaks of a "transcendental" "[*B*-]relation of the representation to the object," where the object, too, is "transcendental" (A 46/B 63). Since Allison's epistemic conditions must be excluded from this transcendental *B*-relation, a mere *B*-relation to an object cannot distinguish between these conditions and his "ontological conditions." And this is not the only place at which Kant speaks of such a *B*-relation in the absence of Allison's epistemic conditions. In the chapter on phenomena and noumena, for example, Kant speaks of such a *B*-relation in the "transcendental employment" of a concept in a principle in which the concept is *B*-related "to things in general and in themselves" (A 238/ B 298).

Furthermore, Kant also says that intuition is *empirical* if it "is in [*B*-]relation to the object through sensation" (A 20/B 34, my emphasis). Yet Allison noticeably omits sensations from his list of epistemic conditions. Moreover, in distinguishing his interpretation of Kant from Bennett's phenomenalistic interpretation, Allison states that it is the "Analogies of Experience, that is, . . . a set of a priori principles or intellectual conditions," that serve as "a criterion . . . of actuality" (33). So, epistemic conditions for Allison seem to be limited to a priori conditions. And Allison makes this explicit when he restricts epistemic conditions to conditions that "must reflect the cognitive structure of the mind (its manner of representation)" (27), assuming, of course, that conditions reflecting such a structure must be a priori. Consequently, since an empirical intuition is *B*-related to an object through sensation, being that through which a representation is *B*-related to an object is too broad a concept for Allison's purposes.

Allison also offers us the difference between epistemic conditions and " 'logical conditions of thought,'—for example, the principle of contradiction" (10)—to explain the distinction he has in mind. But neither concepts of reason for things in themselves nor sensations for states of the subject are themselves such "logical conditions of thought," though it is only such logical conditions of thought that determine the possibility of these concepts of

reason (B xxvi n). If we now eliminate sensations on the previously discussed grounds that seemed to establish that epistemic conditions must be a
priori, we might proceed to distinguish between the logical and the nonlogical a priori conditions of representation, where by "logical" is meant the
logic belonging to formal, or what Kant calls "general," logic. Thus, to get
the distinction he needs, Allison would have to rely on the distinction between transcendental and general logic.

This would seem to do the trick, and it must be close to, if not identical
with, what Allison actually has in mind. Of course, it depends on the work
involved in Kant's distinction between formal, or general, logic and transcendental logic, but it is not my intention to address the question of Allison's success on that score here.[8]

The problem with the formulation just reached is that it leaves Allison
without grounds for his rejection of the "neglected alternative." That is, he
cannot explain why conditions of knowledge cannot be satisfied by objects
that are independent of the mind, since the formulation now contains no
"explicit reference to the mind," no reflection of its "cognitive structure,"
to the exclusion of how things are independently of the mind. There is now
no apparent reason to assert that nonlogical formal conditions cannot be
satisfied both by objects in relation to the mind and by objects that are
independent of the mind.

Perhaps the reason for Allison's apparent failure to motivate Kant's distinction between appearances and things in themselves, a distinction according to which the epistemic conditions cannot be satisfied by things in
themselves, is that Allison thinks the reality to which his identical objects
belong is empirical reality. Why should—indeed, how can—Kant take empirical objects, or appearances, as the identical objects to be viewed in a
twofold manner belonging to his transcendental idealism?

Kant actually addresses this question and provides the basis for an answer
in the negative, and his comments are especially instructive for our purposes. In at least one place he does indeed speak of "two sides" to "appearance" (A 38/B 55). But the two sides to appearance are not the two views
of the object Kant speaks of here and elsewhere. Indeed, in the passage
indicated, it is clear that the object is not "appearance," since Kant speaks
of viewing the object "without regard to the mode of intuiting it," which
Kant himself could not coherently do with respect to "appearance."

There is, of course, the well-known passage in the Aesthetic in which

8. The distinction is critically discussed in Chapter 9.

Kant does speak of appearances as things in themselves, but as has often been noted, he is there speaking of these things in themselves as objects of "the empirical understanding" (A 29/B 45), and thus as distinct from the objects of transcendental knowledge. These things in themselves are what today would be called objects of scientific realism—the objects of physical theory minus the phenomenal properties we predicate of things through sensation.[9]

Finally, in the same passage, Kant speaks of "the transcendental concept of appearances" and asserts that "nothing intuited in space is a thing [*Sache*] in itself," that is, denies that space is a form "inhering in things [*Dinge*]" (substitution of Meiklejohn's "things" for Kemp Smith's "things in themselves").[10] This indicates we might rather look for the identical objects of Kant's transcendental distinction not in his transcendental concept of empirical objects, or appearances, but in his transcendental concept of a distinct object, which here, as well as elsewhere, I have of course been arguing, Kant gives the technical name of "thing." This will, I think, provide us with the grounds that are missing from Allison's unsuccessful attempt to motivate Kant's transcendental idealism. But before we proceed, we owe our representative of the *dualists* among the so-called customary commentators on Kant's idealism a critique of his own.

III

To represent the dualistic customary interpretation of Kant's ontology, I have chosen Paul Guyer,[11] whose work on this topic is prominently featured in the current literature. According to Guyer's version, Kant's dualism consists in his distinction between "things like tables and chairs and our *representations* of them. . . . to deny that the things we ordinarily assume are spatial and temporal really are so, all he has to do is *transfer* spatiality and temporality from objects to our *representations* of them or *confine* asser-

9. Margaret D. Wilson proposes that we interpret Kant's transcendental concept of the empirical object in just this way, namely, as the material object *sans* qualities of sensation. See her "Phenomenalisms of Berkeley and Kant," in *Self and Nature in Kant's Philosophy*, ed. Allen W. Wood (Ithaca: Cornell University Press, 1984), 170.

10. Immanuel Kant, *Critique of Pure Reason*, trans. J. M. D. Meiklejohn (New York: Willey Book Co., 1943; originally published 1855), 28.

11. Guyer will receive further extended critical discussion in Chapters 7 and 12.

tions of spatiality and temporality to the latter" (335).[12] This "transfer" is necessary, Guyer contends, if Kant is to "assume" that we know a priori that the objects we perceive are necessarily subject to space, time, and the categories. This necessity, Guyer contends, is "absolute" and not "conditional." For example, it would be the judgment that perceived objects are necessarily spatial, rather than the judgment that, necessarily, perceived objects are spatial (364). It is in the latter judgment alone that the objects' being spatial is necessary only in relation to the antecedent condition of their being perceived, similar to the way in which a contingent judgment is necessary in relation to an antecedent judgment that implies it. In the former judgment, however, though being perceived is a condition that the objects satisfy, it is not an antecedent condition in relation to which the necessity of their being spatial actually obtains.

Guyer contends that it is only Kant's claim to our having knowledge of certain *absolute* necessities that entails Kant's idealism. Since, according to Guyer, Kant has no good argument for supposing that we have such knowledge—indeed, the supposition is really just an assumption of his—Kant has no good argument for his idealism. Rather, the *Critique* is more defensible as proposing a theory of our a priori knowledge of certain *conditional* necessities, necessities pertaining to certain human capacities for *empirical* knowledge. Such a theory, however, carries no implication regarding transcendental idealism (354ff.).

Kant's assumption of our knowledge of such absolute necessities leads him definitely to assert that when considered apart from their relation to us, objects are not subject to those "subjective" determinations at all. To put it another way, if we were to agree with Guyer against Kant, or, perhaps more precisely, with one "mood" (monistic) of a divided Kant against another "mood" (dualistic) (5–7 *et passim*), and opt for the "neglected alternative" to Kant's dualism, then space, time, and the categories would be determinations of *both* our perceptions of objects *and* the objects themselves independently of us. In that case, however, if anything were necessary, it would be the judgment that if we are to perceive an object, the object will be (contingently, but not necessarily) subject to the determination in question—which would make the necessity involved a mere "conditional" necessity (364). So, according to Guyer, Kant's "assumption" that we have knowledge of

---

12. Parenthetical page references included in the body of this section of the chapter are references to Guyer's book, *Kant and the Claims of Knowledge*. These, too, are to be distinguished from the continuing references to the *Critique* itself.

such absolute necessities drives him to posit his dualistic ontology of representations, or appearances, and things in themselves.

What are Guyer's grounds for asserting that Kant's idealism is due to his "assumption" that we have a priori knowledge of these absolute necessities? One such ground is his attribution to Kant of the "supposition" that properties of things in themselves could not be known a priori, because they could not be known to be necessary (362). That is, only properties of *representations* can be known to be necessary. In support of this attribution Guyer cites an excerpt from a passage in the preface to the second edition of the *Critique:* "If intuition must conform to the constitution of the objects, I do not see how we could know anything of the latter a priori, but if the objects (as object of the senses) must conform to the constitution of our faculty of intuition, I have no difficulty in conceiving such a possibility as this" (B xvii, Guyer's [slightly amended] translation). Presumably, Guyer is taking Kant's remarks about conformity to indicate the transcendental distinction between "in themselves" and "in us." So Kant would be saying that he can see how we could know a priori that something such as space determines an object only if the determination is "subjective." In other words, the a priori nature of the knowledge of the object implies the subjectivity of the determination that is known in regard to it. Unfortunately, this conclusion does nothing to advance Guyer's theory that it is the *absolute* nature of the necessity that is responsible for Kant's idealism. The excerpt from the *Critique,* as well as the larger passage from which it is excerpted, is only concerned with the *a priori* nature of the knowledge, and so far Guyer has not shown that anything in that entails that the necessity is absolute.

Nor does Guyer's theory get any support from another excerpt of his, this one from a passage in the body of the *Critique:* "Space does not represent any determination that attaches to the objects themselves and that remains even when abstraction has been made of all the subjective conditions of intuition. For no determinations, whether absolute or relative, can be intuited prior to the existence of the things to which they belong, and none, therefore, can be intuited a priori" (A 26/B 42). However, this excerpt, too, has nothing to do with the distinction between absolute and conditional necessity, as Guyer's own gloss indicates: "Kant assumes . . . it is not possible to know independently of experience of it that an object genuinely has, on its own, a certain property" (362). In Guyer's own view, the distinction that is really operative here is the one between a priori and a posteriori knowledge, not between absolute and conditional necessity. So we must look still further for the grounds for Guyer's theory.

They might very well be found in what for us will be his penultimate and, apparently for Guyer, decisive argument (357–59, 362). Since his own view against Kant's, or one "mood" of a divided Kant against an opposing "mood," allows us to have a priori knowledge of the properties of "things in themselves," provided the necessity is conditional, Kant, in opposition to Guyer, or in opposition to the other "mood" in himself, must be taking the necessity as absolute (5–7 and 363ff.).

What are Guyer's grounds for the premise of this argument—the argument in support of the "neglected alternative" involving the possibility of a priori knowledge of "things in themselves"?[13] Guyer says,

> [I]t seems at least possible to imagine that we could know, because of certain constraints on our ability to perceive, that any object we perceive must have a certain property: We can perceive only objects that do, and so we can know that whatever objects we perceive will. . . . But then it would seem natural to explain our actual perception of any particular object as due to the very fact that it does have the property in question. . . . My formulation of . . . the conclusion of Kant's argument that spatiality is a necessary condition on our perception of objects . . . yield[s] a result of the form, 'It is necessary that if an object is perceived by us it must be perceived in space. . . .' It is indeed natural to explain perception of an object understood as satisfaction of this conditional necessity by the assumption that any object actually perceived is spatial . . . independently of our perception of it. (363)

In this passage, Guyer first explains our knowledge "that any object we perceive must have a certain property" in terms of "certain constraints on our ability to perceive." He then explains "our actual perception of any particular object," or "perception of an object understood as satisfaction of this conditional necessity," in terms of the "fact that [the object] does have the property in question," "independently of our perception of it." So "cer-

---

13. "Things in themselves" is in scare-quotes in this sentence because it is used more in light of *Guyer's* view of things than of Kant's. It conforms to Kant's use in the sense that the things are considered to have the properties of space, time, and the categories, whether we have the capacity to know them or not, but only in Guyer's sense that we do in fact have the capacity to know them and that this knowledge—that if we have the capacity, we can know them to that extent—*is* a priori. It is a knowledge of that *conditional* necessary truth. See the passage from Guyer and my analysis of it immediately below in the body of the text. Kant, of course, denies we have any knowledge of things in themselves. Hence, the use of scare-quotes.

tain constraints on our ability to perceive" explain our knowledge of the conditional necessity, whereas the perceived object's having the property independently of our perception of it explains the actual perception of the object, or the satisfaction of the conditional necessity. Thus, our subjective constitution explains the conditional necessity, or the possibility of perception, and the object's independent nature explains the actual perception, or the satisfaction of the conditional. This, then, seems to be Guyer's decisive reasoning that we can have a priori knowledge of things in themselves.

It is essential to this reasoning that the object we actually perceive, the satisfaction of the conditional necessity, possesses the property in question independently of our perception of it. Since Guyer intends that independence to hold with respect to our possible as well as our actual perception, that is, to hold with respect to our a priori subjective constitution as well as the empirical conditions surrounding our actual perception of the object, the property in question would be considered to hold with respect to Kant's thing in itself. And since Guyer's argument consists in *contrasting* his theory of the possibility of our a priori knowledge of objects with Kant's, it seems fair to conclude that Guyer intends the object Kant claims we can know a priori to be appearance.

Actually, we need not go through this particular reasoning to reach this conclusion, since Guyer himself is otherwise quite explicit on the subject. An object that is necessarily subject to a category and/or space or time must be an appearance, or a mere representation, according to his reading of Kant (342). Indeed, that is the crux of his dispute with Allison concerning the correct interpretation of Kant's transcendental idealism: Kant needs appearances as objects to account for the possibility of our a priori knowledge only of absolute necessity (334–35 and 362ff.).

The question for us, however, concerning Guyer's absolutist interpretation of Kant is that he does not seem to provide for the distinctness of the object we can intuit or know from the modes of our knowledge of it, that is, space, time, and the categories. The object in regard to which we have a priori knowledge of absolute necessity, being mere appearance, must already be thought through a category and/or an a priori concept of space or time corresponding to an a priori intuition of the same. This object is none other than the empirical object that constitutes what I have called the customary interpretation of Kant's ontology. Consequently, it is subject to the misgivings that I have already expressed with regard to that object.

What we have just seen is that if we agree with Guyer's theory that Kant's employment of the notion of absolute necessity motivates his ontological commitment to "two classes of objects" (335), then, since the ontology is divided between representations, that is, appearances, and things in themselves, we are left without the concept of an object that is distinct from certain constraints on our ability to perceive, where these are understood as a priori conditions (modes) of the possibility of empirical knowledge, and yet is something we can intuit or know. But I have concluded that we need precisely such a concept if we are to provide an adequate interpretation of Kant's ontology.

Finally, it may not have escaped notice that so far I have not addressed what Guyer considers very strong grounds indeed for his theory (that Kant's assumption that we can have a priori knowledge of absolute necessity motivates his transcendental idealism). This is his textual evidence in which Kant explicitly employs that notion of necessity (e.g., A 48–49/B 65–66, cited by Guyer on 365, the discussion of which continues on 366).

Indeed, we can even add the following passage to that evidence: "it [i.e., the form of the intuition of a real object] belongs really and necessarily to the appearance of this object" (A 38/B 55). But this addition only strengthens the response to Guyer I have already given. It is specifically with respect to the appearance that Kant here employs the absolute notion of necessity, if Guyer is right about this. Moreover, in the passage cited by Guyer mentioned above, the notion is employed with respect to an object that stands "in *B*-relation to" the subject of knowledge, whether the object is a triangle, which "[y]ou must therefore give yourself" (A 48/B 65), or a thing that is an outer object "to you" (A 48/B 66). Our interest now, however, is in the concept of an object that is *distinct* from us or the subject ("you"), and thus distinct from the triangle and the outer object, or the appearance. So even Guyer's exegetical arguments fail to provide the concept we are looking for.

IV

If we now turn our attention back to that concept, I can claim that the issue of monism versus dualism that divides proponents of the customary approach can be resolved by the alternative approach I am advocating in this book, namely Kant's ontology of *things*. Since the interpretation of Kant's ontology that has been offered here consists exclusively of things, it is clearly monistic in nature. However, it involves distinguishing things from all other objects, which implies that things are not alone among objects. In regard to Kant's transcendental idealism in particular, I have explicitly distinguished them from appearances and things in themselves, which, of course, for their part, are distinct from one another. My interpretation, therefore, leads to a transcendentally idealistic dualism with respect to things, and in this sense Kant's ontology could be considered dualistic. But this dualism is perfectly coherent with the monism: one set of objects viewed or existing in two ways. Each way provides us with objects that are distinct from one another, namely, the original, or basic, objects—the things— *viewed both ways*. Things thus constitute unqualified, basic reality; when viewed both ways, we get empirical reality and transcendental reality—the sensible world of appearances, that is, phenomena, and the intelligible world of things in themselves, that is, noumena. We get a world (of objects), and not mere objects themselves (things), if and only if the things are thought to be determined *either* according to "qualities" that belong to us or to the subject *or* according to properties or laws that are intrinsic to them. These are properties and laws that belong to things the conditions of whose possibility are thought independently of their being further thought through the conditions of *sensibility,* and hence independently of the *categories* insofar as the latter are conditions of the possibility of our a priori *knowledge* of objects, since they constitute such conditions only insofar as they "can be applied to empirical intuitions" (B 147), or only insofar as they "prescribe to appearances . . . a priori laws" (B 165).

I thus conclude that one of the advantages of my interpretation of Kant's transcendental ontology is that it can reconcile the dispute between these two opposing versions—monistic and dualistic—of the customary interpretation of that ontology. Though I do not side with either Allison or Guyer in this particular dispute, I do nonetheless still agree with Guyer (and, of course, with Strawson before him) against Allison regarding Kant's philosophical motivation for introducing transcendental idealism into his theory of the possibility of knowledge in the first place. It was to accommodate the demands of Kant's theory of the possibility of specifically a priori knowledge as distinct from those of any theory of the possibility of empirical knowledge that Kant was, as Strawson, Guyer, and I argue, led to his doctrine of transcendental idealism. A theory of the possibility of empirical knowledge does not need any such idealism at all, we maintain.

But I have not yet argued for what I believe is specifically responsible for Kant's doctrine of transcendental idealism, namely, *a priori intuition* and the related *V*-relations of intuition. We should thus now turn our attention to the detailed arguments I offer in support of this claim.

THE NECESSITY OF KANT'S IDEALISM

I

I will introduce my explanation of the grounds of Kant's transcendental idealism by beginning more generally than the particular demands of a theory of the possibility of specifically a priori knowledge. A theory of knowledge in general—an epistemology—purports to explain how we can know how things are. But if it delivers on its promise only on the condition that the knowledge it explains is limited to the mere *appearances* of things, in contrast to how they are independently of the senses or how they are whether we observe them or not, we rightly demand a reason for this limitation. For we expect anything rightly called "knowledge" to tell us how things really are, and not merely how they appear to us.[1] If the senses cannot give us the unvarnished truth, we want to know why, and we also want to know why, if that is so, the outcome in which they do have a hand still deserves to be called "knowledge."

We might use this particular notion of appearance *empirically* to point

---

1. Barry Stroud, for example, criticizes Kant for not delivering us the real thing when promising an explanation of the possibility of a priori knowledge of objects and then consigning those objects to mere appearances of things. See his *Significance of Philosophical Skepticism* (Oxford: Oxford University Press, 1984), 116.

out that features of our respective observations of things, say, the sensory conditions of sight or of touch or the standpoints of sight or of hearing, significantly vary from individual to individual and are reflected in the observations themselves. An appearance is then the object of such an observation. As such, it is opposed to the object of an independent thought of how the same thing is, in the sense that the thought is independent of all such observations. Consequently, this contrasting object is also independent of all such variable sensory conditions or standpoints.

This empirical use of "appearance" can be connected with a theory of *empirical* knowledge, or experience. It would be a theory that includes how we can come to have knowledge of sensible qualities of appearances, for example, qualities of sight, touch, and hearing, that vary according to our respective sensory conditions or standpoints. Since all such qualities of the objects can be given to us only through the knowledge itself, that is, empirically, any other sensible qualities that could be given to us but could *not* be given to us empirically would be qualities that could only be given to us *a priori*. In that case, however, the opposition between appearances and how things are whether we observe them or not would not arise in connection with *empirical* knowledge. Yet it would still arise. But it would do so in connection with *a priori* knowledge. A priori knowledge of things in respect of these a priori sensible qualities would again be knowledge of the things only insofar as they are taken as appearances; only now the knowledge would be a priori.

Kant evidently went through such reasoning as this in deciding to use the term "appearance" for the objects to which our specifically *a priori* knowledge is B-related (A 45–46/B 62–63). It is only in regard to the possibility of *a priori* knowledge that he employs what he calls a "transcendental," in contrast to an empirical, concept of appearances, where the former pertains to their sensible *a priori* qualities and the latter their sensible *empirical* qualities (A 11–12/B 25, A 30/B 45, A 45/B 63, A 56/B 81). That is, it is only his theory of the possibility of *a priori* knowledge—his *transcendental* epistemology—that leads him to employ his "transcendental concept of appearances" and thus his transcendental distinction between appearances and things in themselves (e.g., A 30/B 45), which, of course, is the fundamental distinction of his transcendental idealism. Finally, however, when Kant relies on empirical knowledge to demonstrate the objective validity of a priori knowledge, the objects of empirical knowledge exemplify the *transcendental,* not the empirical, concept of appearances, since it is only the B-relation of the a priori knowledge to objects that is being demonstrated. As I have already argued, empirical knowledge and its *B*-relation to objects are involved in the demonstration only for that purpose.

Perhaps the most notable of recent commentators on the *Critique* who also connect Kant's theory of appearances to his theory of a priori knowledge, as I have remarked from the start, is Guyer.[2] His quarry is Allison and those represented by Allison,[3] who hold that Kant's idealism is a consequence of the proposition that conditions of *any knowledge* of objects, whether a priori or empirical, cannot be properties of the objects viewed as they are *in themselves,* that is, viewed as they are apart from those conditions. Guyer claims that Allison and those like him have got Kant's argument backward: the opposition between conditions of knowledge and things in themselves is itself a consequence of a more fundamental proposition in Kant's theory, namely, that we cannot have specifically *a priori* knowledge of things in themselves. And the reason for this, Guyer claims, as already noted in Chapter 6, section III, is that the necessity, and hence the a priori knowledge of the necessity, Kant has in mind in this instance is the *absolute,* rather than the *conditional,* type of necessity.[4] Guyer contends that only Kant's claim to our having knowledge of certain *absolute* necessities entails Kant's idealism. Since, as already remarked, according to Guyer, Kant has no good argument for supposing that we have such knowledge— indeed, the supposition is really just an assumption of his—Kant has no good argument for his idealism. Rather, as I have already stated Guyer's position on this issue, the *Critique* is more defensible as proposing a theory of our a priori knowledge of *conditional* necessities pertaining to certain human capacities for *empirical* knowledge. Such a theory, however, carries no implication regarding transcendental idealism.[5]

As much as I am in agreement with Guyer in his dispute with Allison on this matter, I cannot rest with his treatment of the subject. The problem with Guyer's argument is that it stops short of telling us *why* Kant's theory of our putative a priori knowledge of absolute necessity requires idealism. Specifically, it does not spell out in terms of Kant's theory why Guyer is right and Allison wrong. This chapter is an attempt to make up for that

---

2. Paul Guyer, *Kant and the Claims of Knowledge* (Cambridge: Cambridge University Press, 1987), 343, 354ff. Of course, as I've already noted from Chapter 1 forward, Strawson preceded Guyer in tying Kant's theory of appearances to Kant's attempt to explain the possibility of our a priori knowledge of objects.

3. Ibid., 336–43.

4. Ibid., 363ff.

5. Ibid., 354ff.

lack. In finding in Kant's theory of our apriori knowledge of objects the precise terms that explain the necessity of his idealism, we will discover that his reference to a priori knowledge occurs not in his *assumption* that *we have it* but in his *explanation* of its *real possibility*, that is, his *explanation* of its *B-relation to objects*. His transcendental epistemology consists in just this *explanation*. So the attempt here to make up for Guyer's apparent lack in this matter is also a response to Guyer's objection that Kant actually *assumes* what he should be trying to *prove*. If Guyer had used certain elements of Kant's theory to explain *why* the theory entails idealism, he would have found that Kant indeed tries to *prove* the B-relation of our a priori knowledge to objects. The defense of Kant in this matter, moreover, has rather serious consequences for Guyer's interpretation and defense of that supposed part of the *Critique* Guyer interprets as a theory of our knowledge of *conditional* necessities, that is, as a transcendental theory of experience.

In fairness to Guyer, it should be granted that he does offer an explanation of why Kantian idealism helps us understand the possibility of our a priori knowledge of objects. Where it was "reasonable" for Kant to "assume," with respect to objects considered independently of how we represent them, that we could at best know that as a matter of *contingent* fact they are spatial, it would at least be *necessary*, though surely not *sufficient*, if we are to know of objects that they are *necessarily* spatial, that we consider them only as we can represent them. In other words, since considering objects as independent of us keeps us from understanding the possibility of our knowledge of absolute necessities with respect to them, removal of that impediment would be necessary if understanding the possibility of such knowledge were itself to be possible.

This explanation, of course, does not show how such knowledge necessitates Kantian idealism or his theory of appearances. The first problem is that Guyer fails to explain why he finds Kant's "assumption" in this matter "reasonable." For Kant allows mere *thought* of absolute necessities with respect to independent objects. So what is the difference between thought and *knowledge* in this regard? The only difference I can find is a priori intuition, which is precisely the explanation I offer below for Kant's adopting his transcendental idealism.

It might also be objected on Guyer's behalf that for him Kant's concern is precisely what *I* say it is, namely, finding the conditions of the B-relation of our a priori knowledge to objects. For Guyer ties his discussion of these alleged Kantian absolute necessities to supposed Kantian *de re* necessities,[6]

---

6. Guyer, *Kant and the Claims of Knowledge*, 366.

and the explanation of these latter necessities surely is closely connected to the question I am claiming is Kant's real concern, namely, the *B*-relation of our a priori knowledge to objects. So, Guyer should not be faulted for ignoring the question I claim is Kant's real concern. Guyer's position is simply that Kant has no good arguments in support of his assertion that the *B*-relation obtains, an assertion he just *assumed*.

This objection may very well capture Guyer's intention in this matter. But my response nonetheless remains quite the same: not only did Kant not *assume* the *B*-relation in question, but he in fact provided very good arguments indeed to *prove* it. It is my contention that Guyer just ignores the precise notion in Kant's theory that allows for the proof, namely, the notion of *a priori intuition*. I believe Guyer's neglect of this notion led him to underestimate the strength of Kant's argument in support of the claim that our a priori knowledge *is* *B*-related to appearances. Therefore, I still contend that my defense of Kant in this matter has serious consequences for Guyer's preferred interpretation of Kant's theory of knowledge, consequences that I present later in the chapter.

A final response to this objection that has just been made on Guyer's behalf: Guyer might very well be understood as taking Kant's *appearances* in a manner that can be *contrasted* with my interpretation of Kant's *appearances*. Whereas I take them as representations of *things* and hence as dependent on things, he seems to take them as *independent* of *things*. So, if Guyer were as concerned as I with Kant's interest in the *B*-relation of knowledge to objects and hence with a *de re* relation of the knowledge to objects, he would be concerned with the *B*-relation to appearances *that depend on things*. But, strictly speaking, he is not concerned with that *B*-relation to appearances as I understand them, since for him Kant's appearances *do not* depend on things in the way that I say they do.

To put my response another way, for Guyer *de re* does not actually strengthen the absolute necessity he is concerned with, even though he employs both concepts of necessity, absolute and *de re;* it does not, in any event, strengthen absolute necessity enough to accommodate what I would understand as Kant's *de re* talk about appearances, since I would understand that talk to involve *things*, whereas Guyer does not seem to understand Kant's appearances that way. When it comes to appearances, for Guyer a constraint on representations just is a constraint on objects, whereas for me that is not the case. For me, we need the independent concept of a *thing* to understand the stronger notion of how a constraint on an appearance as a representation is a constraint on an object *of a certain ontological type*—a *thing.* In short, since Guyer's interpretation of Kant's ontology is thus different from mine, so would be his understanding of the *B*-relation of a priori knowledge to objects, and hence his understanding of Kant's supposed *de re* necessities that pertain to appearances.

II

The main argument I am proposing in support of the opposition between a priori knowledge and things in themselves goes as follows:

> (1) A priori knowledge for Kant is understood as knowledge that is "independent of experience,"[7]

which is partly explained by Kant as

> (a) something that "our own faculty of knowledge (sensible impressions serving as the occasion) supplies from itself." (B 1)

He goes on to explain further that it is

> (b) something that one does not "learn through experience." (B 2)

Finally, it is

> (c) something that is possible *a priori,* and not through experience. (B 2)

Moreover, Kant also asserts that

> (2) it is "*experience* in which alone, as given objects, they [i.e., the objects in question] can be known." (B xvii *et passim*)[8]

Since a priori knowledge is independent of experience, in the sense explained so far ((a)–(c)), and since only in being given in experience can objects be known, it follows that

---

7. It is this premise that keeps experience, or empirical knowledge, from being substituted for a priori knowledge in the argument at hand. Consequently, the argument cannot be employed to generate a similar opposition between experience and things in themselves.

8. This is the premise that keeps "being conditioned" and "being thought through a concept" from being substituted for "being known" in the argument at hand. Consequently, the argument cannot be employed to generate a similar opposition between a condition or a concept through which objects are thought and things in themselves.

(3) a priori knowledge is independent of the objects that are given in experience.

If

(4) we attach "intrinsic" to those properties that belong to objects or those laws that govern them independently of their being *given in experience,* that is, whether they are given in experience or not,[9]

then

(5) a priori knowledge is also independent of *intrinsic* properties or laws of the objects that are given in experience, and, conversely, they are independent of it.

---

9. "Intrinsic" would thus exclude qualities and laws that belong to objects *insofar as* they are given in experience. Things that are given in experience have intrinsic properties and laws, which would, of course, be reflected in our experience of them, since their effects on us would be the sensations due to these properties and laws, which make our representations of them empirical (A 20/B 33). Yet these same things would not have their intrinsic properties and laws *insofar as* they are given in experience. They would have them "whether they are given in experience or not."

James Van Cleve, in a discussion of Kant's transcendental idealism, following David Lewis, *On the Plurality of Worlds* (Oxford: Basil Blackwell, 1986), 200ff., also employs a distinction between properties that are "intrinsic" to objects (as here, "intrinsic" signifies that these are properties of things in themselves) and what are here called (extrinsic) qualities of objects, which, because they are *relative* to some other objects(s), really are not intrinsic (relative) properties at all for Lewis and Van Cleve but rather are *relations* between the two sets of objects. See Van Cleve, "The Argument from Geometry, Transcendental Idealism, and Kant's Two Worlds," in *Minds, Ideas, and Objects,* ed. Phillip D. Cummins and Guenter Zoeller (Atascadero, Calif.: Ridgeview Publishing Co., North American Kant Society, 1992), 297–98. This is not to say that Van Cleve himself explains Kant's idealism on these grounds. (At this point in his discussion, he is actually contesting the view of Allison.)

With respect to objects that are given in experience, there is no knowledge of them, including a priori knowledge, unless they are so given. But with respect to those that have intrinsic properties and laws, they have those properties and laws whether they are given in experience or not. This constitutes a sharp distinction between a priori knowledge of objects that are given in experience and their intrinsic properties and laws.

Though a priori knowledge is independent of experience and hence is independent of the objects that are given in experience, it is not knowledge of the objects except insofar as the objects are given in experience. This follows from (2), which eliminates the inference that since a priori knowledge is independent of experience, it is thereby knowledge of properties and laws that belong to objects independently of their being given in experience.

If necessary, the inference to (5) can be clarified by indirect reasoning. Assume

> (not (5)) a priori knowledge is not mutually independent from these intrinsic properties and laws.

Then, first,

> (not (5a)) the concept of a priori knowledge contains the concept of these intrinsic properties and laws.

From (not (5a) and (4), however, we can conclude

> (not (5a*)) a priori knowledge is knowledge of the objects apart from their being given in experience.

But this is contrary to premise 2. Half of the indirect reasoning is now complete. That is, half of the reasoning beginning with (not (5)) entails a proposition, namely, (not (5a*)), that is contrary to premise 2, which presumably is unchallenged. The other half of the indirect reasoning is just as straightforward.

From (not (5)) we can infer

> (not (5b)) the concept of these properties and laws contains a priori knowledge of the objects.

But from (not (5b)) and (2) we can conclude

> (not (5b*)) these properties and laws respectively belong to and govern the objects only if the objects are given in experience.

But this is contrary to premise (4), and this contradiction completes the other half of the indirect reasoning. By indirect reasoning, therefore, we can again conclude (5).

Finally, if

> (6) things in themselves are things that are thought through concepts of *intrinsic* properties or laws

and, therefore,

> (7) are thought apart from the conditions of their being given in experience,

(which is a specification of our previous, more general characterization of things in themselves as objects considered apart from the conditions of our knowledge of objects), we can reach the conclusion that Guyer and I share in opposition to Allison, namely, that

> (8) we cannot have specifically *a priori* knowledge of things in themselves.

If this argument reflects Kant's reasoning, it supports Guyer's contention that reference to a priori knowledge is essential to Kant's transcendental idealism.

Allison might object to my (and Guyer's) conclusion that it is specifically a priori *knowledge* that stands in opposition to things in themselves. He would say it is rather a priori *conditions* of knowledge, whether the knowledge itself is a priori or empirical, that stand in such opposition. For if we substitute "a priori conditions of knowledge" for "a priori knowledge" throughout the argument I have just given, we indeed get the conclusion that these conditions stand in opposition to things in themselves. Since this substitution allows the knowledge itself to be *empirical,* Kant's idealism does not depend on specifically a priori knowledge and, a fortiori, not on the *absolute* type of a priori knowledge referred to by Guyer.

Two impediments block Allison's supposed substitution. In the argument above, being conditioned a priori cannot be substituted for being known, since it is not true for Kant that "it is experience in which alone, as given objects, they [i.e., the objects in question] can be conditioned a priori." Kant speaks of objects as conditioned a priori apart from their being known (e.g., B 150–51). Second, we can ask what happens to the concept of *intrinsic* properties or laws of objects if we make this substitution. How can Allison distinguish between such properties or laws and a priori conditions of knowledge? This rhetorical question is asked in response to Allison's conception of the objects Kant says we can know—a conception, by the way, shared by virtually all other commentators, including Guyer, whom I have characterized as *customary*—namely, *empirical objects* or, more generally, *appearances.*[10] According to Kant, however, these objects have no intrinsic properties or laws, since, on the one hand, intrinsic properties or laws belong to objects independently of their being given in experience and, on the other, empirical objects or, more generally, appearances, have their qualities or laws only insofar as they are given in experience. Since empirical objects, the objects Allison thinks Kant says we can know, have no intrinsic properties or laws, it would be *vacuous* for him to claim that "a priori conditions of knowledge" can be substituted for "a priori knowledge" in my argument in such a way as to yield a conclusion similar to mine, namely, that these *conditions* are opposed to things in themselves. For Allison, the conditions are really opposed to merely an impermissible way of *viewing* these objects. These conditions cannot be opposed to intrinsic properties or laws of objects, so long as the objects are empirical objects, for the simple reason that such objects have no such properties or laws. Yet reference to such properties and laws and to the objects that have them is essential to my argument. In other words, the argument is not even available to Allison for purposes of substitution, since he does not take things in themselves to be what the argument requires in order for it to explain the opposition between whatever is said to be a priori and things in themselves.

For Allison, the objective qualities and laws of empirical objects, those that are independent of any modification of the state of the subject of representation, that is, independent of sensation (A 320/B 366) and hence independent of their being given in experience, must be *identical* with our a priori cognitive constitution; that is, the properties inhere in us, the subjects

---

10. Allison, *Kant's Transcendental Idealism: An Interpretation and Defense* (New Haven: Yale University Press, 1983), 8. See also his "Transcendental Idealism: 'The Two Aspect View,' " in *New Essays on Kant*, ed. Bernard den Ouden and Marcia Moen (New York: Peter Lang Publishing, 1987), 155. As noted in Chapter 6, others have also criticized Allison for failing to make this distinction.

In regard to the present concern, it might be pointed out that knowledge of the conditional necessities favored by Guyer does not entail transcendental idealism, but only if the objects we can know are *empirical* objects. For if they are not (suppose they are *things*), our knowledge of them would entail that they stand under the condition of sensibility. The necessity that would thus be known would be relative to that antecedent condition and hence would be conditional. Yet the objects could be known only as appearances, since that is what *these* objects are under that condition. Consequently, the possibility of this knowledge of conditional necessities *would* entail Kant's idealism. Since Guyer takes our knowledge of conditional necessities *not* to entail this idealism, his objects are not these objects. But these objects constitute the alternative to empirical objects that is here under consideration. Therefore, Guyer's objects must be empirical objects, provided, of course, we have cast the alternative widely enough for the argument to go through. Textual evidence for this reading of Guyer can be found in his *Kant and the Claims of Knowledge*, 335, 364.

to whom the objects are given, or the laws are inherent in all subjects that determine objects through their intuitions (A 42/B 59, B 164–65). If they were not identical, the objects that have them could not be known. For Allison in particular, however, but not for Guyer or myself, things in themselves are really just these empirical objects, only viewed in a way that makes our knowledge of them impossible. The difference here can be put as follows: Whereas Allison's a priori *conditions* of our knowledge of objects *must* be identical with properties or laws that belong to objects independently of their being given in experience, if the objects are to be known, the *contents* of a priori *knowledge* of objects, as Guyer and I view them, *cannot* be identical with properties or laws that belong to objects independently of their being given in experience.

Another substitution, however, might yet keep us from reaching the argument's conclusion—the substitution of "consciousness" or "judgment" and the related expression "thought through the categories" for *"experience"* and its related expression "given in experience," thus yielding "it is consciousness or judgment in which alone, as objects that are thought through the categories, they can be thought." Indeed, in the conclusion of step one of the B-Deduction of the categories Kant does speak in precisely these terms of consciousness, judgment, and the categories without mentioning either knowledge or the opposition between appearances and things in themselves.[11] That is, in speaking of the manifold "given in a single empirical intuition . . . [being] brought into one consciousness" (B 143), there is no implication of an opposition to things in themselves. If there is an opposition in step one of the B-Deduction, it is between appearances, whose contingent unity belongs to derivative, empirical consciousness (B 140), and objects whose necessary unity belongs to original, a priori consciousness (B 141–42). Furthermore, Kant asserts that we do not have any *knowledge of things* unless there is more than a unity of the manifold of a sensible intuition in general, and therefore more than a unity of the manifold of an empirical intuition, in an original consciousness: we need an empirical intuition through which an *object*, not a *manifold*, is given (B 146).[12] And finally, the opposition between the categories and things in themselves does not arise in step two of the B-Deduction until the manifold of nature, that is, the

---

11. As noted earlier, the two-step analysis of the B-Deduction first gained prominence through Dieter Henrich, "The Proof-Structure of Kant's Transcendental Deduction," *Review of Metaphysics* 22 (1969): 640–59.

12. See further discussion of this point in Chapter 13.

manifold of "the sum of all appearances" (B 163), which are "mere representations of things," is combined according to the categories (B 164).

Again Allison is mistaken in his understanding of the opposition in question. He is committed to taking the categories by themselves, apart from their relation to empirical intuitions, to be incapable of being thought of things in themselves, since for him they are "epistemic conditions" and it is a contradiction to think of things in themselves in terms of an "epistemic condition."[13] Yet Kant explicitly says in the second step that categories *can* be thought of things in themselves (B 166 n), whereas in the Aesthetic he explicitly says that space and time can*not* be ascribed to or said of things in themselves (A 27/B 43, A 35/B 52–53).

Matters are completely reversed in the Aesthetic. There we find the explicit opposition between our a priori intuitions and things in themselves. Kant says that the a priori intuitions of space and time do not represent any property of things in themselves (A 26/B 42, A 32/B 49). This reversal suggests the hypothesis that it is solely the idea of an object's being given to us through intuition, and therefore not the idea of its being thought through concepts, that explains the opposition between our a priori knowledge and the properties or laws of things in themselves.[14] Further evidence for the hypothesis can be found in Kant's statement that "the true correlate of sensibility [is] the thing in itself" (A 30/B 45), a statement he makes only after he has abstracted the understanding from the discussion (A 22/B 36).

Further confirmation of the hypothesis can be found in yet another substitution in the argument above that leads to the conclusion that a priori knowledge is opposed to things in themselves. If we substitute "a priori intuition" for "a priori knowledge" and "empirical intuition" or "perception" for "experience" throughout, the argument does go through to the conclusion. And it does so without being blocked by the two impediments that keep Allison's substitute argument from going through. I am referring to Allison's inability to substitute, in the argument, being conditioned for being known and his inability to distinguish between a priori conditions of our knowledge of objects and their intrinsic properties or laws.

I, on the other hand, do not try to make that substitution, and yet I can make the required distinction between a priori *intuitions* and intrinsic properties of things. With regard to the latter, I first argue that the statement

13. Allison, *Kant's Transcendental Idealism*, 11–12 et passim.
14. This hypothesis agrees with a conclusion of Manfred Baum's discussion of space in "Kant on Pure Intuition," in *Minds, Ideas, and Objects*, 314.

(1) Space and time are a priori intuitions

is incompatible with the conjunction of

(2) Things exist in space and/or in time

and

(3) Things are not given to us through intuitions of the senses.

To begin, a priori intuitions cannot be *B*-related to objects that are given to us unless the objects are given to us through intuitions of the senses. But if things exist in space and/or in time, the a priori intuitions of space and/or time *are* *B*-related to objects that are given to us, namely, things as they exist in space and/or in time, that is, appearances. Therefore, given (1), (2) implies not (3). Consequently, the a priori intuitions of space and time cannot be properties of things—that is, things cannot exist in space and/or in time—independently of their being given through intuitions of the senses. Since things are given in experience only if they are given through intuitions of the senses, then, if they are thought through concepts of properties that belong to them independently of their being given through intuitions of the senses, it follows that they are thought through concepts of properties that belong to them independently of their being given in experience. (This allows us now to characterize things in themselves more precisely as objects of the former thought.) Therefore, the a priori intuitions of space and time cannot be properties of things if the latter are taken as things in themselves.

In confirmation of this argument, it should again be noted that Kant does not even speak of space and time as *properties* of things in case the things are given; he rather calls them *Beschaffenheiten,* which, to bring out the contrast with his term for properties, *Eigenschaften,* might better be translated as (extrinsic) *qualities* of things as so intuited, and thus as (extrinsic) qualities of empirical objects, or appearances (*vide,* e.g., A 26/B 42 [b], A 32/B 49 [a], B 164–65, *et passim*).[15]

Missing from Guyer's work is the hypothesis that a priori *intuition* alone, apart from a priori knowledge, which by itself stands in opposition to things in themselves, provides the explanation of the opposition between a priori knowledge and things in themselves. So it seems that Guyer is wrong in

15. See Chapter 5, especially note 2.

claiming that we need the distinction between two types of necessity, absolute and conditional, and, respectively, two types of knowledge of necessity, to explain the opposition in question. Not that Kant does not say that space and time *necessarily* belong to appearances (e.g. A 38/B 55); the point is rather that we need not rely on the idea of absolute necessity to explain the opposition between a priori knowledge and things in themselves. After all, the notion of absolute necessity is just as applicable to predicates of properties or laws that are intrinsic to things, that is, where things are viewed as they are in themselves. So the distinction between absolute and conditional necessity will not do the job of distinguishing between a priori knowledge and propositions about things in themselves in any case. I, however, in contrast to Guyer, need only rely on the opposed ideas of *a priori intuition* and *intrinsic property of objects*. Of course, if Kant's objective were not a theory of our a priori *knowledge* of objects, he would have no use for the concept of a priori intuition, and consequently no use for the opposition between a priori intuition and things in themselves.

What about the laws of nature in general that govern whatever objects of the senses may be given to us? Since they depend on the categories, the explanation of the opposition between our a priori knowledge of the laws and things in themselves must involve the categories as well. Therefore, it seems that the explanation of the opposition between our a priori knowledge of objects and things in themselves cannot be left to the opposition between a priori *intuition* and things in themselves alone.

The answer to this objection is that the opposition between our a priori knowledge of nature in general and things in themselves exists only if the "objects which can be given us in intuition" (B 150) are taken as *appearances*, which are "only representations of things" (B 164) that can be "connected" according to the categories (B 164–65). Therefore, our a priori knowledge of nature in general is opposed to things in themselves only insofar as the categories prescribe a priori laws to *appearances* of things. As necessarily conforming to laws of their own, that is, as conforming to laws apart from their appearances, things are taken as things in themselves.

A reason for this asymmetry between a priori intuition and the categories in the context of an opposition between either of them and things in themselves can be found in my criticism of Allison. Let us return to Allison's inability to explain his purported opposition between a priori *conditions* of knowledge and intrinsic properties of things, an inability due to the fact that "being conditioned" could not be substituted for "being known" in the argument above. We get a similar failure by simply replacing Allison's *con-*

ditions with *categories:* categories *can* represent intrinsic laws of things—that is, they can represent laws of things that are independent of the things' being given in experience—since the categories can represent objects independently of the objects' being given altogether. A fortiori, they can represent things independently of the things' being given in experience, where the things, because they are distinct objects that have intrinsic properties and laws of their own, must be given in experience if they are to be known. On the other hand, not even intuitions that are a priori can represent objects independently of the objects' being given altogether; more specifically, they cannot represent things independently of their being given in experience. Consequently, the categories can represent laws of things apart from the understanding that *knows* them, that is, apart from the understanding that "prescribe[s] to [their] appearances any a priori laws" (B 165, my emphasis). This would be an understanding that can only *think* them. That may be a reason why Kant says that *"for thought* the categories are not limited by the conditions of our sensible intuition" (B 166 n). Of course, in that case, we could only have mere *thought* of objects through the categories, but not knowledge of them, and a fortiori not a priori knowledge of nature in general. We could *think* the intrinsic laws of things, but the only B-relation of the thought to the object would be that of merely logical possibility (B xxvi n); it would lack the B-relation to objects—the relation through intuition—that is a condition of knowledge (B 166 n). In other words, whereas certain laws that would be thought would actually be laws that are intrinsic to things, the thought would lack the required ground of intuition that would make it knowledge.

The argument just presented, that only a priori intuition by itself stands in opposition to things in themselves, has serious consequences for Guyer. His fundamental thesis is that Kant could not make up his mind about which sense of necessity he attached to his notion of a priori knowledge.[16] Accordingly, the *Critique* contains two mutually incompatible transcendental theories. One is a theory of experience, and since it ascribes to us knowledge of mere conditional necessities, it does not entail Kant's transcendental idealism. The other is a theory of a priori knowledge, and since it ascribes to us knowledge of absolute necessities, it does entail transcendental idealism. According to the argument presented here, however, Guyer's division of transcendental theories makes it impossible to attribute to Kant the transcendental theory of experience, which is the one favored by Guyer himself.

16. Guyer, *Kant and the Claims of Knowledge,* 6 et passim.

This is the theory he spends a large portion of his book explicating and defending. In other words, the argument presented here undermines Guyer's interpretation that a transcendental theory of experience is a major objective of the *Critique*.

The reasoning is straightforward. The transcendental theory of experience does not entail transcendental idealism. But the argument presented here concludes that Kant's theory of our a priori *intuition* of objects does entail that idealism. On the assumption that his theory of our a priori *intuition* of objects is essential to any faithful interpretation of the *Critique*, his supposed transcendental theory of experience is not a faithful interpretation of the *Critique* (since it does not entail transcendental idealism). Consequently, Guyer has not succeeded in finding within the *Critique* a transcendental theory that does not entail transcendental idealism. Without that idealism, Kant simply does not have a transcendental theory, and a fortiori, he has no transcendental theory of experience. As I have argued from the start of these investigations, he repeatedly asserts that by "transcendental" he means a theory of the possibility of our *a priori* knowledge, that is, a theory of the B-relation of our a priori knowledge to objects, not a theory of the B-relation of our *empirical* knowledge to objects, no matter how a priori the theory or the B-relation might be. Indeed, as I acknowledged at the beginning of this chapter, Guyer himself would be the first to point out that *a priori* knowledge is simply not *empirical* knowledge, and hence that knowledge of the B-relation of the former to objects is not knowledge of the B-relation of the latter to objects. My point is that knowledge of the B-relation of empirical knowledge to objects is not transcendental, even if it is a priori, as Guyer contends it is. In a word, its being a priori does not make it transcendental, at least not in Kant's sense of the term. It should be noted in conclusion that I will have occasion to use the same form of argument against Guyer in my remarks concluding the additional argument about to be presented below.

Before I turn to this argument, however, I should mention here a troubling consequence for Guyer of my criticism of him. He interprets Kant's notion of our cognitive faculties as being compatible with his own use of conditional necessity, and hence as being free of any entailment of transcendental idealism. But if I am right that Kant's theory of our a priori intuition of objects is not free of that entailment, it follows that Guyer's interpretation of Kant's notion of our cognitive faculties cannot be applied to Kant's notion of the faculty of intuition, namely, sensibility. On the assumption that the latter is essential to Kant's theory of apriori knowledge, we have found a corollary to Guyer's theory of Kant's supposed use of conditional necessity, a corollary that, again, compels us to refrain from accepting Guyer's theory as an interpretation of even part of Kant's theory of our a priori knowledge of objects.

III

There is another way of explaining the opposition between a priori knowledge and things in themselves in terms of the opposition between a priori *intuition* and things in themselves. In the argument that follows, I begin with a passage from the second-edition Aesthetic. In it Kant offers an argument "[i]n confirmation of this theory of the ideality of both outer and inner sense, and therefore of all objects of the senses, as mere appearances" (B 68). Since he has already explained that by "ideality" he means "subjective representation[s] from which we can derive *a priori* synthetic propositions" (B 44), his remarks about "confirmation of this theory of ideality," which I am about to discuss, pertain to the ideality that is involved in his theory of a priori knowledge. So the passage is germane to an explanation of the opposition between a priori knowledge and things in themselves that is our concern in this chapter.

In the passage in question Kant makes heavy use of the term *Verhältnis,* which, as I have explained in Chapter 4, stands for, *inter alia,* the relation of a representation or cognition to a representation or cognition or to a subject or faculty thereof. Following the model of Kant's theory of representation put forward in that chapter, I will continue to call it the V-relation. As already noted, V-relations are specified in both the Aesthetic and the Logic as *forms* of representations, cognitions, or objects. We recall, for example, that that which so determines "the manifold of appearances that it allows of being ordered in certain [V-]relations, I term the *form* of appearance" (A 20/B 34). Or, "General logic . . . considers only the logical form in the [V-]relation of any knowledge to other knowledge" (A 55/B 79).[17]

17. The other term of Kant's that Kemp Smith translates as "relation," as already pointed out in Chapter 4 and as subsequently used by me, is *Beziehung.* Again, this stands for the relation of any given representation(s), cognition(s), or the manifold, faculty, or subject thereof to an object or a subject. Typically, as already noted, Kant speaks of a cognition as being *Beziehung*-related (B-related) to objects through a certain representation of them. And where he calls V-relations *forms* of representations, of the *means* thereof, or of objects, if it is a representation or a cognition that is B-related to objects, he sometimes paraphrases the B-relation as the *content* of the knowledge (*vide* A 55/B 79).

Kant uses his notion of the V-relation in the passage in question to express the opposition between a priori knowledge and things in themselves. The latter, he asserts,

(1) cannot be known through mere [V-]relations.

By "mere [V-]relations" here Kant means the V-relations in *intuition,* which he specifies as including the V-relations "of locations in an intuition (extension), of change of location (motion), and of laws according to which this change is determined (moving forces)." Since he goes on to assert that

(2) everything in our knowledge which belongs to intuition . . . *contains* nothing but mere [V-]relations . . . and if [intuition] *contains* nothing but [V-]relations, it is the *form* of intuition" (B 67, my emphasis),

we can conclude that

(3) that which knowledge *contains* that belongs to intuition, that is, the *content* of knowledge that belongs to intuition, is the *form* of intuition.

And since

(4) knowledge must contain intuition (*vide,* e.g., A 19/B 33),

then, by (3),

(5) the knowledge that must contain intuition, that is, the intuitive content of knowledge, consists in form alone.

In summary, putting the V- and the B-relations together, as determined by the model of representation advanced in Chapter 4, we get the following: A given representation, cognition, or the manifold, faculty, or subject thereof is B-related to an object or a subject through a V-relation that a representation has to it. In that case, this latter representation *represents* the object or the subject that the initial representation, cognition, manifold, faculty, or subject is thereby B-related to.

Furthermore, since

> (6) knowledge that consists in form alone is a priori (*vide*, e.g., A 20/B 34, A 22/B 36),

then, by (5) and (6),

> (7) the specifically intuitive content of knowledge is a priori.

Moreover, since, by (2),

> (8) the intuitive content of knowledge consists in mere V-relations,

then, by (7) and (1),

> (9) things in themselves cannot be known through the intuitive content of knowledge, that is, through a priori intuition.

Finally, since, by (4),

> (10) a priori knowledge must contain a priori intuition,

we reach our desired conclusion, namely, that

> (11) things in themselves cannot be known a priori.

In this particular passage, to summarize the argument, Kant uses the notion of a V-relation to express the opposition between appearances and things in themselves. That opposition is supposed to "confirm" his theory that both outer and inner sense are "ideal"; that is, both provide "subjective representation[s] from which we can derive *a priori* synthetic propositions" (B 44). But Kant has in mind here not all V-relations: he restricts his attention to those that belong to intuition.[18] Kant goes on to assert that what is

___

18. It is true that the V-relations at least among moving forces do involve the understanding as well as our intuition, since they pertain to the *laws* according to which motion is determined (see B 164–65). Still, it is only the V-relations of intuition, not those of thought, that express the *opposition* between appearances and things in themselves, since no such opposition would be expressed if a V-relation of mere thought were present *and* every V-relation of intuition, including, in the present instance, change of location, or motion, were absent.

present in a location or what is operative in things (*Dinge*) themselves in a motion "is not given through intuition," and he immediately goes on to say that "a thing [*Sache*] in itself cannot be known through mere [*V*-]relations" (B 67). Finally, Kant goes on in this passage to make the same point about the opposition between appearances and things in themselves in regard to the *V*-relations of succession, coexistence, and endurance.[19]

In this manner, we have reached a further explanation of why we can have no a priori knowledge of things in themselves, an explanation that was missing from Guyer's account of Kant's transcendental idealism. This time, however, instead of focusing on the opposition between a priori intuition itself and things in themselves, we have widened our focus from mere a priori intuition to include certain *V*-relations that belong to intuition and not to thought.

If we now assume that such *V*-relations are essential to Kant's theory of our a priori knowledge and to its connection to his idealism, we reach the further conclusion that any interpretation that attributes to Kant a transcendental theory that does without his idealism (now explained in terms of certain *V*-relations belonging to intuition), such as Guyer's transcendental theory of experience, is bound to leave out something essential to Kant's theory of our a priori knowledge of objects.

Guyer is subject to further demurral on the basis of the reconstruction I have just provided, though he himself criticizes this argument. First, according to the reconstruction, Guyer is correct in asserting that (1) above is an assumption of the argument. In addition, however, Guyer contends that this assumption is supposed by Kant "to yield the conclusion that space and time are not properties of things in themselves, which in turn implies that they must be mere forms of our representation of things."[20] But it will be noticed that space and time are not mentioned in my reconstruction of the argument. And if one examines the text at B 66, beginning with section "II," no mention of space or time will be found there either. It is true that space and time were mentioned just before this argument, but only as *conditions* of outer and inner sense. In fact, it is only as objects or outer and inner sense, hence of our intuition, that the argument proceeds to distinguish the objects in question from things in themselves. It is on the basis of that consideration, and not because space and time are not properties of things in

---

19. Again, it is clear from the passage that only *V*-relations of *intuition* are relevant to the opposition that Kant is drawing here between appearances and things in themselves and, consequently, the opposition between synthetic a priori propositions and things in themselves.

20. Guyer, *Kant and the Claims of Knowledge*, 352.

themselves, as Guyer has it, that Kant goes on to conclude that these conditions, as Guyer puts it, are "forms of our own representation of things."[21] Considering that the premises involve the concept of our conditions of sense instead of the concepts of space and of time, it is understandable that Kant would conclude that the conditions are "forms of our own representation of things."

IV

It should be noted in conclusion that my main explanation of the opposition between a priori knowledge and things in themselves, namely, the one presented in section II above, presupposes a distinction that was discussed in the Chapter 2. This is the distinction between two types of object that may be *given to us*—appearances and things. The qualities, V-relations, and laws of the former are all to be found in us: *appearances* do not have properties, V-relations, or laws that are intrinsic to them. The case is reversed with respect to *things*, however: they do have their own properties and laws (but not their own V-relations in intuition, as section III above attests). Of course, appearances depend on things, but not the converse. That is, things appear to us if and only if they are given to us—that is, if and only if they stand under the conditions of sensibility. So conditioned, they are represented as appearances. In this manner Kant can speak of an object of either type—appearance or thing—as being given to us. On the other hand, if things are considered as being thought through the concept of their (own) properties or laws—a concept of pure reason—they are then considered as they are in themselves. In that case, they are considered not as being *given to us* but as being merely *thought* by a subject of the understanding. Or, if things exist with their (own intrinsic) properties or laws, they exist independently of us, that is, in themselves.

My concluding note also pertains to the limited scope of this chapter. I have argued for the opposition between a priori knowledge and things in themselves only on the basis of the independence of a priori intuition from the things that can be given to us in experience, and also, in a related way, on the basis of the independence of certain V-relations of intuition from things in themselves. This not only implies the distinction between appearances and things discussed in the paragraph just above, but it also implies a

21. Ibid.

conception of things that is independent of the forms of thought, that is, the categories, as well as of the forms of intuition, that is, space and time. It should therefore be possible to argue for the opposition between a priori knowledge and things in themselves *conversely,* that is, on the basis of the independence of things from a priori intuition and the categories, where the things remain objects that can be given to us in experience and yet are also objects that have properties and laws of their own. That argument, obviously, has already been advanced in Chapter 2. Finally, if we take the results of both chapters together, we get the concluding proposition that our a priori intuitions and the categories, on the one hand, and things, on the other, are independent of each other.

But we should not conclude from this mutual independence that the categories have anything whatsoever to do with Kant's taking things as appearances. Rather, the distinction between appearances and things in themselves can be stated, respectively (and simply), in terms of the relation that things have to sensibility, whether or not sensibility is combined with the understanding, on the one hand, and to the understanding *alone,* on the other. That way of viewing the distinction is presented in the next chapter.

SENSIBILITY AND THE UNDERSTANDING, APPEARANCES AND THINGS IN THEMSELVES

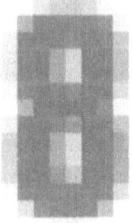

I

Whereas the previous chapter argued that sensibility—whether it occurs apart from the understanding or in combination with it—alone accounts for the possibility of appearances, this chapter, besides providing additional arguments for that earlier thesis, defends the further idea that things in themselves can be understood as objects of the understanding just in case things are taken as standing in relation to it *alone,* that is, apart from any combination with sensibility, and thereby for us can only be objects of concepts alone. (Accordingly, as noted in section II of Chapter 2, things in themselves must be distinguished from things in general, since the latter can be intuited by us.) Appearances, then, are things as they are viewed only in relation to sensibility, whether sensibility is combined with the understanding or not, and things in themselves are the same things viewed in relation to the understanding undetermined by sensibility and thus cannot be intuited by us or perceived. Finally, it will be argued that this way of drawing the distinction between appearances and things in themselves provides a straightforward method of distinguishing between an endorsed and a proscribed notion of things in themselves.

II

We begin with two of the *Critique*'s most famous ideas: its "Copernican Revolution" in philosophy (B xvi, xxii n) and its transcendental idealism. We have already seen Kant use the latter in his explanation of the possibility of our a priori knowledge of objects. And, as already noted in Chapter 2, the former is also employed in Kant's explanation. Its central thesis, we recall, consists in the proposition that the possibility in question requires that the objects of the knowledge conform to the knowledge, and not the other way around. Since for Kant knowledge consists of two distinct elements, intuitions and concepts, which in turn come from two distinct subjective a priori sources or faculties in the mind, sensibility and the understanding, his Copernican Revolution requires that the objects of our a priori knowledge conform to our a priori intuitions and concepts, and hence to sensibility and the understanding. In this manner Kant maintains that the subjective a priori conditions of the possibility of our a priori knowledge consist in the faculties of sensibility and the understanding. In what follows no issue will be taken concerning this part of what we all know about the *Critique*.

The second thesis that concerns us here—transcendental idealism—claims, as we already know, that the explanation of the possibility of our a priori knowledge of objects requires that real objects, that is, *things,* be taken as *appearances,* and hence as "mere representations,"[1] and not as they are *in themselves*. Otherwise, Kant claims, our a priori knowledge would be *impossible,* in the sense that it would not be *B*-related to objects, even though the thought of the knowledge would not be logically contradictory (e.g., B xxvi n). Explanation of this latter, merely logical possibility was not in Kant's interest, not in the *Critique,* anyhow. As with the first thesis, no issue will be taken with this one either.

Finally, these two theses are involved in three points of agreement about the *Critique,* all of which are amply supported by the text itself. The first point is that Kant's Copernican Revolution and his transcendental idealism are connected as follows: the possibility of a priori knowledge cannot entail that things conform to the pure concepts of the understanding as well as to the forms of intuition of sensibility (the Copernican Revolution) unless the things are viewed as mere appearances rather than as things in themselves (transcendental idealism). The second is that since the possibility of a priori

---

1. E.g., A 190/B 235, A 491ff./B 519ff., *et passim*.

knowledge consists of the pure concepts of the understanding (the categories) as well as the forms of intuition of sensibility (space and time), and since a priori knowledge is possible only in B-relation to appearances, the categories are thereby conditions of the possibility of appearances. And the third point is that since objects of possible experience are appearances, and since the categories are conditions of possible experience (as well as conditions of the possibility of a priori knowledge), they are thereby also conditions of the possibility of (these) appearances. Again, no issue will be taken with any of these points.

On the basis of these points it might seem that the understanding by itself, that is, quite apart from sensibility, and hence apart from the full requirements of the possibility of a priori *knowledge,* which depends on sensibility as well as the understanding, has something to do with the possibility of appearances.[2] But though these points are all matters of agreement, it will again be argued that the understanding has nothing whatsoever to do with the possibility of appearances.[3] That is, it will be argued that appearances are possible only with respect to sensibility.[4] Turning the tables on the rather commonly held interpretation that the understanding is at least *a* subjective a priori source of Kant's appearances, it will also be argued that this rather common interpretation actually has matters backward: if things are considered in relation exclusively to the understanding, they are rather for Kant considered as *things in themselves!*

In summary, being considered in relation to the understanding is neither a necessary nor a sufficient condition for things to be appearances. Neither in combination with sensibility (as part of the conditions of the possibility

2. This clearly seems to be the position of Allison's *Kant's Transcendental Idealism: An Interpretation and Defense* (New Haven: Yale University Press, 1983), 25–34, chap. 6, and pt. 4.

3. Cf. Eric Watkins, "Transcendental Idealism and the Categories" (paper delivered at the North American Kant Society Group Meeting, APA Meetings, Pacific Division, April 1996). He holds that the idealism of the *Critique* is not so far removed from that of Kant's inaugural dissertation as is commonly supposed. His thesis accords with my own view that whereas the *Critique* disavows the dissertation's claims to *knowledge* on behalf of the understanding alone, it nonetheless allows one to *think* things in themselves through the categories alone.

4. As noted in the preceding chapter, this stands in opposition to the view of Paul Guyer, who holds that Kant's appearances are entailed by his theory of the possibility of our knowledge of truths that are absolutely necessary, and hence by his theory of the possibility of a priori knowledge, where such knowledge is taken to be knowledge of such truths alone, as distinguished from our knowledge of truths that are only conditionally necessary. See his *Kant and the Claims of Knowledge* (Cambridge: Cambridge University Press, 1987), 5–7, 333–45, 350–54.

of knowledge, whether a priori or empirical) nor apart from it does the understanding contribute anything toward considering things as appearances. On the contrary, when things are considered only in relation to the understanding, they are considered as things in themselves. We might rather go so far as to say that it is *despite* the presence of the understanding in its combination with sensibility that things are still considered appearances, if they are considered in relation to that combination.

A more general lesson to be learned from the arguments to be presented here is that it is not the mere *a priori subjectivity* of sensibility that accounts for the possibility of appearances, since the categories have that property as well and I am arguing that they are not a source of appearances at all. Being an appearance is instead connected to the specific a priori subjectivity that belongs just to sensibility, namely, "the capacity (receptivity) for receiving representations through the mode in which we are affected by objects" (A 19/B 33).[5]

In fairness to certain commentators on these matters, it should be noted that there is a middle ground between the views advanced here and the allegedly mistaken conclusions that others derive from our many matters of agreement.[6] Whereas those who hold the middle ground generally *mention* the relation to sensibility when referring to things as appearances, they tend to be noncommittal on the question whether the understanding makes its own contribution to the possibility of appearances. Because this middle ground does not deal with this question, it will receive no further attention in the discussion that follows.

III

The first point (that the possibility of a priori knowledge, depending as it does on Kant's Copernican Revolution applied to a priori intuition, *inter alia,* entails that things be taken as appearances) actually allows, contrary to the view contested here, that sensibility alone might be responsible for the emergence of appearances in one's view of things. Since the forms of intuition (space and time) are essential to such knowledge, sensibility, as the a priori condition of such forms, might be sufficient to generate appear-

---

5. What this actually means is discussed in Chapter 5, section VI.
6. Included in this group is Patricia Kitcher, *Kant's Transcendental Psychology* (New York: Oxford University Press, 1990), 28, 141, and 258 n. 64.

ances, provided, of course, that things stand in relation to that condition. It follows that sensibility alone might wholly account for the possibility of appearances. So the first point hardly establishes in a conclusive manner that things are appearances if (or only if) they are taken in relation to the understanding.

The second point (that since a priori knowledge can be related only to appearances, the categories, as conditions of the possibility of such knowledge, are thereby conditions of the possibility of [these] appearances) clearly does not imply that the categories themselves are such conditions. It is essential to this point that it is specifically *knowledge* whose possibility depends on the categories. But knowledge depends on the forms of intuition as well. So, sensibility, as the condition of such forms, rather than the understanding, might very well be sufficient for things to be taken as appearances, again provided that they are viewed in relation to sensibility.

With respect to the third point (that as conditions of possible experience, the objects of which are appearances, the categories are conditions of the possibility of [these] appearances as well), it is again possible that sensibility, which is also a condition of possible experience, alone is responsible for appearances. Like the previous two points, this one does not conclusively show that the understanding can be a source of appearances either.

So far we have seen that the three points that have been agreed to allow sensibility alone to account for the appearances that are referred to in those agreements. In other words, they allow that sensibility is a *sufficient* condition for the possibility of appearances. Moreover, in a passage that is very well known Kant is quite explicit that sensibility is indeed such a condition:

> Appearances might very well be so constituted that the understanding should not find them to be in accordance with the conditions of its unity. Everything might be in such confusion that, for instance, in the series of appearances nothing presented itself which might yield a rule of synthesis and so answer to the concept of cause and effect. . . . But since intuition stands in no need whatsoever of the functions of thought, appearances would none the less present objects to our intuition. (A 90/B 123)

It remains to be seen, however, whether sensibility is a *necessary* condition of the possibility of appearances as well. If it is, as we will now try to show, the only remaining question would concern Kant's actual characterization of things when they are considered in relation necessarily only to the understanding alone. As already indicated, it will be argued that under that condition he actually characterizes them as *things in themselves.*

IV

If the understanding were a *sufficient* condition of the possibility of appearances (and therefore, since the understanding and sensibility are distinct from one another, if sensibility were not *necessary*), it could not consistently be used by Kant to distinguish objects of judgment alone from them, where the faculty of judgment is identical with that of the understanding (B 69/B 94, B 141). But it *is* thus used in the concluding stages of the so-called first step of the second-edition (B-) Transcendental Deduction of the categories (B 142). There, Kant distinguishes between "the empirical unity of consciousness, . . . [which] concerns an appearance" (B 140), and the necessary, transcendental unity of apperception (B 142), which therefore, presumably, does not.

To clinch the point, appearances, sometimes referred to as "objects of the senses," reenter the B-Deduction only with the reintroduction of sensibility, or the senses in general (B 145ff.). This is the stage at which Kant is concerned with the "sense and meaning" (*Sinn und Bedeutung*) of the categories (B 149). Kant says that before this stage "we have no intuition at hand" (B 148). Consequently, in step one there is no object of *our* sensible intuition (appearance) either, and a fortiori none to which the categories can be *"applied"* (*angewandt*) (B 146, emphasis added). What we have is a situation in which the categories merely *"extend [erstrecken sich]* to objects in [sensible] intuition *in general"* (B 148, emphasis added). Only sensibility can provide us with the specific possibility of *instances* of such objects, that is, appearances. So the central argument of the entire *Critique* (the Transcendental Deduction) provides seemingly compelling evidence that sensibility is a *necessary* condition of the possibility of appearances. We may fairly conclude, therefore, that sensibility is both a necessary and a sufficient condition of the possibility of appearances. Consequently, the understanding, being quite distinct from sensibility, can be neither.

V

We now must argue for the even stronger thesis in support of the position put forward here, namely, that if things are considered in relation exclusively to the understanding, they are actually taken to be things in themselves. Indeed, if this thesis is added to the earlier thesis that sensibility alone is the criterion (in the sense that it constitutes the logically necessary and sufficient condition) of the possibility of appearances, the result provides a way of understanding transcendental idealism along lines that are strikingly similar to ideas found in Kant's inaugural dissertation.[7]

The dissertation also draws a distinction between sensibility and the understanding. It then attributes to sensibility the possibility of "knowledge" of mere appearances, but reserves to the understanding the possibility of knowledge of things in themselves. A major departure from this position, of course, is the *Critique*'s abjuring any claim to *knowledge* of things in themselves.[8] But it, too, distinguishes between appearances and things in themselves on the same basis as that employed in the dissertation, namely, the distinction between sensibility and the understanding. Appearances and things in themselves thus divide things in two "when things are considered from this twofold standpoint" (B xix). The proposal here is that we should understand the "twofold standpoint" as the view of things (as appearances) from the faculty of sensibility, whether alone or combined with the understanding, and (as things in themselves) from the faculty of the understanding alone.

As part of the twofold standpoint the understanding alone thinks things as intelligible entities (noumena) "in the *negative* sense" that they are "not . . . object[s] of our sensible intuition." As such it belongs to "[t]he doctrine of sensibility" (B 307). This is the sense in which "[t]he concept of a noumenon is . . . a merely *limiting concept*, the function of which is to curb the pretensions of sensibility" (A 255/B 310–11).

The concept is not so narrow, however, that it fails to contain features belonging to the categories. In thinking something as "not an object of our sensible intuition," the understanding "at the same time forms . . . *concepts* of such objects. And since the understanding yields no concepts additional to the categories, it also supposes that the object in itself must at least be *thought* through these pure concepts." So far, Kant does not say that the understanding is "misled" into anything. He immediately goes on to say, however, that it is "[t]hrough this" that the understanding is "misled" into considering the "noumenon" as a determinate concept (B 307).[9] So, Kant is

---

7. See note 3 above.
8. See note 3 above.
9. Translation by Werner S. Pluhar (Indianapolis: Hackett Publishing Co., 1996).

not excluding the categories from the thought of a noumenon in the negative sense; he is instead warning against the understanding's being "misled" by their involvement into thinking that the concept of "noumenon" can be thought in its *positive* sense. This interpretation is borne out by his distinguishing at this point between the mere *extension* of the categories to objects *in general* (negative sense) and their purported *determination* of objects in our *knowledge* of the objects (positive sense) (A 254/B 309–10). This is a significant variation on a distinction that has already been noted above (section IV), namely, that between the mere extension of the categories to objects of sensible intuition in general and their use and application to objects of our human intuition in particular.

Sensibility is not the only faculty that has its pretensions, however; the understanding has pretensions of its own. It may claim that it itself is intuitive and can thus furnish itself with its own objects (B xl a, B 135, B 138–39, B 145, B 308–9, A 255/B 310–11). So, as already noted, there is both a good (negative) and bad (positive) sense of "noumenon" and of "thing in itself." The former, that which Kant himself employs, does not confuse merely subjective conditions, the categories, which belong to the understanding, with properties of objects that might be intuited intellectually (but not by us). "[T]he understanding is well aware that in viewing things in this manner, as thus apart from our mode of intuition, it cannot make any use of the categories" (B 307–8).

When the understanding is "misled" (B 307) by its own pretensions, however, thereby taking itself to be intuitive and thus seemingly providing itself with its own objects, it does think it can *use* the categories with respect to these objects. Noumena would then be objects to which the categories could be *applied* (A 256/B 311). In that instance, the understanding would confuse its merely subjective conditions of thought with properties objects would have independently of those conditions.

The negative sense of "noumenon," and with it the notion of a thing in itself, thus stands as the understanding's counterpart to sensibility's notion of appearance. Just as a thing is an appearance only in relation to sensibility, so a thing is a noumenon in the negative sense, and thus a thing in itself, only in relation to the understanding. As Kant himself characterizes the thing in itself, it is "the true correlate of sensibility" (A 30/B 45). In neither case are a priori subjective conditions of knowledge—space and time, on the one hand, and the categories, on the other—mistaken for objective conditions of the existence of things. The understanding is so far from rendering things appearances that it actually takes them to be the very objects that keep appearances in bounds. The understanding by itself thus curbs its own pretensions to knowledge as it curbs the pretensions of sensibility. In this manner, Kant's fundamental distinction between sensibility and the understanding serves as the basis of the distinction between appearances and things in themselves. The only difference between the two distinctions is that the latter depends on the presence of things, which can be viewed from the twofold standpoint, one belonging to sensibility, the other to the understanding alone.

VI

For Kant, the important thing is not to confuse subjective conditions of the possibility of knowledge with "objective determinations that are attached to things," albeit he issues the warning with respect to time alone (A 37/B 54 a, amended trans.). Toward that end, he tries to curb the pretensions of both sensibility and the understanding.

Commentators, however, have taken this dictum to imply that things in themselves *in general* are distinct from all possible subjective conditions—that the "in itself in general" is distinct from *subjectivity* in general. It is not. There is a sense of a thing in itself in which the notion is thought through the categories; but it must be thought alone—apart from sensibility. When it is so thought, however, the categories do not constitute "objective determinations attached to things." They remain merely subjective conditions of thought. The "in itself in general" is rather distinct from *sensibility* in general, whether the mode of intuition is inner (time) or outer (space).

Besides the official use of the notion of things in themselves, however, there is the prohibited use, in which subjective conditions of the possibility of our knowledge are mistaken for objective conditions of the existence of things. This prohibited use seems to be the one that gets most of the attention from commentators. One of the purposes of this chapter has been to initiate correction of this custom.

This brings to a close my consideration of Kant's transcendental ontology. Since these considerations have covered that part of the Transcendental Aesthetic necessary to my account of his theory of the possibility of a priori knowledge, there now remains that major part of his theory entitled Transcendental Logic. To that we now turn our attention.

PART 3

TRANSCENDENTAL LOGIC

THE CONTENT OF KANT'S LOGICAL FUNCTIONS OF JUDGMENT

I

In the last part of this book I proposed that the ontology of Kant's transcendental epistemology be understood to comprise objects of *transcendental affirmation*. At this stage of the inquiry, what it is to be *transcendental* has been sufficiently discussed, it seems, that it should present no particular problem in our understanding such a characterization of objects. But the same is not true of *affirmation*. This involves one of Kant's *logical functions of judgment* (A 70/B 95ff.), and since such functions are customarily taken to be for Kant logical *forms* of judgment, and since, moreover, Kant takes such *forms* to belong to what he calls "general logic" and we call "formal logic"—a logic that has no content, or (B-)relation (or reference) to an object—it is difficult to see how he could use the concept of such a function (form) to posit certain objects as the particular constituents of his ontology. It would seem that a concept used for that purpose would have to have content. This is to be contrasted with Quine's use of the concept of a bound variable of quantification, taken from the formal logic of quantification theory and offered to us as a criterion of *any* theory's ontological commitment but not as a criterion that itself determines an ontology. I, on the other hand, am indeed proposing that Kant's use of the concept of transcendental affirmation commits his transcendental epistemology to a particular ontology. This chapter tries to explain how that is possible for Kant.

It does so in the course of arguing that all of the logical functions of judgment contained in the Table of Judgments (A 70/B 95ff.), except those of *modality,* have content. This is not to say that this is so apart from an ultimate reference by Kant to intuition (A 68/B 93). But it is to most Kant scholars a nonetheless surprising thesis that these functions make their own contribution to the content of knowledge in general (A 71/B 96, A 72/B 97).

This radical departure from the customary view of these functions also paves the way for a new understanding of why Kant discarded the first-edition Transcendental Deduction of the categories altogether when the time came for publication of the second edition of the *Critique.* My explanation of this is given in the immediately following chapter. And finally, the same reinterpretation of the functions also allows for a new reconstruction of the second-edition Transcendental Deduction that makes sense out of the crucial concluding stage of the so-called first step of the Deduction, a step in which the categories are actually identified with these logical functions of judgment. This last is the job of the two chapters that succeed the next, that is, Chapters 11 and 12.

II

If we direct our attention to what has already been identified as the nub of the difficulties logic supposedly presents for Kant, we find an assumption that seems universal among commentators on the portion of the *Critique* entitled the "Analytic of Concepts." It is the assumption that Kant took the *logical functions of judgment* as *logical forms* that "we give to all our knowledge . . . [through] *general* [or formal] logic" (A 60/B 85, my emphasis).[1] As already remarked above, this is a logic that "abstracts from all

---

1. A distinctive commentator among this group is Klaus Reich, whose *Completeness of Kant's Table of Judgments,* trans. Jane Kneller and Michael Losonsky (Stanford: Stanford University Press, 1992), might be seen as a natural predecessor of the arguments presented here. Though I oppose the assumption he makes concerning the logical functions of judgments (6, 44–45, 47), his reliance on elements that clearly belong to transcendental logic in arguing for the completeness of the Table of Judgments anticipates many of the ideas presented here. The arguments presented here might indeed be seen as merely the next step beyond Reich's concluding remarks concerning the unity of apperception as "the highest point of philosophy" (108–9). Since Reich brings considerations that clearly belong to transcendental logic into his argument for the completeness of the Table of Judgments, why not take the next step, I ask,

content of knowledge of the understanding" (A 54/B 78). In a word, it is customarily assumed that in the Analytic of Concepts these *functions* are taken by Kant as "the mere *form[s]* of knowledge" (A 60/B 85, my emphasis) and therefore not as *contents* of knowledge; that is, they are taken by him as excluded from "all [*B*-]relation of knowledge to the object" (A 55/ B 79). To repeat, it is my contention that the view based on this customary assumption—what I call the customary view—is mistaken. On the view proposed here, it is *transcendental* logic, a logic that abstracts only from the *empirical* content of knowledge, through which these functions belong to the content of our knowledge and thus are not excluded from "all [*B*-]relation of knowledge to the object."

If the customary view is replaced by the view proposed here, we can avoid at least one persistent problem in the defense of a crucial thesis of the Analytic of Concepts,[2] the thesis that "all categories are grounded in logical

and consider the Table of Judgments itself as belonging to transcendental logic? It makes everything so much simpler.

Other philosophers who make the assumption in question include P. F. Strawson (*The Bounds of Sense: An Essay on Kant's "Critique of Pure Reason"* [London: Methuen, 1966], 30, 74ff.), Jonathan Bennett (*Kant's Analytic* [Cambridge: Cambridge University Press, 1966], 76 ff.), Henry Allison (*Kant's Transcendental Idealism: An Interpretation and Defense* [New Haven: Yale University Press, 1983], 125 ff.), Paul Guyer (*Kant and the Claims of Knowledge* [Cambridge: Cambridge University Press, 1987], 30–31, 97–99, 101–2, and "The Transcendental Deduction of the Categories," in *The Cambridge Companion to Kant,* ed. Paul Guyer [Cambridge: Cambridge University Press, 1992], 152), J. Michael Young ("Functions of Thought and the Synthesis of Intuitions," in ibid, 102), and Patricia Kitcher (*Kant's Transcendental Psychology* [New York: Oxford University Press, 1990], 89).

2. I mention here only one problem with one thesis of the Analytic of Concepts. Actually, the customary view is involved in many of the well-known difficulties alleged against Kant's treatment of the logical functions of judgment in the Analytic of Concepts. A good review of these allegations and a useful reference to some of the relevant literature can be found in J. Michael Young, "Functions of Thought and the Synthesis of Intuitions." See also Allison's good discussion of many of the same difficulties and his even fuller discussion of some of the same literature in *Kant's Transcendental Idealism,* 123–29.

If we accept the view presented here, that Kant's treatment of the functions in the Analytic of Concepts belongs to transcendental logic and not to general logic, it will be beside the point to argue against his treatment of the functions on the basis of one's view of the nature of general, or formal, logic, whether it is formal logic as it was known in Kant's time or formal logic as it is known now. Whatever the limitations of formal logic as known then in contrast to what is known now, or merely its limitations as it is known now, the view presented here urges us to turn away from what is distinctive about general logic and instead see his treatment of the functions as belonging to transcendental logic.

This view would allow us to agree with Allison's endorsement (*Kant's Transcendental Idealism,* 350–51) of L. Krüger's position (in "Wollte Kant die Vollständigkeit seiner Urteilstafel bewiesen?" *Kant-Studien* 59 [1968]: 333–56), that for Kant it is merely a fact, like the fact that it just happens to be space and time that are our forms of intuition, that it is just these

functions of judgment" (B 131). The problem we can avoid is the incompat-
ibility of this thesis with Kant's further theses that general logic "can tell us
nothing whatsoever regarding the content of knowledge" (A 61/ B 86) and
that the understanding "introduces a transcendental *content* into its representations [i.e., the categories]" (A 79/B 105, my emphasis). That is, if the

---

functions and not others that constitute the Table of Judgments. Nonetheless, more is required
of the functions than that they produce mere unity in the representations of the understanding,
since that unity is already part of the very meaning of "function" for Kant (A 68/B 93). Yet
that is all that Krüger and Allison require of the functions, so their accounts fall short of what
is needed here. The additional element required is that the unity in the representations in the
understanding be none other than the unity of the pure understanding (A 65/B 89). That is
why, in order to help us "find" the functions, Kant tells us to "consider only the mere form of
understanding" (A 70/B 95).

Allison goes on to agree with Krüger's subsequent observation (made in a further objection
to Reich's interpretation and defense of Kant) "that at this point it is necessary to fall back
upon Kant's presupposition that the understanding is capable of an exhaustive inventory of its
own possessions" (Allison, *Kant's Transcendental Idealism,* 351). That is, Kant should, but
fails to, provide us with grounds for holding that we can fully know the powers of the understanding and also know when our knowledge is complete. But are Allison and Krüger not
demanding too much here? Though it is not self-evident, it is still odd to call it a "presupposition" of Kant's that we can have such knowledge. Kant explicitly says that we should "consider
only the mere form of the understanding." The proposition that the understanding can come
to know all of its own powers through such consideration and know that its knowledge is
complete we guess can be viewed as a "presupposition" of a sort, but if so, it will be seen to
have the unique property of being the supreme "presupposition" that extends over the entirety
of the Analytic of Concepts. For the whole Analytic of Concepts involves arguments that
expressly are supposed to give us knowledge of our understanding based on our consideration
of the mere form of the understanding. Whether these arguments are successful or not is for us
to decide. But that they are successful is hardly "presupposed" by Kant, whatever that might
mean in this context. Obviously, the arguments must answer for themselves. Kant's claim that
the principle he is following will enable him to reach completion, that is, "*an idea of the
totality* of the a priori knowledge yielded by the understanding" (A 64/B 89), should be judged
on its merits and not dismissed as a question-begging "presupposition" of the entire enterprise.

The particular "*idea of the totality* of the a priori knowledge yielded by the understanding"
Kant has in mind is none other than the "*faculty of judgment*" (A 69/B 94, A 79/B 104–5, A
80–81/B 106), that is, the faculty whose functions are the very subject matter of this chapter.
If we "abstract from all content of a judgment in general, and consider only the mere form of
understanding," we can, Kant claims, make the "exhaustive inventory" in question. What
otherwise makes the search for the categories haphazard is that it is "based on induction only"
(A 81/B 107). But the abstraction from all content of a judgment in general and the consideration of the mere form of the understanding eliminate any reliance on such induction. He is
now free to be guided by merely the "common principle . . . [of] the faculty of judgment" itself
(A 81/B 106).

It should also be noted that we find in the second-edition Transcendental Deduction that the
unity of pure understanding is none other than the unity of apperception (B 131 and B 134–
35). We therefore ultimately reach a grand identification of the unity of the logical functions
of judgment, the categories, and apperception. Here I find myself in agreement with much of
what Reich has to say. Ultimately, it is the unity of apperception that is both the unity of the

logical *functions* are *forms* we give to all our knowledge through general logic, and if through general logic we give only *form* but no *content* to our knowledge, how can the categories, which have content, be grounded in mere forms of general logic—a logic that "abstracts from all content of knowledge of the understanding" (A 54/B 78)?[3] The question is even more pressing if we ask how Kant can go so far as to *identify* the categories with the functions, as he does at B 143, if the former belong to transcendental logic and the latter to general logic?[4] The customary view that the functions

---

logical functions of judgment and the unity of the categories. This places the view of the logical functions of judgment presented here between the positions of Reich, on the one hand, and Krüger and Allison, on the other, with respect to the issue of the relation between the functions and the unity of apperception. That is, I agree with Reich that the unity of the functions is the unity of apperception, but I also agree with Krüger and Allison that it is merely a given fact that we have just the functions we have. So it is my position that it is a given fact that the unity of apperception is involved in just these logical functions of judgment.

Those familiar with this controversy might ask where I would position Richard Brandt in relation to Krüger/Allison and myself. Although I did not have the benefit of Brandt's book *The Table of Judgments: Critique of Pure Reason A 67–76; B 92–101*, trans. and ed. Eric Watkins (Atascadero, Calif.: North American Kant Society, 1995), when I wrote this chapter, I can now, in an admittedly cursory manner, venture the idea that Brandt could probably be placed somewhere between Krüger and Allison, on the one hand, and myself, on the other, in at least one respect. Like me, he goes further than they do, in the sense that they just rest with the idea that the functions produce unity in the representations of the understanding, whereas both he and I develop the analysis. But I then side with Reich in identifying that unity with the transcendental unity of apperception, whereas Brandt rejects this identification, partly on the ground that it is based on textual material that extends beyond A 76/B 101 (16–17).

At this point, Brandt pursues his fundamental interest in the grounds that were available to Kant for the claim that the Table of Judgments exhibits a systematic unity and completeness. Here, again, Brandt departs from Krüger, Allison, and myself. Whereas we are content to leave Kant with his admission that he cannot explain why we have just the functions we have, just as he cannot explain why we intuit things in space and time, Brandt attempts to provide such an explanation, on Kant's behalf. Though this explanation would stop short of trying to provide "more ultimate reasons" for the functions, Brandt does extend his analysis to include Kant's "essential elements of the doctrines of concepts, judgments, inferences, and method" (7). Brandt's actual detailed analysis of these elements is given in the third chapter of his book.

Any evaluation of Brandt's position would therefore depend on an assessment of his analysis of these elements. Whatever the outcome of that assessment, his position would still be at odds with mine regarding the question whether the Table of Judgments belongs to general or to transcendental logic. For despite many of his observations that support my stand on this question (see, e.g., 5–6), he, like all other commentators on this subject, is adamant that at least the Table of Judgments itself belongs to general logic (see, e.g., 71).

Brandt would take exception to my views in several other important respects, but this is not the place to explore his position further.

3. One philosopher who makes this criticism of Kant is Guyer, in "The Transcendental Deduction of the Categories," 152.

4. A commentator who presses this question is J. Michael Young, "Functions of Thought and the Synthesis of Intuitions," 103, 108. At the beginning of the second-edition Transcenden-

are forms of general logic thus makes it impossible to ground the categories in these functions or identify the categories with them. It puts Kant in the impossible position of trying to ground the categories in, or identify them with, elements of the very logic he himself takes to be incapable of providing those grounds or identifications. In this manner the customary view reduces Kant's arguments in both the Metaphysical and Transcendental Deductions of the categories to absurdity. The view proposed here saves Kant from that incoherence. Once we discard the customary view, we may proceed to more fruitful interpretations of both deductions.

III

The misunderstanding inherent in the customary view did not arise for no reason at all. Kant did say things that evidently led to this misunderstanding, and it behooves us to clarify what he said before we propose a new view. Otherwise it would seem a total mystery why whole legions of Kant commentators have gone so far off the track.

First, he tells us to "abstract from all content of a judgment in general" (A 70/B 95, amended trans.), This seems to suggest that we should abstract from all content of *knowledge,* and hence that we should deal with "knowledge in general, *irrespective of content"* (my emphasis). We would thus be engaged in *general* logic (A 151/B 190, see also A 54/ B 78). But I submit that the seeming suggestion should be resisted, as I emphasize toward the conclusion of the last section (IV) of this chapter. For there I refer to the second-edition Deduction's employment of the objective (transcendental)

---

tal Deduction the categories are said to be "grounded in" the logical functions of judgment, presumably in the sense in which, earlier, Kant says that concepts "rest on" functions (A 68/B 93). At this beginning stage of the Deduction (B 131) it has not yet been demonstrated that the manifold of a sensible intuition must be brought into a "determinate combination" (B 138) through its determinate relation to the unity of consciousness (B 137). So the concepts are only "grounded in" the logical functions of judgment. The demonstration itself takes place later, at B 143. Once it does take place, the categories can no longer be distinguished from the logical functions of judgment, but must rather be "identified with" them, since otherwise the key passage at B 128, where Kant specifically addresses the relation between the categories and the functions, would be contradicted. So, in terms of what Kant says at B 128 and what has preceded the present stage of the argument at B 143, Kant has laid the grounds for his statement that "the *categories* are these functions of judgment" (B 143). This point will be developed further in the next chapter and in Chapter 12.

unity of apperception as the source of the B-relation that any judgment has to an object. This interpretation of that B-relation is then developed in the immediately following Chapters, 10, 11, and 12. Finally, in Chapter 12 (in section III, specifically in proposition 12 of a portion designated "stage III") I complete the development of this interpretation of what Kant means by the B-relation of any judgment to an object. The basic idea is that the V-relation between or among representations in a judgment "consists in" the transcendental unity of apperception, from which arises the B-relation of the representations in a judgment to objects (B 141), and thus arises the very content of *the judgment as such* or of *a judgment in general*. So, abstracting from the content of a judgment in general suggests abstracting what that V-relation "consists in," namely, the transcendental unity of apperception. In other words, any *judgment* is objective, or has content, because, besides the given representations that are contained in it, it also contains the V-relation, or copula, consisting of the transcendental unity of apperception. And since the content of a judgment in general consists of this B-relation, we can fairly conclude that it is none other than the transcendental unity of apperception that Kant is abstracting when he abstracts from all content of a judgment in general at A 70/B 95.

This makes strategic sense for Kant, since he wants to abstain from any explicit mention of the transcendental unity of apperception until the Transcendental Deduction of the categories. It will be argued in the next Chapter, 10, section III, that in preparation for the Transcendental Deduction Kant merely alludes to the transcendental unity of apperception in the Metaphysical Deduction. This interpretation thus allows the logical functions of judgment to be part of the content of *knowledge* while at the same time abstracting from the content of *a judgment in general*.

We can conclude discussion of this first factor that is probably responsible for the customary view of the logical functions of judgment with the following argument. The function of a judgment is a unity of an action of the understanding through which knowledge is B-related to an object (A 69/B 94). Since, as already noted, that through which knowledge is B-related to an object constitutes content of knowledge (A 55/B 79), the function of a judgment constitutes such content, even though it is knowledge in general with which we are dealing. The point is that we are dealing with knowledge in general with respect to the quantity, quality, and relation of a judgment (but notice that the functions of modality are exceptions that receive special treatment [A 74/B 100]). Consequently, knowledge in general need not be wholly "irrespective of content," as the passage at A 151/B 190 might suggest. And this is so, even if we are abstracting all content from *a judgment in general*, as the passage at A 70/B 95 instructs us to do.

A second factor probably responsible for the customary view is Kant's instruction preceding the Table of Judgments that we "consider only the mere form of understanding" (A 70/B 95). Previously Kant had said that general logic "deals with nothing but the mere form of thought" (A 54/B 78), "that form which the understanding is able to impart to the representations, from whatever source they may have arisen" (A 56/B 80). So his instructions that precede the Table of Judgments seem to suggest that we are engaged in general logic. Nonetheless, our considering the form of a faculty of knowledge does not imply that we are thereby not dealing with content of knowledge. Space and time are the forms of sensibility, for example, but they also constitute content of knowledge.

Furthermore, strictly speaking, Kant does not say that in general logic he is *considering* the mere *form* of understanding; he rather says that "general logic . . . only *considers representations*, be they originally a priori in ourselves or only empirically given. . . . It [i.e., general logic, instead] *deals* therefore only with that *form* which the understanding is able to impart to the representations, from whatever source they may have arisen" (A 56/B 80, my emphasis). It is noteworthy, moreover, that in general logic we are to *consider* empirical as well as a priori representations, whereas in the instructions preceding the Table of Judgments we are told to *consider* "*only* the mere *form* of understanding" (my emphasis). This restriction of our *consideration* to the "origin of the modes in which we know objects, in so far as that origin cannot be attributed to the objects" (A 55/B 80), suggests that Kant is indeed engaged in transcendental, rather than general, logic. It is from the *restricted consideration* of the mere *form* of understanding (in transcendental logic) that he finds the logical functions of judgment. On the other hand, it is from the *unrestricted consideration* of "*any* knowledge [in (*V*-)relation] to other knowledge" (A 55/B 79, my emphasis), of "all knowledge," of "all our knowledge" (A 60/B 85), that we give to knowledge the *form* of understanding.

The difference I am pointing to in the present instance is that in general logic we *consider* all knowledge, empirical as well as pure, and *deal* only with the *form* of the understanding, whereas in the instructions that precede the Table of Judgments, Kant tells us to *consider* only the *form* of understanding so that we can find the functions of judgments that are involved in all our knowledge. In general logic we abstract from all content of knowledge to find the form of the understanding and thus the a priori principles that belong to a *"canon of understanding* and of reason" (A 53/B 77), that is, "a *canon* of judgment" (A 61/B 85). In transcendental logic we rather "abstract from all content of a judgment in general" so that we can "consider only the mere form of understanding" to "find . . . the function of thought in judgment" (A 70/B 95). In transcendental logic, after the abstraction from all content of a judgment in general, the function of thought in judgment remains as the content through which knowledge is *B*-related to an object (A 69/B 94). In the case of general logic, however, once we abstract all content from knowledge of the understanding, not even the function of thought in judgment remains: no content of knowledge remains.

A third factor perhaps responsible for the customary view is two of Kant's remarks immediately preceding the Table of Categories. The first is his remark that "[b]y means of analysis different representations are brought under one concept—a procedure treated of in general logic. What transcendental logic, on the other hand, teaches, is how we bring to concepts, not representations, but the *pure synthesis* of representations" (A 78/B 104). This remark may give the appearance that only now is Kant engaged in transcendental logic, that the preceding Table of Judgments contained merely the forms of analysis in which "different representations are brought under one concept." Two things might lend some basis to the appearance. First, leading up to the Table of Judgments, Kant defines "function" as "the unity of the act of bringing various representations under one common representation" (A 68/B 93). So "the act of bringing various representations under one common representation" that is specifically involved in judgment may seem to be the analysis by means of which "different representations are brought under one concept." Thus, the logical function of the act of judgment may seem to be the unity of the analysis. Consequently, the logic involved in drawing up the Table of Judgments would be general, not transcendental. Second, Kant does not explicitly introduce *synthesis* into the discussion until well after he draws up the Table of Judgments and, to reinforce the point, almost immediately before the remark at A 78/B 104 presently under discussion (A 77/B 102). Furthermore, when he does introduce *synthesis* in the passage just cited, he goes on to state that it is synthesis that "unites [the elements of knowledge] to [form] a certain content" (A 78/B 103). This may suggest that Kant considers synthesis, and therefore a certain content, to be missing from the functions of judgment.

In response to the first point, an indirect argument is in order. The point being made is that the logical function of judgment is the unity of the *analy-*

sis by means of which "different representations are brought under one concept." So the discussion leading to the Table of Judgments is only concerned with this unity of analysis, rather than with the unity through which *synthesis* of different representations is brought to concepts. But this would exclude from the discussion Kant's concern with how concepts are *B*-related to objects through their use in judgments. More precisely, it would exclude discussion of the idea that it is through judgments that concepts comprehend other concepts and, ultimately, intuitions, where the comprehension is brought about through the subordination of lower-level concepts and, ultimately, intuitions to higher-level concepts (A 69–70/B 93–94). But this consequence is contradicted by the entire discussion. Clearly, Kant's concern throughout the discussion is to show the role of judgment, or the use of concepts, in the *B*-relation of concepts to objects. Ultimately, that use is constituted by their subordination of intuitions.

With respect to the second point, the one concerning the place at which the term "synthesis" is explicitly introduced into the discussion, two distinct responses can be made. First, though the term "synthesis" is used explicitly neither in the definition of "function" nor "the functions of unity in judgments" (A 69/B 94) or in "the logical function of the understanding in judgments" (A 70/B 95), a closely related term is used in Kant's characterization of judgment. It is through judgment, he says, that "much possible knowledge is collected into one" (A 69/B 94). The German word translated as "collected" is *zusammengezogen.* When at two of the places he explicitly uses "synthesis" in the second-edition Deduction, he uses *Zusammensetzung* (B 160) and *Zusammenfassung* (B 160 n). The common connotation of the prefix *zusammen-* as something being done "jointly" or "together" indicates that Kant's notion of synthesis is present as something that is at least incipient in the discussion of the logical functions of judgment, even though the term "synthesis" is missing and is not introduced until the discussion immediately preceding the Table of Categories. After all, in the discussion leading up to the Table of Judgments we do not yet have "the synthetic unity of the manifold in intuition in general" that allows for the introduction of the categories (A 79/B 105), nor do we have "the objective unity of apperception" that allows for both an "objectively valid" relation among representations in a judgment (B 142) and the possibility of "the unity of intuition" (B 143).

The second response to the second point made above concerning synthesis is that in the passage quoted synthesis is only said to be required for "a *certain* content," that belonging to "*our* knowledge" (A 78/B 103, my emphasis). So, if we consider the mere form of understanding, as we are instructed to do preceding the Table of Judgments, we abstract from what is distinctive in *our* (human) knowledge and rather deal with the content of knowledge in general. Consequently, no specific manifold involving space or time, either empirical or a priori, would have to be considered as given. Sensibility, and therefore synthesis of a specific manifold, would thus be abstracted from the entire discussion in which the logical functions of judgment are originally set forth.

This does not imply, however, that we have thereby abstracted from the distinction between "representations, be they originally *a priori* in ourselves or only empirically given" (A 56/B 80).[5] We are still considering only the mere form of understanding, which will lead us only to a priori concepts. The point is that the logical functions of judgment on which these concepts rest are independent of sensibility. Being thus independent, no *certain* content of knowledge is indicated by the logical functions of judgment. We can thus speak of their contribution to the content of knowledge in general.

The second remark I alluded to above as perhaps being somewhat responsible for the customary view of the functions occurs just before the Table of Categories. After stating that the understanding introduces a transcendental content into its representations, Kant says we are now entitled "to regard them as applying [i.e., extending] *a priori* to objects [a priori *auf Objekte gehen*]—a conclusion which general logic is not in a position to establish" (A 79/B 105). This may have led commentators to think that Kant is contrasting the present position with the one we were in when he laid out the Table of Judgments.

But Kant is here talking about the *representations* of the understanding, that is, the categories, and he is saying that general logic cannot establish that *they* extend a priori to objects. His point, I think, is that all that general logic can establish is how representations can be involved in *V*-relations to other representations or to the understanding itself. He does not seem to be indicating any restrictions concerning what can be established regarding the logical functions of judgment, since they simply are not representations. They are rather the functions on which certain representations, that is, the categories, rest.

Indeed, it would be odd for him to be indicating any such restriction here

---

5. This is important to remember later on when we distinguish between general and transcendental logic on the grounds, *inter alia*, that only general logic abstracts from the just-mentioned distinction between representations.

when he immediately goes on to say, "In this manner there arise precisely the same number of pure concepts of the understanding which apply [i.e., extend] *a priori* to objects of intuition in general, as, in the preceding table, there have been found to be logical functions in all possible judgments" (A 79/B 105).

If, because the logical functions of judgment belong to general logic, they cannot be involved in establishing the extension of the categories to objects of intuition in general, why should Kant immediately thereafter say that "[i]n this manner" there arises the correspondence between the categories and the logical functions of judgment? To echo the problem of Kant interpretation with which this chapter began, why would something (i.e., the functions) belonging to a logic (i.e., general logic) that cannot establish the extension of the categories be involved in any manner in a correspondence between the categories, *with their extension,* and the functions?

A fourth factor probably responsible for the customary view of the logical functions of judgment in the Analytic of Concepts is that the *same* form of understanding is involved in both general logic and in the instructions preceding the Table of Judgments.[6] This identity of form entails that the division in the Table of Judgments, though it belongs to transcendental logic, does not "depart . . . in any essential respects" from the technique recognized by logicians in general logic (A 70–71/B 96). This latter remark itself might very well have been a major cause of the customary view and as such might be numbered as a fifth factor contributing thereto. In any case, even the inessential apparent departures of the table from the technique recognized by logicians in general logic do not involve distinctions that are unfamiliar to logicians. The very expression of the issues between Kant and the logicians uses the same technical terms, that is, "singular judgment," "infinite judgment," and so forth, that are used in general logic. So the fact that it is inessential that the table departs from the technique recognized by logicians seems to suggest that the issue between Kant and the logicians is a controversy that belongs to *general* logic, and hence that the table itself belongs to general logic.

This factor deserves two distinct responses. First, a question may arise concerning what is left for general logic if I am right that the logic in which

---

6. Allison employs the same identity, that is, the form of the understanding, for the different purpose of explaining the identification of the logical functions of judgment and the categories; *Kant's Transcendental Idealism,* 126. I try to explain that identification differently in Chapter 12.

the Table of Judgments is drawn up belongs to transcendental logic.[7] The answer is that transcendental logic takes nothing away from the interest that general logic has in the *V*-relations that representations have to one another and to the understanding itself. Transcendental logic is concerned with these *V*-relations only insofar as they are involved with the quite distinct *B*-relation that cognitions have to objects. Perhaps it was a failure of commentators to keep the two sets of relations distinct, and hence a failure to appreciate the significance of the *B*-relation in the discussion surrounding the Table of Judgments, that as much as anything else was responsible for the customary view. According to the view presented here, general logic continues to have the set of *V*-relations belonging to judgments included in its field of work. Confusion in interpretation of the Analytic of Concepts, resulting in the customary view, arises only when these same relations figure in Kant's discussion of the *B*-relation of cognitions to objects and when the significance of that connection is not appreciated by the commentators. In that instance, I maintain, Kant is engaged in transcendental logic.

The other response concerns the misunderstandings to which Kant alludes in his observations immediately following the table. What misunderstandings are Kant's observations supposed to guard us against? That because of the apparent *inessential* departures of the table from the technique recognized by logicians, we might think Kant is *not* here engaged in general logic? That is, are the observations meant to assure us that he is *not* engaged in transcendental logic? On this interpretation, Kant's observations amount to an admonition that in general logic we ought not to continue the custom of conflating certain of the distinctions in the Table of Judgments. Are these conflations committed by *logicians* the possible misunderstandings of the Table of Judgments that Kant is warning *his readers* against?

This interpretation is contradicted by the very observations themselves. Kant says that in general logic logicians are "justified" in conflating, for example, the singular and the universal judgments (A 71/B 96) and are "right" not to distinguish the infinite and the affirmative judgments (A 72/ B 96). So, recommending *changes* in the technique of general logic hardly seems to be Kant's intention in making these observations. Furthermore, if the departures from general logic are *in*essential, why would they lead Kant's readers to make the mistake of thinking that he is *not* engaged in general logic? That makes no sense. It would rather seem that because the departures from the recognized technique of general logic are *in*essential,

---

7. This question was actually raised by Charles Parsons in discussion.

Kant's reader might mistakenly think that he is here engaged in doing just that—general logic. It is much more plausible to conclude because the same form of understanding is involved in both general and transcendental logic, Kant must guard against the possible misunderstanding that he is here engaged in the same logic that had been the only logic previously recognized, namely, general logic.

It might be objected that these "justifications" are meant by Kant to be limited to just certain concerns of general logic, concerns involving such items in general logic as the extension of a concept (A 71/B 96). The objection might continue that Kant is actually concerned to widen the scope of general logic beyond its recognized boundaries to include "moments" (A 70/B 95) of the mere form of understanding heretofore neglected or conflated. So the table and the accompanying observations would still teach us nothing whatsoever regarding the content of knowledge. The possible misunderstanding then remains that we might be taking Kant to be engaged in transcendental, rather than general, logic (as I, in particular, am taking Kant) when he insists on his tabular distinctions, which admittedly are conflated in the technique then recognized by logicians.

Unfortunately, this objection amounts to nothing more than a mere reiteration of the customary view, whose validity is the issue before us. That is, the objection amounts to a begging of the question whether Kant's discussion of the logical functions of judgment in the Analytic of Concepts is meant by him to belong to general logic. One advantage of the view proposed here is that instead of being question-begging, it is fully in line with another of Kant's differentiations between his work in the Analytic of Concepts and that of logicians. In the second-edition Transcendental Deduction Kant cannot be intending to make an assertion in *general* logic when he notes the failure of logicians to tell us what it is in which the V-relation of two concepts in a judgment in general consists (B 141). His theory that it consists in the objective unity of apperception cannot be said to be included in general logic, unless, of course, one is prepared to erase altogether his distinction between general and transcendental logic as it appears in the Analytic of Concepts.

Finally, a further set of remarks by Kant may have misled commentators to believe that he took his discussion of the logical functions of judgment in the Analytic of Concepts to belong to general logic. In these remarks Kant asserts that we have Aristotle to thank for having provided us with a complete science of (general) logic (B viii). Kant asserts, moreover, that he wants his Table of Categories to be systematically complete (A 67/B 92). For this purpose he claims that it is "developed systematically from a common principle, namely, the faculty of judgment." It is this that distinguishes his method, he says, from Aristotle's in the search for the categories (A 80–81/ B 106). So the traditional interpretation puts all these remarks together and concludes that the Table of Judgments provides the systematic completeness of the Table of Categories because the Table of Judgments is taken from Aristotle's complete science of general logic.

But Kant nowhere claims that the completeness of the Table of Judgments is the same completeness that belongs to Aristotle's general logic. Indeed, if Kant even implicitly made that claim, would he not have chided Aristotle for having overlooked the principle of completeness he himself had discovered in his own science of general logic? Kant would probably have said something like, "Aristotle unnecessarily proceeded 'haphazardly' in search of the categories, when the material for a complete, systematic search lay quite at hand in the form of his own general logic." No, the completeness of general logic and that of the Table of Judgments should rather be viewed as quite distinct things for Kant.

To sum up, several remarks Kant himself makes may account for the hold the customary view continues to have on our understanding of the role of the functions in the Analytic of Concepts. I have tried to provide an interpretation of his remarks that allows us to consider another view of the functions. From this position I can now argue directly for the view that his discussion of the functions in the Analytic of Concepts belongs to transcendental logic. In doing so, I, of course, cannot but cover some of the same ground just traversed in this section.

IV

Kant first tells us to "abstract from all content of a judgment [in general]" (A 55/B 80). However, since we are still dealing with judgment, albeit a judgment in general, we have not abstracted an essential property of judgment. Of all knowledge, judgment is the knowledge by means of which a concept "can [B-]relate to objects." And it would not constitute this means unless the concept itself or another concept to which it is B-related in the judgment comprehended an "immediate representation" (A 69/B 94), that is, "an intuition" (A 68/B 93). So the functions of judgment are the specific types of unity of the action of the understanding in which a concept can comprehend an intuition. Therefore, Kant's concern with the B-relation of a concept to an intuition in a judgment (A 68–69/B 93–94) implies a concern with the means by which a concept "can [B-]relate to objects" (A 69/B 94), and this is the concern with "concepts, as predicates of possible judgments, [that] [B-]relate to some representation of a not *yet* determined object" (A 69/B 94). Moreover, Kant immediately hereafter says that as a representation "comprehending other representations" a concept is "the predicate of a possible judgment." And just before he lays out the Table of Categories he speaks of the Table of Judgments as consisting of "logical functions in all possible judgments" (A 79/B 105). Finally, in the second edition of the *Critique* he concludes the transition from "the clue to the discovery of the categories" to the Transcendental Deduction proper with the remark that "it remains undetermined" to which of the functions of a judgment concepts are to be assigned if the concepts are not brought under the categories (B 128).

It seems fair to bring these passages together with the conclusion that the logical functions of judgment are conditions of concepts as predicates of possible judgments. Though the concepts in possible judgments are not yet B-related to determined objects, the possible judgments, and thus the functions that are "in" them, are conditions of the possibility of that B-relation. Since Kant considers the content of all knowledge to be none other than the B-relation of knowledge to objects, possible judgments are conditions of the possible content of concepts; that is, they are conditions of the possibility of the B-relation of concepts to determined objects. Since the logical functions of judgment belong to possible judgments, in the sense of being "in" them, as Kant puts it, they ultimately stand as conditions of the possibility of the content of concepts. As such, they can be alluded to by Kant as the "first seeds and dispositions" of the categories (A 66/B 91). Here, then, we find support for his claim that the categories are grounded in these functions (B 131).

The picture that emerges is that judgments are possible, or B-relate to objects, if objects are represented through concepts as predicates that can be B-related to intuitions. So far, however, the objects of the intuitions are not yet determined. Nonetheless, the condition of the possibility of these concepts with respect to determined objects consists in the logical functions of judgment. Therefore, these functions are only conditions of the possibility of the content of knowledge of the understanding. They themselves are not yet content if the objects are determined. They become content only insofar as concepts are B-related to determined objects through them. But in that case they are identified with the categories (B 143). This last step, however, involves the *B*-relation of representations to the objective unity of apperception (B 142), bringing the manifold in a sensible intuition "under one apperception" (B 143).

For our purposes here, however, it is enough to have established that the logical functions of judgment are conditions of the possibility of the content of knowledge of the understanding—the possibility of the *B*-relation of knowledge of the understanding to determined objects. Even if they are conditions of the mere possibility of the *B*-relation of knowledge to determined objects, however, they still should be included in transcendental, and not general, logic, since transcendental logic alone is concerned with "the *B*-relation of knowledge to the object," whereas the concern of general logic is restricted to the quite distinct *V*-relation of "any knowledge to other knowledge" (A 55/B 79). That is, it is my contention that the discussion belongs in transcendental logic even though so far I have only established that it concerns merely the possibility of the *B*-relation of knowledge to determined objects. To include the discussion in general logic is to mistake the nature of the relation whose possibility is under discussion: it is mistakenly to identify the *B*-relation belonging to transcendental logic with the *V*-relation to which general logic is restricted.

We need not leave the logical functions of judgment as belonging merely to the possible content of knowledge, or the possible *B*-relation of knowledge to objects. Since the functions are "in all possible judgments" (A 79/B 105), and since these judgments "[*B*-]relate to some representation of a not yet determined object" (A 69/B 94), that *B*-relation must constitute content even though the object is not yet determined. Otherwise, all content of knowledge would exclude the *B*-relation of knowledge to "the undetermined object of an empirical intuition [that] is entitled *appearance*" (A 20/B 34). However, knowledge must be *B*-related to the undetermined object of an empirical intuition if knowledge is to have *any* content, or *any B*-relation to an object. So the logical functions of judgment belong to judgments that are *B*-related to undetermined objects of knowledge. As such, they have content, and consequently their discussion in the Analytic of Concepts belongs to transcendental logic.

This conclusion can be reinforced if we again direct our attention to Kant's observations appended to the Table of Judgments. There he speaks of "a singular judgment . . . as knowledge in general, according to its quantity in comparison with other knowledge" (A 71/B 96), and, as we have also noted, he later states in these observations that quantity, along with quality and relation, "constitutes the content of a judgment" (A 74/

B 100). This indicates that he is here dealing with knowledge in general in respect to its content. Since he later says that general logic is concerned with "knowledge in general, irrespective of content" (A 151/B 190), I think it fair to surmise that he takes these observations to belong to transcendental logic.

Other remarks Kant makes in the observations immediately following the Table of Judgments provide further support for the view of the functions presented here. He tells us to "estimate" the singular, as compared to the universal, judgment "as knowledge in general, according to [its] quantity" (A 71/B 96). He also says we should consider "what may be the worth or content of a negative predicate in a logical affirmation, and what is thereby achieved in the way of addition to our total knowledge" (A 72/B 97). Here he actually contrasts the worth of the function with "the logical form" of the affirmation. Shortly thereafter, he explicitly refers to "the content of that [i.e., the judgments'] knowledge" (A 73/B 98). Finally, though he says that modality "contributes nothing to the content of the judgment" (that contribution's having been exhausted by the first three functions), he says, nevertheless, that it involves "the value [i.e., worth] of the copula in [*B*-]relation to thought in general" (A 74/B 99–100). He explains his use of "value" here by saying that the judgments may thereby be "conditions of the *knowledge* of truth" (A 75/B 100, my emphasis). We should contrast this remark with his earlier statement that "the general rules of thought . . . concern only the *form* of truth," which belongs to general logic (A 59/B 84, my emphasis).

It is also noteworthy that in the Analytic of Concepts Kant does not once speak of the logical functions or moments as "logical forms" of thought or understanding. Moreover, if they were such forms, Kant would use them to *V-relate* judgments to one another (in the sense of "relation" to which general logic is restricted), since that is the role of the logical forms that we give to cognitions through general logic (A 55/B 79). However, in his observations following the Table of Judgments, Kant employs the functions to *distinguish* judgments from one another according to their contributions to knowledge.

Furthermore, Kant actually calls both the logic employed in his discussion of the functions (A 71/B 97) and the Table of Judgments itself (A 73/B 98) *transcendental*.[8] Kant's characterization can be seen to be correct in

---

8. In a discussion following her presentation of "The Conditioned Formalism of General Logic in the *Critique of Pure Reason*" (MIT, November 20, 1992), a paper concerned with the

light of a further asymmetry between the two logics. Through general logic "we give [a certain *form*] to all our knowledge" (A 60/B 85, cf. A 56/B 80). If the logic is transcendental, however, what we give to our knowledge is *content:* "For no knowledge can contradict it [i.e., transcendental logic] without at once losing all content, that is, all [*B-*]relation to any object" (A 62/B 87, cf. A 55/B 79). Since "intuition without concepts . . . can[not] yield knowledge" (A 50/B 74), and since a representation is " a concept solely in virtue of its comprehending [i.e., "containing" (*enthalten*)] other representations, by means of which it can [*B-*]relate to objects," Kant concludes that the concept "is therefore the predicate of a possible judgment" (A 69/B 94). So all knowledge requires concepts as predicates of possible judgments. Without such predication in possible judgments, we therefore lose "all content, that is, all [*B-*]relation to any object." Since the table is supposed to be "an exhaustive statement of the functions of unity in judgments" (A 69/B 94), every possible judgment is covered by the table. That is, the possibility of judgments involves the logical functions of the understanding in judgments. Without these logical functions, therefore, our knowledge loses all content. To sum up, whereas general logic gives form to all our knowledge, transcendental logic gives the content of the logical functions of judgment.

Kant also speaks of "transcendental philosophy" as "the hitherto rarely attempted *dissection of the faculty of the understanding* itself, in order to investigate the possibility of concepts *a priori* by looking for them in the understanding alone" (A 65/B 90). Since he asserts that "these [logical] functions [of judgment] specify the understanding completely, and yield an exhaustive inventory of its powers" (A 79/B 105), it would seem that such specification belongs to the dissection of the understanding for the purpose indicated, and therefore that the Table of Judgments belongs to transcendental philosophy.

One might also observe of the content inherent in the logical functions of judgment that its essential involvement in the logical employment of the understanding in judgments thereby involves the functions in the specific requirements of a judgment in general itself. Such a requirement is that the objects of judgment be given (A 62–63/B 87–88, A 68/B 93). Since objects are only given to us through intuitions of the senses, judgments ultimately involve "appearances that present themselves to us" (A 69/B 93). As such,

---

nature of formal logic in the *Critique*, Sally Sedgwick acknowledged this point against the customary view of the functions.

the logic involved here is "a canon for passing judgment upon the empirical employment of the understanding." Consequently, the logic is transcendental (A 63/B 88). General logic, on the other hand, is that through which "we give to all our knowledge . . . the form of understanding" (A 60–61/B 85). Abstracting from the distinction between "representations, be they originally *a priori* in ourselves or only empirically given" (A 56/B 80), general logic does not require that objects be given in empirical intuition.

The penultimate argument in support of the view of the functions presented here is that if the customary view were the correct view, the transcendental unity of apperception would also belong to general logic. In the opening section of the second edition of the Transcendental Deduction of the categories (§ 15), Kant says that combination is "already thought" in the logical functions of judgment (B131). Since "the concept of combination includes, besides the concept of the manifold and of its synthesis, the concept of the unity of the manifold" (B 130), and since that unity is the unity of apperception (see B 135),[9] it would be in *general* logic that Kant accounts for "the [V-]relation of given cognitions in any judgment" (B 141). This would place the entire first step of the second-edition Transcendental Deduction (§ 15–§ 21) in *general* logic. In addition, it would, of course, do the same thing with the entire segment of the transcendental logic entitled "The Clue to the Discovery of All Pure Concepts of the Understanding" (A 66/B 91ff.). Of course, the latter assignment is the very assumption on which the customary view of the functions is based. What would remain for *transcendental* logic would thus be confined to the relation between sensibility and what has been found in general logic. But this approach would not be adequate for Kant to explain the possibility of a priori knowledge. The second-edition Transcendental Deduction was necessary, I submit, precisely because the first-edition Deduction did not treat the understanding's contribution to such knowledge independently of sensibility. That independence, I maintain, constitutes the significance of the first step of the second-edition Deduction.[10]

The last and simplest argument in favor of the view of the functions presented here is that even if the respective arguments in support of the two views weighed equally, the preference should still be given to the view presented here, on the grounds that it is the view that makes a coherent interpretation of the Metaphysical and Transcendental Deductions possible. This might be called the principle of charity applied to Kant interpretation.

9. This argument is laid out in greater detail in Chapter 12.
10. The case is made for this last point in Chapter 10.

In summary, in making it possible for Kant to ground the categories in the logical functions of judgment, the view presented here allows Kant the theoretical consistency to work toward the stated purpose of the entire *Critique*, namely, the a priori demonstration of the possibility of a priori knowledge.[11]

11. Beatrice Longuenesse's *Kant and the Capacity to Judge* (Princeton: Princeton University Press, 1998) appeared only after I completed writing this book. To give it the detailed attention it deserves would take us into areas that extend beyond not only the present chapter but other chapters as well, not to mention areas involving Kant's philosophy that are not covered in the book at all.

Nevertheless, the following observation on her book in relation to the present chapter can be made. The two of us are in agreement on a major thesis, one that stands in opposition to recent commentary and, in my case, to Anglophone commentary in particular. This is the thesis that for Kant the logical functions of judgment provide for the relation (which I designate the B-relation) of representations to objects (Longuenesse, *Kant and the Capacity to Judge*, 5, 12, 78). They therefore fall outside the domain of modern formal logic (5, 74).

The manner in which we separately arrive at this thesis and that in which we move on from it point up some divergences between us, however. Longuenesse leaves Kant's discussion surrounding the Table of Judgments and the logical functions of judgment within the science Kant calls "general logic." She just makes that a richer, more psychological, or mentalistic, logic than other commentators, now including myself, are inclined to do. She puts it in the tradition of the richer Port-Royal logic. Accordingly, now like other commentators and excluding myself, she continues to call the logical functions of judgment "logical *forms* of judgment." In this manner she is able to attribute to the logical functions of judgment the capacity to provide for the B-relation of representation to objects. I, on the other hand, argue against that practice, since I contend that the functions have *content*, which Kant's logical *forms* of judgment clearly do not have. The content is precisely that which B-relates a representation or a cognition to objects. So, since she and I agree that the logical functions of judgment provide for this B-relation, I would invite her to agree that these functions are not logical *forms* of judgment. I am aware, of course, that that would create problems for the other of her main theses that I have already mentioned, namely, that commentators have misunderstood Kant's notion of general logic. We recall that according to Longuenesse they have failed to appreciate the richness of the logic that Kant understood to stand in the tradition of Port-Royal logic. So, in the end, it does not seem that our respective positions on these issues are fully compatible, though we do agree on at least one important thesis, namely, that the logical functions (for Longuenesse, logical *forms*) of judgment provide for the B-relation of a representation to an object.

There are other important points of agreement between us as well. Some of these extend to topics covered in Chapters 10 and 12. In particular, though we do not share the same explanation of why Kant completely rewrote the Transcendental Deduction of the categories for the second (B) edition of the *Critique* and do not agree on the value of reading the B-Deduction in light of the first-edition (A-) Deduction (as she rightly notes Kant himself suggests), we nevertheless do see that certain propositions in the Metaphysical Deduction are actually precursors of certain major theses Kant attempts to prove in the B-Deduction. Foremost among these are the propositions asserted at A 79/B 104–5 in the Metaphysical Deduction.

KANT'S CATEGORIES
RECONSIDERED

I

The customary view of the logical functions of judgment, namely, that they are logical *forms* of judgment and, consequently, have no content, gets support beyond that which is provided by Kant's own language surrounding the Table of Judgments—language I have just finished reinterpreting according to the view of the functions as having content. This support can be found in the first-edition (A-) Transcendental Deduction of the categories.

The A-Deduction argues on behalf of both the transcendental unity of apperception—the unity to which all representations and cognitions must be brought if they are to be *determinately B*-related to objects (B 138), that is, *B*-related in such a way that escapes whatever vagaries belong to any individual's perceptions—and the categories on the grounds that they are necessary conditions of the possibility of *experience*. But if that were the possibility for which the categories and the transcendental unity of apperception were required, the functions on which the categories supposedly rest (A 68/ B 93) would belong to general, or formal, not transcendental, logic, since the latter is the specific logic of *a priori* knowledge *alone* (A 55/B 80). In that case, however, the logic could not provide the content for the categories (through the functions [i.e., forms] of judgment). Consequently, the

Metaphysical Deduction would fail as an argument in support of the idea that it is just these concepts, that is, the categories, that we must employ if we are to think of objects in general.

Without Kant's grounds in the Metaphysical Deduction for taking the categories as necessary for our thought of objects in general, we are forced to look to his more direct dependence on possible experience for these grounds. Only now they must be taken to be objects of possible experience. But Kant does not provide such grounds in the A-Deduction; they are rather to be found in the Analytic of Principles. Charting this route through the undermining of the A-Deduction is the task of the present chapter.

It also points the way toward a more successful Transcendental Deduction of the categories. That would be an argument for the categories that connects them to the transcendental unity of apperception independently of considerations pertaining specifically to the possibility of experience. The argument here will have to be more abstract than that. Such an abstraction will allow the Deduction to continue with the employment of the transcendental logic that was begun in the discussion surrounding the Table of Judgments—something the involvement of possible experience in the initial stages of the A-Deduction does not permit. Consequently, the chances of a successful second-edition Deduction are much improved.

That the indispensability of the categories to our thought of objects in general must be argued for beyond the confines of the Metaphysical Deduction and yet independently of the possibility of experience is the negative thesis of this chapter and a negative thesis of this book as well. This negative thesis suggests a positive one that also is part of the main thesis of this book, namely, that the categories should be argued for as necessary conditions of the possibility of a knowledge that is distinct from experience, namely, a priori knowledge. Only in the context of such an argument can it be shown that the categories are required for possible experience as well.

Before we turn our attention to my separate arguments in support of the two theses I attribute to Kant, we should first consider an objection that applies to both attributions. It might be noted that for Kant the objective validity of the categories is not completely established until they are shown to be necessary conditions of the possibility of experience (e.g., B 161). It might then be asked why the demonstration of this necessity cannot be separated from that necessity pertaining to the possibility of a priori knowledge, as Strawson and Guyer recommend.[1]

1. P. F. Strawson, *The Bounds of Sense: An Essay on Kant's "Critique of Pure Reason"* (London: Methuen, 1966), 86ff. *et passim*; Paul Guyer, *Kant and the Claims of Knowledge* (Cambridge: Cambridge University Press, 1987), 73ff. *et passim*.

The answer is that in demonstrating that the categories are necessary for possible experience, Kant takes the objects of possible experience to be *appearances* (e.g., B 159ff.). However, as Guyer himself would be the first to agree, Kant's appearances are intelligible only in a context in which the possibility of a priori knowledge, not experience, is under discussion. *Appearance* is a transcendental, not an empirical, concept for Kant (Cf., e.g., A 45/B 62ff.). Therefore, that is the context in which the categories are also shown to be necessary for possible experience. That is, apart from that context, Kant has no argument for the view that the categories are necessary for possible experience. All this, of course, is predicated on the proposition that Kant's appearances are to be understood in terms of his theory of the possibility of a priori, not empirical, knowledge—admittedly a proposition to which only some of us subscribe, yet one for which I have already argued in Chapters 7 and 8.

I am now in a position to argue for the two theses separately.

II

Kant himself disposed of his first-edition Transcendental Deduction of the categories on the grounds of its "obscurity" (B xxxviii). What does this "obscurity" actually consist in? After I offer my interpretation of it, we shall find (in section VI below) that it actually rests on an underlying inconsistency at the very heart of the A-Deduction.

The question confronting the Transcendental Deduction, let us recall, is whether appearances, given by means of sensibility, must be subject to the conditions of the unity of the distinct faculty of the understanding (A 89–90/B 122–23). In the A-Deduction Kant thought he could answer the question affirmatively if, having already (in the Metaphysical Deduction) identified the categories as the conditions of the unity of the understanding, he merely took the extra steps of (1) identifying that unity with the transcendental unity of apperception and (2) laying down that unity as the principle to which all objects must be subject if they are to be taken up into the necessary unity of knowledge (A 103ff.). So the transcendental unity of apperception is the principle of the possibility of all objects with respect to our knowledge of them, that is, the epistemic possibility of objects, insofar as that knowledge contains the necessary unity of thought.

One would expect, therefore, that in advancing beyond the Metaphysical Deduction to prove that all appearances must be subject to the categories if they are to be known, Kant would explicitly show the pivotal item in that advance—the transcendental unity of apperception—to be connected to the categories.

But that is not done in the A-Deduction. Rather, Kant argues "that the categories . . . are nothing but the conditions of thought in a possible experience" (A 111) and that it is as the unity of a possible experience that the transcendental unity of apperception depends on the categories (A 110, A 116). But precisely how the transcendental unity of apperception as a necessary condition of a possible experience depends on exactly the categories is left unexplained, or "obscure."

We can reconstruct the A-Deduction as follows: First, it lays down the argument for the unity of apperception in terms of a need belonging to what Kant calls "all reproduction in the series of representations" (A 103, cf. A 119–20), where the representations have already been identified as "appearances" (A 101) or "objects of the senses" (A 119). Next, it argues that this need is met, first, by "a pure transcendental synthesis of imagination (A 101, cf. A 124). This is understood to be the "means" by which "we bring the manifold of intuition, on the one side, into connection with the condition of the necessary unity of apperception, on the other" (A 124).[2]

The first problem with the A-Deduction solution as so far reconstructed is that this "means" by which "we bring the manifold of intuition . . . into *connection with* the conditions of the necessary unity of apperception" (my emphasis) does nothing to explain how through these conditions we bring to the unity of apperception the manifold of intuition that is *distinct from,*

---

2. Many recognize that this indeed is Kant's solution to the problem in the A-Deduction. For example, Allison mentions Heidegger as a commentator who not only recognized this feature of the A-Deduction but in Allison's opinion mistakenly criticized Kant for allegedly having abandoned it in the B-Deduction. According to Allison, Kant did no such thing. See Henry E. Allison, *Kant's Transcendental Idealism: An Interpretation and Defense* (New Haven: Yale University Press, 1983), 163. I am prepared to show not only that a defense of a solution such as Allison's, that is, having the imagination explain the relation of the categories to appearances, is fundamentally flawed, but that his rejection of Heidegger's view that the role of the imagination in the B-Deduction is significantly less than the role it enjoyed in the A-Deduction is also mistaken. Against Heidegger, however, I would argue that he, too, is wrong, but in his own way. His mistake in my view is to regret the change Kant makes in the B-Deduction with respect to the role of imagination. That is, Kant's solution in step one of the B-Deduction, at least in the reconstruction of it that I am about to offer, seems to me much better than the corresponding A-Deduction solution, which consists of "pure imagination." For reasons of economy, instead of going into detailed criticisms of either Allison or Heidegger in this regard, I should like my general criticism of the A-Deduction solution, which I am about to give below in the body of the text, to stand as my grounds for claiming that both Allison and Heidegger are mistaken in their shared commitment to "pure imagination" as the preferred solution to the problem of the Deduction.

and so far unconnected with, the conditions. The explanation must first consist in the particular *V-relations* in which the conditions are so *V*-related to the distinct manifold that the manifold is *B*-related to the objects through the conditions, that is, to the very objects that are represented through the conditions. It is only in regard to a manifold that is *distinct* from the conditions, and not to a manifold of intuition that is *connected* with the conditions (through the pure imagination), that the very problem of the Transcendental Deduction even arises. In relying on the pure imagination to prove that the categories are *B*-related to appearances, Kant is relying on something that presupposes the a priori conditions of sensibility, although the question before him is how the categories can be applied to appearances when the latter are first determined through these very conditions of sensibility. Reliance on pure imagination causes Kant to go in a circle and leave unanswered the question he set before himself.[3] In other words, after going through the Deduction he is back where he started, namely, facing the task of accounting for the particular *V*-relation of the categories to a manifold of intuition that is *distinct from* and *unconnected with* them and nonetheless—indeed, thereby—*B*-related to the objects that are represented through them.

Let it not be imagined that Kant already assumes the *V*-relation of the categories to the manifold in intuition in general in the Metaphysical Deduction, and hence relies on an implicit account of that *V*-relation in that Deduction. When he speaks of the categories and of the objects of intuition in general in that Deduction he definitely does *not* speak of the *B*-relation of the categories to the objects; he rather says that the categories *extend to* these objects *(auf Objekte gehen;* A 79/B 105). The *extension* of a concept does not provide Kant with the notion he needs to explain the *B*-relation of a manifold of representations or cognitions to an object; for that he needs the particular *V*-relation that is still in question. The extension of the categories fails to so *V*-relate them to the distinct manifold of representations that the manifold is *B*-related to the objects that are represented through the categories, that is, to the objects of intuition in general.

---

3. Allison is aware of this issue and considers it an example of question-begging; see *Kant's Transcendental Idealism*, 161. But he seems to think it a problem facing the *B*-Deduction, which is puzzling, since we both agree that the issue can be resolved in terms of certain features of step one of that Deduction, the step that *precedes* the introduction of pure imagination into the B-Deduction. So the issue does not even arise in the B-Deduction. I also think mistaken the way in which Allison tries to keep pure imagination in the picture in the B-Deduction, because it wrongly assumes that for Kant the unity of time ("a single all-inclusive time") involves the categories (ibid., 162). But Kant explicitly *excludes* this involvement at B 160 n.

Having begun an analysis of the trouble with the A-Deduction with the simple expedient of putting the entire blame on the role played by imagination in the Deduction, I can now advance to a more detailed diagnosis of the difficulty. The necessity of bringing appearances under the rules of the understanding stems from the fact that otherwise they might be in such disarray that the unity of our thought of these objects, and hence our knowledge of them, would be impossible (A 89–91/B 122–23, A 100–101). The problem facing the Deduction, then, is: how are we to understand the necessity that the manifold of appearances must be brought to that unity of the understanding without which our thought, and hence our knowledge, of objects would be impossible? If that necessity can be explained as the requirement that, as a matter of *principle*, apart from which objects could not even be *thought*, all of a subject's representations must be subject to that unity (i.e., the principle of the transcendental unity of apperception), then the *first step* of showing that the manifold of *appearances* must be subject to the *categories* would consist in showing that the categories are the conditions of bringing the manifold of *a sensible intuition in general* to that unity.

But the A-Deduction does not take this *first step*. Throughout, the Deduction is concerned with the unity in the synthesis of *appearances*, not objects of a sensible intuition in general. The difference between them, we recall, is that our a priori intuition is present in the former, but absent in the latter. In the Deduction, if appearances are taken *collectively*, the unity in their synthesis is represented by two notions, both of which are grounded in the synthetic unity of apperception (A 110, A113, A 122). First, appearances are said to represent a single object, namely, *the transcendental object*. This is the object that alone is supposed to "confer upon all our empirical concepts in general [B-]relation to an object, that is, objective reality" (A 109). Second, appearances have an *affinity* with one another. That is, in the synthetic unity of the manifold of appearances the synthetic unity of apperception is entitled *affinity*. So we have two notions that are equally grounded in the synthetic unity of apperception, the first providing objective *reality* for all our empirical concepts and the second providing objective *validity* for the categories by providing for the objective validity of our a priori knowledge of objects.

The trouble with these two notions, and perhaps the reason that Kant made no use of them in the B-Deduction, is that they can throw no light whatsoever on why it is specifically the categories—the concepts that the Metaphysical Deduction tells us are in "agreement" with the logical functions of judgment—that the understanding must employ in bringing the manifold of representations or cognitions to the unity of apperception. And the reason, I suggest, like my reason for rejecting pure imagination in the A-Deduction, is that they cannot help us find the grounds of the categories in the purely *intellectual* functions of the understanding, namely, the logical functions of judgment, the so-called "moments of thought in general" (A 71/B 96).

Kant must have come to realize that the problem of any Transcendental Deduction of the categories would be insoluble so long as the proposed solution was restricted to a manifold of *our* sensible intuition. For that restriction is none other than pure imagination itself under a translucent guise, since pure imagination consists in the determination of *our* intuition by the understanding (B 151–52). That is, it consists in the *connection* of the categories with the manifold of *our a priori* sensible intuition without providing any explanation of what the *V*-relation of the categories to the manifold of a sensible intuition *in general* consists in. So, as noted just above, any solution to the problem of the Deduction requires that the manifold be a manifold of a sensible intuition *in general,* that is, an intuition from which sensibility and its two modes of intuition, space and time, have been abstracted. The solution must therefore be independent of sensibility.[4] Indeed, Kant explicitly stipulates this requirement in the *Metaphysical* Deduction. There he introduces the categories as the representations of the understanding that have got their "transcendental content" "by means of the synthetic unity of the manifold in intuition *in general*" (A 79/B 105, my emphasis). It is the ubiquitous *überhaupt* ("in general") itself that creates the very problem of the Deduction in the first place and renders the A-Deduction solution to it a nonstarter, since it is the very generality of the categories that separates them from sensibility and in so doing raises the very question the Transcendental Deduction is supposed to resolve, namely, that of their B-relation to the given objects of sensibility, that is, to objects of the senses. To borrow a phrase from the B-Deduction, no "beginning is made of a *deduction* of the pure concepts of the understanding" (B 144) in the A-Deduction. This is not to deny an essential role to the imagination at a *later* stage of the Deduction. It is only, again, to say that the A-Deduction is no substitute for an essentially prior argument that so *V*-relates the categories to the manifold

---

4. I say "independent of sensibility," and not just "independent of our sensibility," because I so interpret Kant's use of "sensibility" that reference to us (human beings) is already present in the use, implicitly. That is, I understand Kant's use of the term to be anthropocentric, or if broader than that, it involves a reference to sentient beings who are just like us in the particular respects that are adumbrated in the Aesthetic.

of an intuition *in general* that the latter is determinately *B*-related to objects in general, since the *distinctness* between appearances and the categories requires that the categories *first* be thus *V*-related to the distinct manifold of an intuition *in general* if they are eventually to be *B*-related to appearances.

A certain objection might be leveled against this criticism of the A-Deduction. It might be argued that since the categories are rendered intellectual through their connection with the logical functions of judgment, the only task left for a Transcendental Deduction of the categories is to demonstrate that they, and thereby, through them, the transcendental unity of apperception, have a *V*-relation to a manifold of an intuition (or to objects) that for the sake of the demonstration is (are) regarded as independent of any *B*-relation the categories might have to it (them). So, there is no need to abstract sensibility from the argument, even as early as step one, for any other purpose than to demonstrate that the relevant synthesis in question, that is, a synthesis through the categories, is an intellectual synthesis.

In response, I would draw attention to the fact that the objection offers no argument whatsoever in support of the claim that the unity of apperception is actually *V*-related to a manifold of intuition (or to objects) through the very *V*-relation of the categories to such a manifold (or objects). After all, a basic connection between the categories and the logical functions of judgment has already been laid down in the Metaphysical Deduction. So, the objection just assumes, as I think the A-Deduction just assumed, the very thesis that I think Kant came to see actually requires proof in the Deduction, namely, the proposition that the categories are necessary conditions of the possibility of a manifold of sensible intuition in general being brought to the transcendental unity of apperception.

This takes us to the ultimate question of what drove the A-Deduction into this impasse, where it seems it cannot free itself of imagination, and consequently sensibility. To answer this question, I can only repeat what I have said above: Throughout, the Deduction is concerned with the unity in the synthesis specifically of *appearances*, since they are the objects that present the entire problem of the Deduction in the first place, namely, that appearances might be in such disarray that experience would be impossible. This statement of the problem creating the need for such a deduction seems very likely to have led Kant to the mistaken view that *possible experience* itself must mediate the connection between the categories and the unity of apperception and that possible experience entails the involvement of the imagination.

To briefly recapitulate the analysis thus far of the A-Deduction: First, as the A-Deduction lays down the argument for the unity of apperception, it does so in terms of a need belonging to what Kant calls "all reproduction in the series of representations" (A 103, cf. A 119–20), where the representations have already been identified as "appearances" (A 101) or "objects of the senses" (A 119). After the introduction of the pure imagination to synthesize these appearances, Kant argues that the need of "all reproduction in the series of representations" can only be met by the transcendental unity of apperception. It in turn depends on "rules" governing the "reproduction of the manifold" of intuition (A 105). But the burden of specifying which rules at bottom they must be falls entirely on the Metaphysical Deduction (cf. A 119, A 125), in which case the rules must in some way rest on the logical functions of judgment. Moreover, since the rules required by the transcendental unity of apperception are to provide for the *reproduction* of appearances, they condition appearances through *empirical* concepts or laws, which makes the conditioning itself *empirical*. In this manner the necessity of the rules is relative to the requirements of empirical, not a priori, knowledge—as it is in psychology. Consequently, if this were the knowledge whose possibility Kant is trying to explain, he could not argue for the necessity of *the logical functions of judgment* on the ground that the possibility of a priori knowledge *alone* requires them. That is, if the possibility of empirical knowledge were his concern, the discussion surrounding the Table of Judgments would belong to general logic, not *transcendental* logic. So his argument for the categories in particular would have to be shifted from the Metaphysical Deduction to the Analytic of Principles, where they should be shown to be necessary for possible experience. And this is precisely what most recent commentators think he indeed should have done, namely, shift the argument as indicated.

To sum up, although the A-Deduction has advanced beyond the Metaphysical Deduction through the introduction of the transcendental unity of apperception, that which mediates between the categories and the unity of apperception is *possible experience*. But not until the Analytic of Principles does the first edition of the *Critique* demonstrate, beyond the argument of the Metaphysical Deduction, that it is the categories in particular that contain the rules required for possible experience.

Now, it is no coincidence that so many of those who criticize Kant for failing to bring the categories up to the distinctive demands of the Transcendental Deduction brought about by the introduction of the transcendental unity of apperception into the argument are commentators who are actually sympathetic to what I consider to be the unfortunate method the A-Deduction seems to follow. This is the method of trying to prove the necessity of the transcendental unity of apperception on the grounds that it is a presupposition of the possibility of experience. These commentators would be among the first to notice that since Kant is arguing for its necessity on these grounds, he needs further argument that would serve to connect it to the categories on the additional grounds that the categories themselves are necessary for the possibility of experience. And these further grounds are provided, they claim, only later on, in the Analytic of Principles. Such commentators are legion.[5]

III

To see what it would take to upgrade certain propositions in the Metaphysical Deduction so that they can adequately serve as premises in the Transcendental Deduction, we should first notice that it is following the Metaphysical Deduction that Kant raises the question facing the Transcendental Deduction in terms of "the functions of the understanding" (A 89/B 122) or "the functions of thought" (A 91/B 123), as well as in terms of the categories (A 85/B 117, A 88/B 120). That is, he refers to the conditions of the unity of the understanding as such functions as well as the concepts that "rest on" the functions, that is, the categories (A 68/B 93). It is therefore evident that the functions referred to are the logical functions of judgment, since the Metaphysical Deduction has just tried to establish that these are the functions that stand in isomorphic relation to the categories and that "specify the understanding completely, and yield an exhaustive inventory of its powers" (A 79/B 105).

So let this isomorphism between the categories and the logical functions of judgment provide a clue toward discovering what must be done to make the premises given by the Metaphysical Deduction suitable for the Transcendental Deduction and its distinctive reliance on the transcendental unity of apperception. Since the grounds of this isomorphism consist in two identity propositions that are crucial to both the Metaphysical and the Transcenden-

5. A sample of such commentators might include Jonathan Bennett (*Kant's Analytic* [Cambridge: Cambridge University Press, 1966], 94–95), Patricia Kitcher (*Kant's Transcendental Psychology* [New York: Oxford University Press, 1990], 89), and Paul Guyer (*Kant and the Claims of Knowledge* [Cambridge: Cambridge University Press, 1987], 98–99, and "The Transcendental Deduction of the Categories," in *The Cambridge Companion to Kant,* ed. Paul Guyer [Cambridge: Cambridge University Press, 1992], 127).

tal Deductions, let us identify them here. First: "The same function which gives unity to the various representations *in a judgment* also gives unity to the mere synthesis of representations *in an intuition,* and this unity, in its most general expression, we entitle the pure concept of the understanding" (A 79/B 104–5). Kant is thus asserting an identity between the function (i.e., "the unity of the act [i.e., action (*Handlung*)] of bringing various representations under one common representation" [A 68/B 93]) that is the source of the unity in a *judgment* and the function that is the source of the unity of a synthesis in an *intuition.*[6] We thus look forward to further argument for an explanation of this identity between the source of the unity in a judgment and that of the unity of a synthesis in an intuition—that is, an explanation of the relation between a unitary judgment and a unitary synthesis in an intuition.

The other identity Kant asserts is between the two *actions* (*Handlungen*) that contain the identical function just mentioned: "The same understanding, through the same operations [i.e., actions (*Handlungen*)] by which in concepts, by means of analytic unity, it produced the logical form of a judgment, also introduces a transcendental content into its representations, by

6. Moving back just a bit in the Metaphysical Deduction, we find that the pure concept of the understanding is given by "pure synthesis" (A 78/B 104). So, the same function that gives unity in a judgment and in an intuition thus depends on the previously mentioned pure synthesis. Therefore, it is pure, not empirical, synthesis that gives unity to the representations both in a judgment and in an intuition. This should eliminate any role for the synthesis of the "reproduction of the manifold" in an explanation of the common source of unity in a judgment and an intuition, since that synthesis "is merely empirical" (A 121; see also B 152). But that is part of the explanation of the unity of the manifold of intuition that we find in the A-Deduction (A 105, A 121). So the A-Deduction is already at odds with the Metaphysical Deduction.

These concluding remarks may prove perplexing to readers who are recalling that being empirical did not prevent the synthesis of *apprehension* from being carried over from the A- to the B-Deduction (B 160, B 162 n). So why should it be responsible for eliminating the *reproduction* of the manifold of intuition from the B-Deduction? The answer is that it is not *merely its being empirical* but instead its being *merely empirical* that eliminates the synthesis of reproduction from the argument. The difference between the two is that the concepts, even the necessary ones, that is, the laws, governing the *merely* empirical synthesis of *reproduction* are themselves *empirical* (A 100, A 121, B 152), even though they must rest on a priori grounds (A 101–2, A 122), whereas the forms to which the empirical synthesis of *apprehension* must conform are a priori (*vide* A 99, B 160). The problem with the merely empirical synthesis of reproduction is that what immediately conditions it is itself empirical and thus psychological (B 139–40). The Transcendental Deduction must be rid of *all psychological* conditions on synthesis, including all *associative* ones, if it is to establish the possibility of *a priori* knowledge. The B-Deduction does just that, even though it holds over from the A-Deduction the empirical synthesis of apprehension. This empirical synthesis is not a psychological phenomenon.

This position is at odds with the entire approach to the *Critique,* including, therefore, the Transcendental Deduction, of Patricia Kitcher in her *Kant's Transcendental Psychology.*

means of the synthetic unity of the manifold in intuition in general" (A 79/ B 105). Now, it seems universally agreed among commentators that the expression "the logical form of a judgment," as Kant employs it here, is a generic term for the logical forms of judgment that are given by the Table of Judgments, which has been laid down earlier in the Transcendental Logic (A 70/B 95). In line with this reading of the passage is the corollary that the transcendental content Kant is referring to here consists in a synthetic unity of the manifold of intuition in general that is independent of these logical functions (i.e., forms) of judgment.

Both readings, however, are dubious. Presumably, the expression in the passage "its representations" refers to the categories. One reading would thus have the content of the categories be independent of the logical functions of judgment. But this cannot be, since it is through these "functions of unity in a judgment" that "concepts, as predicates of possible judgments, [B-]relate to some representation of a not yet determined object" (A 69/B 94). And surely we can understand this B-relation of concept to object as the content of the concept (see A 55/B 79). So, for this reason, as well as the others given in the previous chapter, we might rather view the transcendental content in question as belonging to the logical *functions* of judgment.[7]

Where does this leave Kant's reference to the logical *form* of a judgment? A clue can be taken from the B-Deduction. There, this form is identified as consisting in "original apperception and its *necessary unity*." As a principle that gives rise to "the objective determination of all representations," it is none other than "the transcendental unity of apperception" (B 142). But the necessity of this unity is the very issue before us! It is with respect to this unity that we are looking to an upgrading of the identity propositions from the Metaphysical Deduction for the conditions under which objects or representations may be brought to it.

Well, the passage from the Metaphysical Deduction we are presently reading tells us that the same action that produces the transcendental unity of apperception in concepts also introduces the content of the logical functions of judgment into the categories. So, since the issue before us is how, independently of the Analytic of Principles, Kant can support his thesis that the categories are the conditions under which objects or representations may be brought to the transcendental unity of apperception, we have only

---

7. This interpretation of "transcendental content" seems to dispute that given by Darrell Johnson, namely, that it refers to the concept of an object in general. See his "Kant's Metaphysical Deduction," in *Proceedings of the Eighth International Kant Congress* (Milwaukee: Marquette University Press, 1995), vol. II, pt. I, 273.

to look for an argument that spells out the relation between the logical *form* of a judgment that is produced in concepts and the *transcendental content* that is introduced into the categories. But, under the present proposal, this is a relation between the transcendental unity of apperception and the content of the logical functions of judgment. Furthermore, Kant asserts that the relation obtains through an *action* that is identical to both of them. It is thus an argument that establishes a relation between this form and this content through an identical action that is involved in each. Precisely this relation through this identical action (which Kant entitles *combination* [B 130ff.]) finally gets spelled out in the conclusion of the "first step" of the B-Deduction, §§ 19 and 20.[8] And, necessarily, this is done as the B-Deduction also explains the identity asserted in the *first* identity proposition considered above, namely, the identity between the unity in a judgment and that of a synthesis in an intuition. Of course, this identical unity is none other than the transcendental unity of apperception itself. In a word, these two identity propositions from the Metaphysical Deduction set the initial tasks for the Transcendental Deduction.

These explanations are precisely those missing from the A-Deduction. By sliding over the need for such explanations, the A-Deduction fails to tell us how the transcendental unity of apperception depends on the categories for objects or representations to be brought to it.

IV

It is the contention of this chapter that the role assigned to possible experience causes the A-Deduction to rely on, instead of explain, the two identity propositions from the Metaphysical Deduction, mentioned above, that are crucial to the Transcendental Deduction. Since both editions of the Transcendental Deduction advance beyond the Metaphysical Deduction through their respective applications of the concept of the transcendental unity of apperception, if that advance has us return to the Metaphysical Deduction for certain premises, namely, the identity propositions in question, that have not themselves been brought forward as they should have been, to meet the

8. As already noted, the now widely accepted division of the B-Deduction into two steps was first introduced into the current commentary on the Deduction by Dieter Henrich in his "Proof-Structure of Kant's Transcendental Deduction," *Review of Metaphysics* 22 (1969): 640–59.

demands of the new concept, then the argument has in effect returned us to its starting point despite its ostensible advance through its introduction of the new concept.

To put this charge another way, since the Transcendental Deduction adds the concept of the transcendental unity of apperception to the premises given by the Metaphysical Deduction, it cannot simply rely on these premises as they are given in this Deduction for support of the new concept. The Transcendental Deduction must work with those premises to make it clear that and how they support the new concept. It is proposed here that this reliance on these identity propositions, without any accompanying truly clarifying explanation—indeed, the explanation it offers in terms of possible experience only further obscures matters—is characterized by Kant as "an obscurity." The explanation of exactly these identity propositions must have been what Kant had in mind when he announced in the preface to the *Metaphysical Foundations of Natural Science* that he had found a new, simple proof for the Deduction of the categories,[9] which he actually presented in the so-called first step of the B-Deduction.

Both the preface to the *Metaphysical Foundations of Natural Science* and step one of the B-Deduction make it clear that the relation between the categories, which are given in the Metaphysical Deduction, and the new concept of the transcendental unity of apperception, which is introduced in the Transcendental Deduction, should be understood as mediated by *the logical functions of judgment*.

But these functions cannot be clearly understood as bringing about this relation so long as possible experience interferes with this task. This brings us once again to the conclusion of the argument for the negative thesis, that the A-Deduction's particular reliance on possible experience creates the "obscurity" to which Kant refers in the second-edition preface. Since the logical functions of judgment do not have any content if the knowledge whose possibility they are supposed to determine includes empirical as well as a priori knowledge (in which case they do indeed become mere logical *forms* of judgment and are thereby comprehended within general logic), the reliance on possible experience to mediate between the categories and the transcendental unity of apperception actually "obscures" our understanding of how the logical functions of judgment can play their necessary role in that mediation.

---

9. Immanuel Kant, *Metaphysical Foundations of Natural Science*, trans. James Ellington (Indianapolis: Bobbs-Merrill, 1970), 13–14 n.

V

A priori knowledge alone is the sort of knowledge that allows the readings of these two identity propositions from the Metaphysical Deduction that are required for a successful Transcendental Deduction. The logical functions of judgment can have the content attributed to them on the proposed reading of the second identity proposition if and only if the discussion of these functions that surrounds the Table of Judgments belongs to *transcendental*, not formal, or general, logic (A 55/B 79). Moreover, logic is thus transcendental if and only if any knowledge of which it is the logic is a priori knowledge (A 55/ B 80). Therefore, the logical functions of judgment have the content required for the proposed reading of the second identity proposition just in case any knowledge that contains them is a priori knowledge. Consequently, they can contribute to the content of empirical knowledge only in the context of their contribution to the content of a priori knowledge.

The proposed reading of the first identity proposition is also affected accordingly. I have already proposed that the identical function that gives unity to a judgment and to a synthesis in an intuition, that is, the transcendental unity of apperception, is the very unity of the identical action, combination, that is involved in the second identity proposition. This combination is none other than that involved in a judgment. "[W]e can reduce all acts of the understanding to judgments" (A 69/B 94). And "the understanding . . . is nothing but the faculty of combining *a priori*, and of bringing the manifold of given representations under the unity of apperception" (B 135). So, the unity of the identical action in the second identity proposition is the very unity that is referred to in the first identity proposition. Of course this must be the case, since a judgment and a synthesis in an intuition are both *combinations* (B 135, B 142, B 143, B 150, B 162b) and the unity belonging to all combinations is the transcendental unity of apperception (B 131, B 132, B 134–35).

VI

It might be objected that the structure of the proposed interpretation of the B-Deduction does not follow the actual structure of the Deduction itself. The interpretation seems to tie the triadic interrelation among the categories, the logical functions of judgment, and the transcendental unity of apperception too closely to a priori knowledge, when, in fact, that interrelation is laid down in the first step of the Deduction quite independently, not just of experience, but of a priori knowledge as well. Worse, a priori knowledge of mathematics aside (B 154–55), the possibility of a priori knowledge of the laws of nature in general is established in step two (B 164–65) only after, and indeed on the basis of, the proof of the possibility of experience (B 161). So, either the interrelation in question is established independently of knowledge altogether (step one), or its involvement in a priori knowledge (in step two) does indeed depend on first proving its necessity with respect to experience, which is precisely the proposition contested in this chapter.

In reply, though the logical functions of judgment are not yet contained in any knowledge in step one, that step, were it not to belong to a demonstration of the possibility of a priori knowledge, would not belong to a logic that is transcendental. This would locate it in formal, or general, logic, if in any logic at all. But that would confound the employment of the categories and the transcendental unity of apperception, not to mention the logical functions of judgment, in step one. Surely they contribute to the B-relation knowledge has to objects; yet that B-relation is of no concern to formal, or general, logic whatsoever (A 55/B 79).

The objection that the reference to the possibility of experience precedes the reference to the possibility of a priori knowledge of the laws of nature in general takes us back to the beginning of this chapter. As noted there, the categories are shown to be necessary for the possibility of experience only in a context in which the objects of possible experience are taken as appearances. But this implies that it is actually the possibility of a priori knowledge that is being proved in that context. Consequently, the proof of the necessity of the categories for possible experience rather belongs to that context and does not stand alone apart from it.

VII

So long as Kant views the transcendental unity of apperception as a presupposition of possible experience and the proof of the categories as conditions for objects or representations to be brought to that presupposition, he is bound to miss the "obscurity" in his reasoning and overlook the considerations adduced above for moving beyond the confines of the Metaphysical Deduction to demonstrate the necessity of the categories, without, however, going all the way to the arguments contained in the Analytic of Principles. As the A-Deduction has been described above, it takes the rules required by the transcendental unity of apperception as conditions of the possibility of experience. More precisely, the rules are taken as conditions of the reproduction of the manifold of intuition, which the Deduction also considers to be the manifold of appearances. However, this leaves the A-Deduction egregiously incomplete and shifts the burden of proof of a connection between the categories and the transcendental unity of apperception to the Analytic of Principles, where, it is claimed by most commentators, it is possible experience, not the logical functions of judgment, that is supposed to bring the two items together.

We can now bring the discussion to a close by summarizing all three positions considered in the chapter. The position of the A-Deduction itself is untenable because, first, it is "obscure" in the manner indicated, and worse, inconsistent. Its "obscurity" consists in its failure to explain the assertions in the Metaphysical Deduction of (1) an identity of the unity in a judgment and that in an intuition and (2) an identity of the action that produces the unity of apperception in concepts and that which introduces the content of the logical functions of judgment into the categories. Once the argument advanced to the pivotal concept of the transcendental unity of apperception in the Transcendental Deduction, it was no longer sufficient just to assert (1) and (2). These identities should have been upgraded as they became requirements for objects or representations to be brought to the transcendental unity of apperception.

Uncovering this "obscurity" also reveals the inconsistency mentioned above. On the one hand, the argument relies on the Metaphysical Deduction as an exercise belonging to transcendental logic. This implies that the discussion surrounding the Table of Judgments belongs to that same logic, not to general logic. Consequently, the logical functions of judgment are argued for on the basis of requirements of a priori knowledge alone, not empirical knowledge. With respect to the latter, a significantly reduced table of the logical *forms* of judgment belonging to the general logic practiced by the logicians of the time would have sufficed. Nevertheless, the A-Deduction proceeds to consider the transcendental unity of apperception and its required rules as presuppositions of possible experience, and hence as conditions of empirical knowledge. But this is an exercise in theory of empirical, not a priori, knowledge. Therefore, reliance on results the Metaphysical Deduction draws from transcendental logic, which abstracts from all empirical conditions of synthesis, such as the reproduction of appearances, makes the A-Deduction inconsistent. From the vantage point of the A-Deduction, the reasoning of the Metaphysical Deduction appears to belong to general logic. So independent arguments for the necessity of the categories with respect to objects or representations brought to the transcendental unity of apperception must be provided.

This is precisely the position of so many present commentators on the *Critique*. The A-Deduction's characterization of the transcendental unity of apperception and the categories as conditions of possible experience supports their contention that the discussion surrounding the Table of Judgments belongs to general logic and, consequently, that the adequate arguments for the specific categories can be found only in the Analytic of Principles.

The third position is found in the B-Deduction and is the one advocated in this chapter. It is that the Metaphysical Deduction is in order because the discussion surrounding the Table of Judgments belongs to transcendental logic. To rely on it, the Transcendental Deduction must establish the categories as entailed by the act of bringing the manifold of an intuition in general to the transcendental unity of apperception independently of considerations pertaining to the conditions of the possibility of experience. Possible experience enters the picture only as the knowledge that gives a priori knowledge the empirical employment of its concepts and principles that is required for its (their) objective validity. Finally, the main point of the chapter is that the Transcendental Deduction cannot thus rely on the Metaphysical Deduction unless the relation between the categories and the unity of the understanding is upgraded to keep pace with the argument's advance through its employment of the pivotal concept of the transcendental unity of apperception. It is therefore the first order of business of the B-Deduction that it address this issue, which it does in the so-called first step of the Deduction.

THREE ISSUES IN STEP ONE
OF THE B-DEDUCTION

I

Having cleared away the false steps, or, better, having exposed the lack of good ones, of the A-Deduction, we can consider how in the B-Deduction Kant upgrades the two identity propositions of the Metaphysical Deduction (A 79/B 104–5) so that we can understand the connection between the categories and the transcendental unity of apperception, a connection made through a reliance on the logical functions of judgment. This initial task of the B-Deduction is the primary job of the so-called first step of the Deduction, the step that is brought to a conclusion in subsection 21.

What distinguishes this first step of the B-Deduction from the initial stages of the A-Deduction, in both the latter's so-called subjective and objective versions, is that it contains no reference to the possibility of experience in its explanation of the objective validity of the categories. In fact, there is an explicit distinction of the object of a judgment or of an intuition, including an empirical intuition, from the object of an individual's perceptions insofar as the latter is subject to the vagaries of empirical conditions and circumstances (B 139–40, B 142). Only the former is an object to which a manifold of cognitions has a determinate *B*-relation either through the representation of the transcendental unity of apperception, namely, the "I think" (B 132) (as an object of a judgment [B 142]), or through the categories (as an object of a sensible intuition [B 137, B 141ff., B 143]).

Before I lay out my positive account of the first step of the B-Deduction (in the next chapter), however, I must deal with three issues that have given rise to serious criticism of the Deduction and that would keep my positive account from going forward if I failed to deal with them. As I do so, however, the importance of the distinction of a priori knowledge from empirical knowledge will again be evident. It will be seen that the issues have proved troublesome for Kant only because the *Critique*'s defensible theory of knowledge has mainly been restricted to *empirical,* rather than a priori, knowledge. My take on the theory, on the other hand, allows me to rebut the particular criticisms surrounding these three issues and thereby to present my positive account of his theory of knowledge. The issues will be represented by Kitcher, Allison, and Guyer.

II

The first of these issues concerns the relation of Kant's theory of judgment to his theory of the unity of apperception. Though Kitcher defends Kant's claim that we make judgments about objects on the basis of a synthesis of intuitions,[1] and further defends his claim that that synthesis involves the unity of apperception,[2] she stops short of defending his "analysis of making judgments," insofar as it is "intertwined with considerations about the requirements of apperception."[3] What are these "requirements of apperception" that she wants to remove from her account of his "analysis of making judgments"?

They seem to be the logical functions of judgment listed in the Table of Judgments and their "alleged connections" with the categories. They also seem to be the categories themselves, for immediately after her mention of "the requirements of apperception," she criticizes Kant's "One-Step Deduction" for "mov[ing] quickly from this analysis [of making judgments] to an argument for a special status for the categories."[4] This surmise is borne out by her later criticism that Kant "believes that the unity of apperception is

---

1. Patricia Kitcher, *Kant's Transcendental Psychology* (New York: Oxford University Press, 1990), 88–89.
2. Ibid., 115–16.
3. Ibid., 88.
4. Ibid., 89.

brought about by syntheses that are guided by rules associated with the categories"—a belief of Kant's based on arguments of his that Kitcher contends do not "succeed."[5] These are the arguments he alludes to "[i]n a well-known footnote to the preface of *The Metaphysical Foundations of Natural Science* (1786), [where he] estimates that the Deduction of the categories could be carried out 'almost by a single conclusion' from an exact definition [or analysis] of the act of judgment."[6]

She aligns her first criticisms of these arguments of Kant's with those criticisms already advanced by such commentators as Jonathan Bennett.[7] And among these, her first complaint is that Kant "does not adequately defend the table of judgments,"[8] wherein he lists the logical functions of judgment (A 70/B 95). Perhaps she is demanding of Kant a defense such as that provided by Klaus Reich, discussed in Chapter 9.[9] If so, as already argued, I would agree with Allison that such a demand is misguided, since Reich tries to derive the functions from the unity of apperception, and Allison cites the already much discussed passage in the second-edition Deduction in which Kant explicitly disavows any such derivation:[10] "This peculiarity of our understanding, that it can produce *a priori* unity of apperception solely by means of the categories, and only by such and so many, is as little capable of further explanation as why we have just these and no other functions of judgment, or why space and time are the only forms of our possible intuition" (B 145–46).

We must acknowledge, however, that this passage probably would not satisfy Kitcher's demand of Kant for an adequate defense of the table, since Bennett, for one, cited the very same passage,[11] and this did not block his criticism of the Table of Judgments; and since Kitcher is aligning herself with Bennett, it should not block hers either.

Bennett persists in his criticism because he claims that the view repre-

---

5. Ibid., 105.

6. Ibid., 86. This footnote of Kant's would not be especially troublesome to the view of the logical functions of judgment advanced in Chapter 9.

7. Ibid., 89. In an endnote she cites Bennett's well-known criticism in *Kant's Analytic* (Cambridge: Cambridge University Press, 1966), chap. 7, not 6, as Kitcher has it.

8. Kitcher, *Kant's Transcendental Psychology*, 89.

9. See his *Completeness of Kant's Table of Judgments*, trans. Jane Kneller and Michael Losonsky (Stanford: Stanford University Press, 1992).

10. Henry E. Allison, *Kant's Transcendental Idealism: An Interpretation and Defense* (New Haven: Yale University Press, 1983), 128. In this regard Allison is following the lead of L. Krüger in his "Wollte Kant die Vollständigkeit seiner Urteilstafel bewiesen?" *Kant-Studien* 59 (1968): 333–56. See Chapter 9 for a discussion of Allison's relation to this article of Krüger's.

11. Bennett, *Kant's Analytic*, 83.

sented in the passage above "is surrounded by the swarm of difficulties which beset the outer-sense theory . . . construed as an account of the mode of operation of a noumenal outer sense."[12] "The swarm of difficulties" Bennett alludes to are developed in a sustained argument of his that is finally summed up in his statement that since "a genetic theory of outer experience requires a reified outer sense," that sense, "inevitably, must be noumenal."[13] Similar reasoning about a genetic theory of judgment making presumably would require a reified understanding, which, "inevitably," would also have to be noumenal. In what sense is Bennett using "noumenal" here?

We can answer the question if we turn to the actual argument that leads to this summation of Bennett's. We find in Bennett's argument the premise that "[a] noumenon is anything which is not phenomenal, i.e., which is not a sensory state and which cannot be known through the senses. The 'things in themselves' of which Kant also speaks can for present purposes be equated with noumena."[14]

The trouble with this premise is that it extends the concept of a noumenon over too many elements of Kant's system that Kant himself obviously had no intention of considering as such, including, to mention just two, space and time. So we must look for a better way of understanding what Kant meant when he disavowed any attempt to explain "why we have just these and no other functions of judgment."[15]

12. Ibid.
13. Ibid., 27.
14. Ibid., 24.
15. Though this question will not be examined further here, one line worth pursuing is suggested by Dieter Henrich in his "Kant's Notion of a Deduction and the Methodological Background of the First *Critique*," in *Kant's Transcendental Deductions*, ed. Eckart Förster (Stanford: Stanford University Press, 1989), esp. 37. For a valuable comment on this line, with a suggestion of a further way of understanding Kant's position, see, in the same volume, P. F. Strawson, "Sensibility, Understanding, and the Doctrine of Synthesis: Comments on Henrich and Guyer," 69–74. For my own part, I, of course, take a completely different tack on the entire question, arguing that in the Analytic of Concepts Kant did not intend the logical functions of judgment to be taken as logical *forms* of judgment belonging to *general* logic. Rather, they have *content*, and consequently belong to *transcendental* logic. My position, which is spelled out in Chapter 9, is that Kant considers the functions different specifications of the unity of apperception that is involved in all acts in which "much possible knowledge is collected into one" (A 69/B 94). We simply "find" the differences, Kant says, once "we abstract from all content of a judgment [in general], and consider only the mere form of understanding" (A 70/B 95). The sense in which he uses "find" here accords with the sense in which he says that it is just a fact, without further explanation, that "space and time are the only forms of our possible intuition" (B 146). In other words, he is not prepared with any explanation of why we have the forms of knowledge we in fact have, whether the forms belong to sensibility or to the understanding. The forms are nonetheless there, in those two faculties, awaiting to be "found" by us in our analysis of the faculties.

If we turn now to Kitcher's second complaint against Kant that is aligned with Bennett's criticism, a complaint she shares with Guyer,[16] we find that she alleges that Kant has not adequately defended "the alleged connections between these forms [i.e., the logical functions of judgment] and the categories."[17] Of these alleged connections, Bennett is actually critical only of those under the head of "relation."[18] Bennett contends that the argument in support of the a priority of these relational categories is to be found in the "Principles" chapter and not in the deductions, Metaphysical or Transcendental.[19]

It must be admitted that Kitcher's, Guyer's, and Bennett's criticisms of the alleged connections between the logical functions of judgment and the categories *would* be in order if an intuition in which a manifold is given *might be* represented through a category *without* being "regarded as determined in respect of one of the logical functions of judgment" (B 128). But this possibility contradicts Kant's conception of the categories as "concepts of an object in general, by means of which [i.e., through which (*dadurch*)]

16. Kitcher, *Kant's Transcendental Psychology,* 89. Guyer, *Kant and the Claims of Knowledge,* 98–99.

17. Kitcher, *Kant's Transcendental Psychology,* 89. As is by now to be expected, I would of course dispute her characterization of Kant's logical functions of judgment as the logical *forms* of judgment.

18. Bennett, *Kant's Analytic,* 94–95.

19. Ibid. Kitcher actually extends this contention of Bennett's to cover *all* the logical functions of judgment. That is, she holds that the *entire* Deduction, including the *second* step, "derives its force from two principal sources: the analyses of cognitive tasks, including the doctrine of the forms of intuition, and the arguments of the Principles, in particular the careful reasoning of the Analogies"; *Kant's Transcendental Psychology,* 168. But this cannot be right. For the principles in question are judgments (A 132/B 171), which contain concepts involving intuitions or appearances, not to mention the categories themselves. But we "find" the logical functions of judgment, Kant says, only by "abstracting all content from a judgment [in general]" (A 70/B 95). Therefore, as long as Kitcher insists that the force of the argument in the Deduction is to be found in part in the arguments pertaining to the principles, she will be prevented from appreciating what Kant himself considers to be the distinctive contribution of the logical functions of judgment to the Deduction of the categories. After all, the *judgments* that are the principles to which Kitcher refers on Kant's behalf *presuppose* the very *functions* of judgment that on my view provide the "force," to use Kitcher's term, for the decisive, concluding stage of step one of the Deduction. Since they are presupposed by the principles, Kitcher cannot legitimately look to the principles to play the role only the functions themselves can play in the Deduction. All attempts to postpone the decisive arguments for the categories to the Principles chapter will be guilty of the same shortcoming. This applies to Guyer's arguments that Kant's best arguments in support of the categories are to be found in his "Refutation of Idealism" and in his "Principles" chapter. For example, see his contention to this effect in his article "The Transcendental Deduction of the Categories," in *The Cambridge Companion to Kant,* ed. Paul Guyer (Cambridge: Cambridge University Press, 1992), 127.

the intuition of an object is regarded as determined in respect of one of the logical functions of judgment" (B 128). So the criticisms in question are outright rejections more than mere criticisms of Kant's conception of the role of the categories in the determination of an intuition in respect of one of the logical functions of judgment. Those rejections would be unnecessary, however, if a positive place could be found for that conception in the Deduction. So a desideratum of a defense of the "One-Step Deduction" alluded to in *The Metaphysical Foundations of Natural Science* is that it find a place for that conception in the actual second-edition Deduction in the *Critique*. I therefore try to meet that demand in my own reconstruction of Kant's argument, which is given in the next chapter.

Kitcher's final criticism of Kant's "One-Step Deduction" is that "nothing in the analysis of making judgments establishes that the rules of synthesis [which admittedly are involved in the analysis] are even a priori$_o$," where "[a] proposition or concept is a priori$_o$ if it includes elements that do not derive from sensations."[20] The validity of this criticism, however, depends on her prior contention that the analysis of making judgments should be separated from "the requirements of apperception." For if the logical functions of judgment are included among those requirements, they would constitute "rules of synthesis that are a priori$_o$," in Kitcher's sense of that whole expression. But since I have not accepted that prior contention of hers, I need not accept this final criticism either.

III

The second issue that is central to my reconstruction of Kant's argument is whether Kant has clearly distinguished between the objective and subjective unity of consciousness. For if that distinction is obscure, we can expect obscurity in the distinction, crucial to the Deduction, between, on the one hand, a combination of representations in a judgment, and therefore "*in the object,* no matter what the state of the subject may be," and, on the other hand, a mere conjunction of the same representations in the perception of the subject, which does depend on what "the state of the subject may be" (B 142).

Allison charges Kant with just this obscurity in his use of the notion of subjective unity of consciousness that is related to the idea that representa-

20. Kitcher, *Kant's Transcendental Psychology,* 89, 15.

tions are merely conjoined in the perception of the subject. That is, he finds fault with the way in which, in §§ 18 and 19, Kant distinguishes between the subjective unity of consciousness in the conjunction of representations in perception and the objective unity of consciousness in the combination of the same representations in judgment.[21]

Allison's problem with Kant's notion of the subjective unity of consciousness is that it can be given two interpretations, only one of which is defensible. Yet even after presenting the defensible version, Allison maintains, Kant still occasionally employs the indefensible version.

The *indefensible* version takes the unity to be "a unity through which we represent to ourselves our own subjective states or condition."[22] Allison asserts that this version is indefensible because it cannot but employ what is supposed to be the *contrasting* notion of the *objective* unity of consciousness.[23] Unfortunately, Kant's statements that Allison offers in support of this assertion in fact do not support it. A passage from a letter of Kant's to Herz contains material that actually undermines the assertion: "assuming that I am conscious of each individual representation, but not of their relation to the unity of representation of their object, by means of the synthetic unity of apperception."[24] This quotation shows Kant thinking that he *can* be conscious of his "own subjective states or condition," to use Allison's expression for an individual representation, without being conscious of their relation to the synthetic unity of apperception.

The point here is that appearances may be objects of inner sense or of original consciousness, with its objective, a priori unity. As objects of the former, they may also be objects of empirical consciousness, but not objects of original, a priori consciousness as well, even though the latter is still the original consciousness from which the empirical consciousness is "derived" (B 139–40), unless inner sense is determined by the understanding. The reason that they are not objects of the latter even though the former is "derived" from the latter is that in this situation "the manifold of intuition . . . is empirically given" (B 139); that is, the former is "derived" from the latter "under given conditions *in concreto*" (B 140). As objects of inner sense, unless inner sense is determined by the understanding, as described at § 24, B150—that is, if inner sense is determined by *empirical*, instead of a priori, conditions (B 139–40)—they lose the objectivity accorded them through

21. Allison, *Kant's Transcendental Idealism.*
22. Ibid., 154.
23. Ibid., 153–54.
24. Ibid., 153.

original, a priori consciousness alone, that is, independently of sensibility and inner sense. It is for § 24 to remedy the situation by bringing sensibility and inner sense under the a priori conditions of the possibility of a unitary sensible intuition, namely, the categories (B 143). Only if sensibility and inner sense are determined through the categories can the objects of inner sense—appearances—be objects of "the synthetic unity of apperception" as well (B 150). It is this necessary condition, which is only introduced into sensibility and inner sense at § 24, that Allison leaves out of his account of the matter.

We can interpret Kant's talk of the "derivation" of the empirical unity of apperception from the transcendental unity of apperception as an expression of the view that "under given conditions *in concreto*" the unity of consciousness is no longer signified by the copula of the V-relation that belongs to a judgment. A judgment thus depends on the abstraction of such given concrete conditions in which a subject happens to find itself on any particular occasion of representation. The objectivity of a judgment consists in this abstraction, so that what remains after abstraction is the consciousness with which we begin, that is, objective consciousness. The "derivation" of empirical consciousness in this context therefore consists in thus adding what is concrete to the consciousness that originally is abstract. The resulting *subjective* unity of consciousness is therefore *not* subject to the original consciousness from which it is "derived," and consequently, it has only *subjective* validity.

Allison also claims that in a passage from the *Reflexion* Kant asserts an implication between the proposition that a "purely subjective play of representations can be brought to consciousness and represented as an object" and the proposition "that such representation is objectively valid and categorially determined."[25] Unfortunately, Allison's paraphrase of Kant's assertion omits Kant's qualification in his use of "object." According to Allison's own quote from the *Reflexion*, Kant speaks of becoming conscious of the object "as such an object," where the "such" specifies an object of *inner sense*. But consciousness of an object as an object of *inner sense* is precisely the consciousness whose unity §§ 18 and 19 say has only *subjective* validity. So the implication of Kant's assertion seems to be just the opposite of what Allison takes it to be.

It might be objected on Allison's behalf that for Kant even a representation of something as merely an object of inner sense is still a representation

---

25. Allison, *Kant's Transcendental Idealism*, 153–54.

that is "objectively valid and categorially determined." But I would reply that if this were a correct reading of Kant's position, then, first, a subject's assertion that objects of its inner sense "are connected according to laws of association" would not itself be based on laws of association but rather on the understanding. This indeed, I think, captures at least part of Allison's position on this matter. In being objective about objects of inner sense, one's consciousness must thereby be objective. But, second, I would also point out that this is a proposition that is transcendental in nature, since it employs the transcendental concept of inner sense, as distinguished from the similarly transcendental concept of objective consciousness, as that distinction is drawn in §§ 18 and 19. Yet what Allison is interested in is the possibility of one's empirical, if not a priori, judgments about one's own states of mind. So, if this were Allison's objection to my criticisms of his position on this matter, I would conclude my response by pointing out that now he would simply be mistaking transcendental propositions as nontranscendental judgments.

The *defensible* version of the notion of subjective unity, according to Allison, holds that "nothing is represented, not even our subjective states," through such a subjective unity. The problem now, Allison claims, is that Kant occasionally backslides into the indefensible version in one of two ways. Either the subjective unity of consciousness is again taken as a consciousness "of one's subjective states,"[26] or the subjective unity is an "empirical unity [of consciousness, which] is derived from the transcendental unity 'under given conditions *in concreto* (B 140)."[27]

The problem alleged in the first sort of backsliding can be resolved on the basis of my replies to Allison's discussion of Kant's letter to Herz and the *Reflexion*. In brief, I consider defensible the version Allison judges indefensible. With respect to the derivation of the empirical unity of consciousness from the transcendental unity, one of its problems, according to Allison, is that it in turn can be given at least two interpretations, neither of which is defensible. The interpretation Allison finds "most plausible" makes empirical unity "subject to the transcendental conditions of unity." The problem with this interpretation, he correctly claims, is that it makes it impossible to predicate subjective validity of an empirical unity without contradiction. Obviously, this interpretation must be discarded. The other interpretation

26. Ibid., 156.
27. Ibid., 156–57. See also Aquila's analysis of Kant's talk of the derivation of the empirical unity of apperception, *Representational Mind* (Bloomington: Indiana University Press, 1983), 137.

of the derivation is said by Allison to encounter the problem "that the order in which perceptions occur in inner sense is determined by causal laws and is in that sense subject to the transcendental conditions of experience."[28] Clearly, this interpretation must also be discarded.

In the end, we are left with either the version of Kant's notion of subjective unity that Allison considers indefensible but I judge otherwise or the version according to which the subjective unity of consciousness does not even represent one's subjective states. But if such states are considered objects of inner sense, it is difficult to see how Allison can take this latter alternative as Kant's actual view of the matter. So, finally, we are left with the version Allison considers indefensible and I consider otherwise.

It might now be objected, again on Allison's behalf, that Kant might rather be adopting the view that a subjective unity of consciousness does not actually represent one's subjective states or objects of inner sense, since such states or objects need not be actually represented for one's consciousness of them to have a merely subjective unity. In reply, I must say that the difficulty I find in this position would nonetheless remain, for it is hard to understand how a consciousness whose unity is only subjective is a consciousness of these states, while the states themselves are not even represented in consciousness. It would seem they would have to be represented just to be states of which one is conscious.

What Allison has unfortunately rejected is the view that the important question is whether "the same representations" are "combined *in the object*" (B 142).[29] Kant's position is that they are if and only if they are brought to the objective unity of consciousness through a judgment that belongs to the understanding. According to this view of the matter, there is no problem in understanding the sense Kant gives to the subjective unity of apperception. It is a unity of representations that are not "combined in the object," because they do not satisfy Kant's criterion of such combination. This does not imply, however, contrary to Allison's interpretation of Kant's statements, that representations in a subjective unity cannot represent objects; they can, provided the objects are objects of inner sense.

Perhaps what in my opinion is Allison's fundamental error is that he believes §19 presents a conception of judgment in general that applies to such "judgments" about the subject itself and its states or conditions as are expressed by "If I support a body, I feel an impression of weight" (B 142). His

28. Allison, *Kant's Transcendental Idealism*, 157.
29. Ibid., 157–58.

mistake, then, is a conflation of sorts, as expressed by his assertion: "Both [i.e., "The body is heavy" and "If I support a body, I feel an impression of weight"] involve the relation of representations to an object."[30]

The distinction I am claiming Allison conflates is based on a difference in meaning between the two German words that, since Chapter 4, I have argued Kant uses as distinct technical terms but that, unfortunately, Kemp Smith translated with just one English word. As already explained, he uses the word "relation" for both *Verhältnis* and *Beziehung*.[31] Following the model of representation put forward in Chapter 4, I will continue to call the former relation the *V*-relation and the latter the *B*-relation.

Now, only the *V*-relation in "The body is heavy" has a *B*-relation to an object through a combination that is a judgment. Though the same representations can be related to each other in a *V*-relation of the association "If I support a body, I feel an impression of weight," in that *associative V*-relation they do not have the *B*-relation to an object through a combination of a judgment. So when Allison says that "If I support a body, I feel an impression of weight" involves "the relation of representations to an object" and that "[t]he difference between them [i.e., between 'The body is heavy' and 'If I support a body, I feel an impression of weight'] is not relevant to the conception of judgment which Kant is here trying to explicate,"[32] he reveals a conflation of a distinction that I would maintain lies at the bottom of Kant's thought on this matter.

Despite its hypothetical form, "If I support a body, I feel an impression of weight" is not a judgment for Kant in § 19, since it is not a *V*-relation among representations that "indicates their [*B*-]relation to original apperception, and its *necessary unity*" (B 142). It is, rather, an expression of a law of association.[33] Finally, Allison does make note of this distinction of Kant's between a law of association and a judgment, but he criticizes it by saying, "Kant also attributes subjective validity to this association or subjective unity."[34] His criticism is that this distinction between a law of associa-

30. Ibid., 158.

31. In their translation of Reich's *Completeness of Kant's Table of Judgments*, 125 n. 2, Kneller and Losonsky observe that though *Verhältnis* and *Beziehung* are "generally" used synonymously, Reich takes note of the distinction between Kant's use of *Verhältnis* in the categories and his use of *Beziehung* overall. For my part, I take Kant's distinction between the two terms as extending beyond the categories, as it does here.

32. Allison, *Kant's Transcendental Idealism*, 158.

33. In this particular regard I am in agreement with Aquila on this issue. See his *Representational Mind*, 123. But see Chapter 12, where I disagree with him on this matter, but, of course, in a different respect.

34. Allison, *Kant's Transcendental Idealism*, 157.

tion and a judgment depends on the earlier distinction between subjective and objective unity, which Allison believes he has by now discredited. I will close this discussion of Allison by replying that there is nothing here for him to be critical of, for although he is right that the distinction between a law of association and a judgment does depend on the earlier distinction between a subjective and an objective unity of consciousness, there is nothing wrong with that earlier distinction.

IV

The third and final issue I will deal with before I propose my own account of Kant's argument concerns the strategy of the entire portion of the Deduction with which I am concerned. It is with respect to this issue that we turn our attention to Guyer's criticism of this portion of the Deduction.

Guyer contends that the entire first step of the Deduction fails to deliver on its promise to provide conditions of knowledge of objects, namely, the categories, which are supposed to have been discovered independently of a conception of such knowledge—discovered, that is, in the supposedly independent conception of "the unity of *self*-consciousness."[35] He further contends that the Deduction actually does just the reverse of what it suggests it is going to do; that is, it finds the conditions of the unity of self-consciousness in the conditions of knowledge of objects.[36] He says,

> These claims may seem surprising, since the second-edition text of the Deduction begins with remarks about the transcendental unity of apperception which seem more clearly than any of Kant's other texts to identify this concept, and thus the chief premise of Kant's argument, with the unity of *self*-consciousness rather than the representation of an object. In spite of this initial promise, however, Kant effects his goal in this version of the Deduction by nothing other than a direct exploitation of a strong conception of objectivity itself.[37]

Since § 19 asserts that even empirical judgments, such as "Bodies are heavy," involve a claim to synthetic necessary truth (Guyer actually makes the stronger assertion that Kant holds that when we assert that judgment,

---

35. Guyer, *Kant and the Claims of Knowledge*, 108–9.
36. Ibid., also 117, 120. See also his "Transcendental Deduction of the Categories," 149–55.
37. *Kant and the Claims of Knowledge*, 108–9.

we "assert that a body '*must* be heavy' "),[38] Kant holds that all knowledge of objects involves such a claim. One such claim to necessary truth is our alleged claim to know that the categories are related to objects. But since such a claim cannot now be supported by an independent reference to the conditions of the unity of self-consciousness, and since that reference is Kant's only support of that claim, Kant has no argument at all to support his view that even empirical judgments involve a claim to necessary truth, in particular the truth that the categories are related to objects. Consequently, the Deduction of the categories fails to the extent that it depends on such a claim to necessary truth.

According to Guyer, the offending passage in which the reversal occurs can be found in § 17, at B 137. There, Guyer says, "Kant first defines the faculty of understanding, which has thus far simply been conceived as the faculty of *combination,* as the *'faculty of knowledge,'* where knowledge 'consists in the determinate relation of given representations to an object' and an *'object* is that in the concept of which the manifold of a given intuition is *united.'* "[39]

Kant's procedure may not seem so dubious, however, if we direct our attention to an argument in § 17 that immediately precedes the passage in question. In this preceding argument Kant claims to establish the principle that "the manifold representations of intuition [that] are *given* to us" are "subject to conditions of the original synthetic unity of apperception" (B 136). The argument turns on his concept of *combination.* He says that "without being *combined* in one consciousness," "given representations [of a manifold of intuition] would not have in common the act of apperception 'I think,' and so could not be apprehended together in one self-consciousness," in which case "nothing can be thought or known" (B 136–37). So, if anything can be thought or known, the manifold "must allow of being combined in one consciousness." We finally get back to the principle that the manifold is subject to the conditions of the original synthetic unity of apperception, with the further premise that "insofar as [the manifold] must allow of being *combined* in one consciousness, [it is] subject to [the principle]" (B 137).

We might also reconstruct the argument as follows. The manifold of intuition is subject to the conditions of the original synthetic unity of apperception because it must allow of being combined in one consciousness, and this is necessary if the given representations of the manifold are to be accompa-

38. Ibid., 120.
39. Ibid., 117.

nied by the "I think" of original apperception, an act without which nothing can be thought or known (B 132). Consequently, to the extent that, and in the sense in which, it is necessary that all my representations be able to be accompanied by the "I think"—the extent and the sense being that otherwise "nothing is thought or known"—the given representations must be subject to the conditions of original apperception.

This is an argument in which there is no trace of the reversal in strategy alleged by Guyer. It does not include any bald or question-begging assertion to the effect that all knowledge or judgment about objects implies a claim to necessary truth—a claim Guyer is right to characterize as something empiricist-minded philosophers would reject at the start. It rather stays within the framework of the conditions of the "I think" itself and thus belongs to the fulfillment of Kant's suggested promise to establish the necessity of the categories as conditions to which the manifold of intuition must be subject if the manifold is to be brought to the unity of original apperception. It is hard to see how the offending paragraph, which immediately follows the one that contains the argument I have just reconstructed—the paragraph in which the alleged reversal occurs—introduces any material that contradicts my characterization of Kant's argument. Kant's characterization of the understanding as the faculty of knowledge, and his conception of an object as that in whose concept the manifold of a given intuition is united, can be read as fully in line with the argument that immediately precedes it, without containing any unsupported assertion to the effect that knowledge involves a claim to necessary truth.

Of course, Guyer is right that so far Kant has not yet specified or established just what the conditions of the unity of original apperception are. But, it seems, Kant never suggested that he would do so at this particular stage of the Deduction. We should not find it surprising that he waited until §§ 19 and 20 to do so. It is in these later sections, of course, that he argues those conditions consist of, first, *judgments* belonging to the understanding and, second, *concepts* belonging to the understanding—that is, the categories. And that is where my own reconstruction of Kant's argument comes in.

Finally, I might comment on Guyer's whole approach to the problem he claims to have found in the strategy Kant actually pursues in the *Critique*, as opposed to the strategy Kant allegedly promises us. Though I have defended here that school of thought which takes the second-edition Deduction as an argument *from* the principle of the transcendental unity of apperception *to* the categories as conditions of the possibility of any knowledge of objects, I have *not* done so under the stipulation that Kant must state the conditions of the unity of self-consciousness independently of the conditions of the cognitions of objects.

Indeed, it seems misguided of Guyer to demand that independence. The conditions of knowledge of objects just *are* the conditions of the unity of self-consciousness. For Kant, self-consciousness of the sort that we humans have supplies no manifold unto itself. The manifold can only be supplied by a sensible intuition—that is, an intuition that is *given*, that is independent of the understanding (B 135, B 138–39, B 145, B 159). Therefore, to speak of the conditions of the unity of self-consciousness apart from the conditions under which a manifold of representations is brought into that one consciousness and thus is knowledge is to speak of a self-consciousness whose "identity . . . cannot be thought" (B 135). It is to speak of an understanding that is unlike ours, "whose whole power consists in thought, consists, that is, in the act whereby it brings the synthesis of a manifold, given to it from elsewhere in intuition, to the unity of apperception" (B 145).

Guyer himself tells us what might very well have misguided him, as I see it, in his studies of this issue in Kant. It was his understanding of Dieter Henrich, in particular Henrich's *Identität und Objektivität*.[40] It is Henrich, Guyer says, who argues that Kant's texts contain two different kinds of deduction, which he calls the "objectivity" deduction and the "identity" deduction.[41] And Guyer states that he interprets §§ 19 and 20 as belonging to the "objectivity" deduction.[42] What my reconstructed argument shows, however, is that the "objectivity" deduction is indeed a noncircular argument in support of Kant's claim that even an empirical judgment such as "Bodies are heavy" involves categorial a priori knowledge of objects. It only appears circular if one approaches it along Guyer's version of Henrich's line, a version that distinguishes between the conditions of the cognitions of objects and the conditions of the unity of self-consciousness. On my reading of Kant, the possibility of cognitions of objects, that is, their possibility with respect to the understanding, just *is* their B-relation to the unity of self-consciousness. The conditions through which given cognitions are B-related to that unity are therefore the conditions of their possibility. And there could be no unity of consciousness—and thus the identity of the subject could not be thought (B 143)—unless the manifold of representations and ultimately the manifold of intuition (B 132) were brought to the unity of consciousness.

40. Ibid., 86. Guyer cites Dieter Henrich's *Identität und Objektivität: Eine Untersuchung über Kants transzendentaler Deduktion* (Heidelberg: Carl Winter Universitätsverlag, 1976).
41. Guyer, *Kant and the Claims of Knowledge*, 86.
42. Ibid., 102ff., esp. 119–21.

JUDGMENT, CONSCIOUSNESS, AND THE CATEGORIES

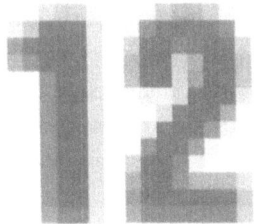

I

My positive account of step one of the B-Deduction can begin with an observation on Kant's own remarks about the possible success of a deduction of the categories. It does not seem accidental that his ostensible reasons for completely rewriting the Deduction for the second edition, mentioned in both the preface to the second edition of the *Critique* (B xxxviii) and in the preface to *The Metaphysical Foundations of Natural Science*, are given in exactly the same terms in which he warned his readers in his preliminary remarks to the Deduction itself in both editions about the hazards of failing to understand the very *need* of a deduction before embarking on such a study. These hazards consist in the possible obscurity one may find in the material and the futility of wandering in a circle as one tries to make one's way through it. Whereas obscurity is always a danger in the study of any difficult subject, and though it often leads to circular reasoning, it need not be an impediment to an independent understanding of what the obscurity consists in. And the matter is no different for us who might be interested in the precise nature of the obscurity Kant confesses to have created in the course of composing the A-Deduction. If my proposal in Chapter 10 about the nature of the obscurity and that of the inconsistency it hides in the A-

Deduction is on the right track, it should help us understand the strategy Kant adopts for the B-Deduction.

His official reason for the need for a Transcendental Deduction, let us remind ourselves, is that the distinctness between the faculties of sensibility and the understanding implies a distinctness between, on the one hand, intuitions of the senses and their objects, or the given objects of sensibility—the objects that are given to us in space or in time, that is, appearances—and, on the other hand, "the conditions which the understanding requires for the synthetic unity of thought" (A 90/B 123). In other words, the problem for such a deduction to solve is why empirical intuitions and their corresponding appearances in space or in time must be subject to the concepts of objects of sensible intuition in general, that is, the categories.

So, the work before us is well defined. Since the Metaphysical Deduction leaves us with the problem of accounting for the V-relation of the categories to a distinct manifold of a sensible intuition in general that B-relates them to objects in general, we need some pure representation, to which the manifold is necessarily subject, that is *both* mutually distinct from, or unconnected to, the manifold of intuition *and* yet "precedes *a priori* all concepts of [the act of understanding entitled] combination" (B 131), and thus a representation that can be distinguished from the conceptual acts themselves. Indeed, it is a representation that "cannot itself be accompanied by any further representation" (B 132).[1] The faculty of the understanding represented through this *further*, purely *intellectual* representation, the "I think" (B 132), and thus represented without the interposition of the imagination between the manifold of an intuition of the senses and the categories alone can be the principle that solves the problem of the Deduction. So represented, the faculty of the understanding is none other than that entitled *apperception* (B 134 n). In other words, the A-Deduction goes in a direction exactly opposite to the one it should have taken. Instead of moving toward sensibility, thereby becoming *imaginative,* it should have moved away from sensibility and thus become as *intellectual* as the categories themselves. It thus should have V-related the categories to the manifold of a sensible intuition in general, that is, quite independently of sensibility.

Having already laid down in the Metaphysical Deduction the intellectual act of synthesis itself, or the category, as extending to objects of intuition in

---

1. See the analysis of proposition 16 (my number) of the Deduction, below. According to this analysis, in (16) Kant identifies the *act* of the understanding with the very *unity* of the act itself.

general, the task at hand is to so show that the *necessary B*-relation of the manifold of an intuition in general to the unity of the act of synthesis (the unity of apperception) requires that the manifold be subject to the act (the category) itself. But the success of this demonstration in turn depends on showing that the unity to which the manifold must be *B*-related (i.e., the unity *of* the manifold, which is the unity of apperception) is none other than the unity of the very act to which the manifold is supposed to be necessarily subject, even though the unity is distinct from the act itself.

These three features—the manifold, its synthesis, and the unity of the manifold—are included, Kant says, in the concept of *combination* (B 130). So the first stage of step one of the Deduction, after abstracting sensibility and the two modes of sensibility from the argument, must show that the unity to which the manifold of intuition in general is brought (the unity of apperception) is none other than the unity of the very act (the category) to which the manifold must be subject. This means that the initial stage of step one of the Deduction must show that the "I think," which represents the unity to which the manifold of intuition must be brought, that is, the "I think" to which the manifold must be subject, represents the unity of the very act (combination) through which the manifold is brought to the unity. We now turn our attention to Kant's attempt to show that the act of combination has the very unity of apperception.[2]

At the beginning of the Deduction, in § 15, Kant distinguishes the understanding from sensibility as the faculty of representation involved in the spontaneous act of synthesis entitled *combination*. This action, he says, "is originally one and is equipollent [i.e., equivalent (*gleichgeltend*)] for all combination" (B 130). Such unity and equivalence of all combination is not meant to deny that we cannot find different species of the unity and equivalence in the logical functions of judgment (B 141, 143). This remark allows Kant to conclude that the same consciousness is involved in all acts of the understanding. It thus provides the grounds for what might otherwise seem to be a dubious proposition about the unity of consciousness. For Kant himself acknowledges that "when the manifold [of representations] is under consideration," "[t]he *consciousness* of the one [representation] . . . has

---

2. The importance of Kant's notions of an act, action, or activity of the understanding has been duly recognized in analytic commentary on the *Critique*, notably at a time when it was not especially fashionable to acknowledge that a faculty of the mind might be said to engage significantly in such things. See Robert Paul Wolff, *Kant's Theory of Mental Activity* (Cambridge, Mass.: Harvard University Press, 1963).

always to be distinguished from the consciousness of the other [representation]" (B 131 n). So Kant has to shift our consideration from the manifold of representations to the unity and equivalence of all the acts of the understanding through which all the manifold is combined, if he is going to conclude that the same consciousness is involved in all acts of the understanding.[3]

As I have already noted, Kant proceeds to explain that a *combination* consists of not just a manifold and its synthesis but the unity of the manifold. In § 16 he also asserts that "It must be possible for the 'I think' to accompany all my representations" (B 131). Otherwise, he says, a representation "could not be thought at all, and that is equivalent to saying that the representation would be impossible, or at least would be nothing to me" (B 132). As already indicated, he goes on to call the "I think" *pure apperception* and say that it has a certain unity.

If we bring these assertions together, we can lay out an argument that consists of the following premises:

(1) The distinctive action of the understanding, that is, combination, is always the same.

(2) This action always involves a unity of the manifold.

(3) All the representations of a subject that can be thought by the subject can be accompanied by the "I think."

(4) The "I think" is identified with the unity of apperception.

The conclusion of this argument is the proposition that

(5) The unity involved in combination can be none other than the unity of apperception.

And Kant formulates this conclusion as follows:

(6) Combination . . . is an affair [or doing (*Verrichtung*)] of the understanding alone, which itself is nothing but the faculty of combining *a priori*, and of bringing the manifold of given representations under the unity of apperception. (B 134–35)

---

3. The importance for the B-Deduction I here ascribe to the unity and equivalence of all action of the understanding is a feature of that unity and equivalence that hitherto seems to have gone largely unnoticed in the literature.

From this passage, by abstraction and detachment, we can infer the following proposition:

(7) The understanding is nothing but the faculty of bringing the manifold of given representations under the unity of apperception.

Furthermore, I have a specific understanding of Kant's use of "mode" in the passage in which he says "a judgment is nothing but the mode [*Art*] of bringing given cognitions to the objective unity of apperception" (B 141, my translation). I take Kant to be using "mode" at B 141, as he does elsewhere, to signify that in which a representation, R, is so *V*-related to an S that the S is a *cognition* that is thereby *B*-related to the object, O, that is represented through R. In other words, a mode is a form belonging to one of the two sources of *knowledge,* sensibility and the understanding (A 50/B 74), that provides for the *V*-relation(s) of a representation, an R, to an S that provides that the S is a *cognition* that is *B*-related to the O that is represented through the R. It thus distinguishes among representations those that are *cognitions* that are *B*-related to objects represented through the mode. A mode thus serves to satisfy a condition for something to be a *representation* that is itself a *cognition.* Cognitions are thus *B*-related to the objects that are represented through the mode of the cognitions.[4]

Given this understanding of Kant's use of "mode" at B 141, we would expect that if a manifold of given *representations* is brought to the unity of apperception through a mode, the representations are *cognitions*. Since at B 141 Kant does speak of a judgment as a *mode,* it is understandable that he there speaks of what is given as *cognitions,* and not merely as *representations,* which is how he speaks of them at B 134–35. It is true that at B 134–35 Kant speaks of *representations* that are "given in intuition," and hence he must be speaking of *cognitions,* or *knowledge,* since "intuition is that through which it [i.e., a *cognition*] is in immediate [*B*-]relation to them [i.e., objects]" (A 19/B 33). But he does not call these representations *cognitions,* or *knowledge,* until he entitles *"[u]nderstanding . . . the faculty of knowledge"* at B 137. He thereupon asserts, "This knowledge consists in

4. A mode, as I understand it, would thus qualify as an "epistemic condition," or a "condition of human knowledge," of Allison's, if that notion of his can be so characterized that it really serves to explain Kant's transcendental idealism (see Henry E. Allison, *Kant's Transcendental Idealism: An Interpretation and Defense* [New Haven: Yale University Press, 1983], 10 *et passim*).

the determinate [B-]relation of given representations to an object; and an *object* is that in the concept of which the manifold of a given intuition is *united*" (B 137). Since he has previously said that "besides intuition there is no other *mode* of knowledge except by means of [i.e., through *(durch)*] concepts" (A 68/B 93, my emphasis), and since he has just said that "it is the unity of consciousness that alone constitutes the [B-]relation of representations to an object," he is now in a position, at the conclusion of this paragraph at B 137, to speak of representations that are B-related to an object through a concept as *cognitions (Erkenntnisse)*, and not merely as *representations*.

Returning now to the topic paragraph at B 141–42, we must note that immediately preceding his use of "mode" in this context, he speaks of the V-relation of the given cognitions in any judgment "as belonging to the understanding" (B 141). His subsequent reference to the V-relation of a judgment is therefore governed by this condition, namely, that the V-relation belongs to the understanding. Consequently, his subsequent reference to a judgment as something that contains that V-relation is also governed by this condition.

But this condition also governs Kant's use of "judgment" in the *Prolegomena to Any Future Metaphysics,* where he recognizes so-called judgments of perception,[5] which have the same merely subjective validity that in the *Critique* belongs to the mere conjunction of representations "in my perception" (B 142). That is, it is only in the *Critique* that the V-relation of given cognitions in *any* judgment is objectively valid. So, in the *Critique* there is a restriction that excludes the "judgments of perception" of the *Prolegomena.* Since the *Prolegomena* considers these judgments to belong to the understanding, and since the *Critique* does not consider them to be judgments at all, the restriction in the *Critique* must be a restriction on Kant's use of "the understanding." That restriction is none other than the requirement expressed by proposition 7 above, namely, that the understanding is the faculty of bringing the manifold of given representations to the unity of apperception, a proposition that itself is derived from propositions 1–6. So the difference between the *Critique* and the *Prolegomena* in this matter is the role of "combination" in the former and its absence in the latter.

In addition to noting this restriction of his use of "the understanding,"

---

5. Immanuel Kant, *Prolegomena to Any Future Metaphysics,* ed. Lewis White Beck, trans. Paul Carus (Indianapolis: Bobbs-Merrill, 1950), § 18, pp. 45ff.

we should also note that when Kant introduces judgments into the Logic he says,

> (8) we can reduce all acts [or actions (*Handlungen*)] of the understanding to judgments. (A 69/B 93)

This proposition permits us to "reduce" the actions of the understanding involved in (7) above to *judgments*. But since all judgments belong to the understanding, and since in the *Critique* all acts of the understanding are combinations, we can conclude this stage of the argument with Kant's assertion that

> (9) a judgment is nothing but the mode of bringing given cognitions to the objective unity of apperception. (B 141, my translation)

The assertion in (9) can therefore be seen as a valid inference from premises previously laid down by Kant; it is not an *ad hoc* assertion inserted into the Deduction merely for the purpose of assuring its formal validity and without any integration into surrounding theory.

If exception is to be taken to (9), therefore, it must also be taken to at least one proposition included in (1)–(8), my understanding of what Kant means by "mode" at B 141, or the restriction he puts on his use of "the understanding" in this portion of the *Critique*. That is, since the inference is valid, the only possible legitimate exception to the argument that leads to (9) is that it is unsound. For my part, I find it difficult to refuse Kant, in his commitment to (1)–(6), the use of his notion of combination or his conception of consciousness as the condition under which a representation can be thought by the subject whose representation it is. With respect to the latter, it seems evident that in respect of its content a thought could not be ascribed to a subject that the subject could not ascribe to itself and, moreover, that the subject could not ascribe to itself if it did not understand the (content of the) thought.[6] I also cannot refuse him the restriction on "the understanding" that is involved in (7), the use of his theory of the understanding that is involved in (8), or his use of "judgment" in (9). And I of course subscribe to my own interpretation of his use of "mode" at B 141. So I find the argument that leads to (9) to be valid and its premises warranted within the system Kant develops up to that point in the *Critique*.

6. Tyler Burge employed this Cartesian-like principle in the first of his two Alfred North Whitehead Lectures at Harvard University, April 14, 1994.

II

So far Kant has only argued that a judgment is necessary if given cognitions are to be brought to the objective unity of apperception, but he has not yet demonstrated a priori that the very V-relation that ties representations together in a judgment is itself B-related to an object, or has "objective validity." This is the V-relation according to which "what we are asserting is that they [i.e., the representations in a judgment] are combined *in the object*, no matter what the state of the subject may be" (B 142). That is, (9) only asserts that through a judgment given cognitions are B-related to the objective unity of apperception; it does not assert that the V-relation between or among given representations in a judgment is itself objectively valid, or B-related to that unity. This distinction between the V-relation that ties representations together in a judgment and its own B-relation to an object, that is, its own objective validity, may not be clear to us, however, if we are reading the Kemp Smith translation without consulting the German text. So let us keep the distinction before us as we proceed with the positive account of the argument.

Since we have already discussed Kant's use of "representation" instead of "cognition" in cases in which given representations are not yet *determinately* B-related to an object,[7] we can understand Kant's use of "representation" instead of "cognition" in the present context. For he wants to speak of "the same representations" in two specifically different V-relations, one that gives rise to a judgment, the other to an association. Only in the former sort of V-relation are they B-related to an object of knowledge, for the former V-relation alone "belongs to the understanding" (B 141), which is *"the faculty of knowledge"* (B 137). That is, as we have already noted, in the present context a judgment is a mode of knowledge. So only insofar as given representations are interrelated in a V-relation that gives rise to a judgment are they B-related to the objective unity of consciousness, and hence B-related to an object of knowledge. The associative, or subjective, V-relation, on the other hand, is the relation through which the manifold of representations is only brought to "the empirical unity of consciousness," which "has only subjective validity" (B 139–40).[8] Kant considers association to be the

---

7. See the discussion in section I above.
8. See Chapter 11, section III, for the distinction between two types of object to which the same given representations may be B-related. On the one hand, representations may be B-related to the empirical unity of consciousness and, on the other hand, may also be a B-related to the objective, transcendental unity of consciousness. If we consider the B-relation in respect

work of what he calls the "reproductive imagination" (B 141). So the question with which we started the present section concerns Kant's claim that a V-relation that gives rise to a judgment is itself objectively valid, or—what I take that to mean—that it is necessarily B-related to an object. What are his grounds for this claim?

Before I lay out these grounds, one might ask for the sense in Kant's claim that the V-relation in a judgment itself is objectively valid. From the passage in question it is clear, if one adopts my account of a B-relation to an object, that he considers the claim to consist in the proposition that the representations in a judgment are B-related to an object. This entails "that they [the representations] are combined *in the object*" (B 142). And, as we shall see at the end of this particular stage of the Deduction, the representation through which this is possible is the representation of the unity of apperception, that is, the "I think." So, the claim whose grounds I am about to lay out is precisely the *converse* of the claim already established up this point in the argument. That is, whereas I have already reconstructed Kant's argument in support of the proposition that a manifold of representations is brought to the unity of apperception through a judgment, I am now about to reconstruct his argument in support of the converse proposition, namely, that the V-relation in which the manifold of representations is combined in a judgment is itself B-related to the unity of apperception, in the just given sense that the manifold combined in a V-relation in a judgment is B-related to the unity of apperception and is thus combined "in the object." We shall now see that that B-relation obtains through the representation of that unity, that is, through the "I think."

Before Kant makes the claim in question, he says that in the judgment "Bodies are heavy"

(10) [the representations involved in the judgment] belong to one another *in virtue of the necessary unity* of apperception in the synthesis of intuitions. (B 142)

So he must be considering the judgment to involve a synthesis in the intuition to which the concept of body corresponds, provided that the concept of heavy refers to the concept of body (if his earlier analysis of a logically

---

of the *object* to which the given representations are thereby related, the B-relation itself will of course vary according to the type of the object. In any case, it is clear that a B-relation *simpliciter* that given representations have to an object is not sufficient to provide for objective validity. The object or the B-relation must be of the type that provides for the objective validity.

similar judgment is to be our guide [cf. A 68/B 93]). Proposition 10, however, is a particular statement of a more general proposition he asserted
earlier in the Deduction, namely,

> (11) all unification of representations demands unity of conscious-
> ness *in the synthesis of them.* (B 137, my emphasis)

The objective validity of a *V*-relation in a judgment, or the *B*-relation to
objects in which any judgmental *V*-relation itself stands, thus seems to consist in the unity of consciousness in the synthesis of representations that are
V-related to one another in the judgment. It should be remembered, however, that the representations involved in a judgment are also involved in a
subjective mental state "according to laws of association" (B 142). It is the
same set of representations in both cases. The difference resides in the *V*-
relation, that is, whether or not it has objective validity.

My view on this matter can be developed further by first noting its opposition to Aquila's view on the same subject.[9] According to his view, the
reason that the same representations can be both merely associated in a
subject's mental state and combined in an objective judgment is that the
latter "arises out" of the former. In contrast, I hold that the latter is quite
distinct from the former, and that *if* one were to arise out of the other, it
would have to be the other way around. This accords with my interpretation of what Kant means by the "derivation" of the empirical unity of consciousness from the original consciousness.[10]

Aquila has also questioned my account's explanation of how representations can be both comprised in a subject's mental state and combined in an
object.[11] I should note that on my view of this stage of the argument, Kant
does not distinguish the object (which by assumption is not the self) from
the combination of representations in a judgment. The object is instead distinguished from the association of the same representations in a state of the
subject. The object is thus none other than the object in one consciousness.

On my interpretation of the Deduction, an *object* (which is not the self or
an object of inner sense) distinct from the nontranscendental understanding
(henceforth simply called "the understanding") is not introduced into the
Deduction until § 22, B 146, where Kant explicitly refers to *things* (which,
it will be recalled, I consider the true denizens of Kant's ontology, as they

9. *Representational Mind* (Bloomington: Indiana University Press, 1983), 138.
10. See Chapter 11, section III.
11. He has done so in correspondence with me.

are defined in Chapter 2); and the actual *distinction* from the understanding is not made explicit until § 24, B 151, where Kant refers to appearances; and finally the transcendentally idealistic distinction between appearance and thing in itself is not introduced into the Deduction until § 26, B 164.[12] Of course, throughout the first step of the Deduction it is repeatedly made explicit that the *manifold* combined through an act of the understanding can only be given independently of the understanding, in intuition (B 135, 138–39, 145). So, if mere independence from the understanding is what is in question, the manifold of sensible intuition in general, instead of an object, fills the bill.

From (11) Kant immediately infers

(12) it is the unity of consciousness that alone constitutes the [*B*-]relation of representations to an object. (B137)

And it seems that on the basis of (12), and hence on the basis of what we have drawn (12) from, we can reach Kant's conclusion of § 19, namely:

(13) Representations that are *V*-related in a judgment "are combined *in the object,* no matter what the state of the subject may be." (B 142)

In summary, the argument in the second paragraph of § 19 can be accounted for in two stages. First, proposition 9 is asserted on grounds that have previously been laid down. Second, it is also claimed, again on the basis of propositions already asserted or argued for by Kant, that through the objective unity of apperception the *V*-relation in a judgment has objective validity. Thus, in one respect a *V*-relation in a judgment is a condition of the unity of consciousness to which a manifold of given cognitions is brought through the judgment; that is, it is a condition under which a manifold of given cognitions is brought to that unity and without which it would be a unity of nothing. Yet in another respect the unity of consciousness is a condition under which proposition 13 holds good, and hence that unity is the condition under which the objective validity of the *V*-relation in a judgment obtains. In a word, judgment and the unity of objective consciousness are conditions of one another in the different respects indicated.

---

12. This later, second step of the Deduction is discussed in the next chapter.

III

Once the relation between judgment and original, hence unitary, consciousness is established in § 19, Kant is in a position to demonstrate that "all sensible intuitions are subject to the categories" (B 143), in the sense that their manifold of representations is so subject, since the role of the categories is to bring the manifold to the unity of apperception, that is, to unite the manifold in one consciousness. This distinction between a given sensible intuition in general and its manifold rests on the idea that the mode in which a sensible intuition is given is also the mode in which the intuition consists of a plurality, or diversity, of representations. That is, the mode provides a representation for distinguishing not only the intuition from other intuitions but also the representations in which the intuition consists. This demonstration at B 143, Kant makes clear, is only "a beginning . . . of a *deduction*" of the categories (B 144). The completion, he says, is not reached until § 26 (B 159).

In the first sentence of the proof in § 20, Kant says that since

> (14) "the *unity* of intuition is possible" only through the original synthetic unity of apperception (B 143),

it follows that

> (15) [t]he manifold given in a sensible intuition is necessarily subject to the original synthetic unity of apperception. (B 143)

In effect, Kant is arguing that the representation through which the unity of a single intuition is possible is included among the very representation(s) to which the manifold of representations in a single intuition is necessarily subject. That is, Kant is arguing that the representation or condition through which the unity of a single intuition is possible is a representation or condition to which the manifold of a single intuition is necessarily subject. We can abbreviate this inference by saying that for Kant the condition of the unity of intuition is a condition for a manifold to be given in a united representation. For example, the manifold of representation in a united intuition, say, an intuition of a body (B 142), must be subject to the synthetic unity of apperception.

At the end of this first sentence of the proof in § 20, Kant cites a previous section, § 17, as justification for the assertion of (14) and the inference from (14) to (15). Section 17, however, does not explicitly mention the unity of *intuition* as such. It rather speaks of the *manifold* of intuition: "the manifold representations of intuition . . . must allow of being *combined* in one consciousness" (B 136). It likewise speaks of "a determinate combination of the given manifold" (B 138). Moreover, it asserts that "an *object* is that in the concept of which the manifold of a given intuition is *united* [*vereinigt*]" (B 137). Finally, it asserts that "without this synthesis [i.e., the synthesis involved in the synthetic unity of consciousness], the manifold would *not* be united in one consciousness" (B 138).

Thus, in § 17 Kant speaks of combination or unification, or says that something is united, only with respect to the *manifold* of intuition or the *manifold* of an intuition, but not with respect to *intuition* as such. So when Kant refers to § 17 in support of (14) and of his inference from (14) to (15), he must be thinking that his grounds are to be found in his statements in § 17 about the combination, unification, or uniting of the *manifold* of (an) intuition. We can thus conclude that the possibility of the unity of intuition is the B-relation that the unification of the manifold given in intuition (i.e., the judgmental V-relation) has to objects, where that unification is possible through the original synthetic unity of apperception.

With respect to Kant's use of "unity" in "unity of intuition" in § 20, the very words for unification and uniting in § 17 obviously connote unity. Regarding his reference to combination in § 17, that in turn is based on his assertions in § 15 of propositions 1 and 2 above. Indeed, he characterizes it, if he does not actually define it, as "representation of the *synthetic* unity of the manifold" (B 131).

To sum up, his talk of "the unity of intuition" in the first sentence of § 20 seems to be based on his talk in § 17 of the combination, unification, or unity of the manifold of intuition or of the manifold of a given intuition. Consequently, any exception one might take to the first sentence should be based on an exception to the relevant passages in § 15 or § 17. Since the transition from § 15 to § 17 is through § 16, one should also take exception to the relevant assertions in § 16 to the extent that one takes exception to an assertion in § 17 that involves the transition through § 16, as the assertions in § 17 about combination surely do. Consequently, a critic would need to address at least one of the propositions 1–13. The point is that the argument in § 20, like that in § 19, consists of propositions whose assertions are based on earlier assertions or positions taken and that criticisms of either the validity or soundness of the argument in § 20 must address the grounds on which § 20 is based.

Having made reference to the *B*-relation of the manifold of an intuition to the original synthetic unity of apperception in the first sentence of § 20, Kant proceeds to identify the *action* of the understanding through which the *B*-relation is made with the logical *function* of judgment:

> (16) [T]hat action of the understanding by [i.e., through (*durch*)] which the manifold of given representations (be they intuitions or concepts) is brought under one apperception, is the logical function of judgment. (B 143)

The great significance of (16) is Kant's identification of the *action* of the understanding with its own *unity*.[13] Kant bases his assertion of (16) on § 19, the section we have already analyzed. But we have only analyzed § 19 with respect to the grounds for its assertion of (9) and (13), propositions concerned with what "The Logical *Form* of All Judgments" consists in (my emphasis), and hence with "the Objective Unity of . . . Apperception" (B 140). In this context, "logical form" does not mean what is meant by "logical function of judgment."[14] So, though we have already examined Kant's employment of his concept of the logical form of all judgments (as consisting in the objective unity of apperception), we have not done the same with respect to his use of his concept of the logical function of judgment. Consequently, our present task is to provide an *analysis* of (16), where our concern is now with the logical *function* of judgment, instead of with what the logical *form* of all judgments consists in, even though the form consists in the same unity that is "thought" in this function (cf. B 131), that is, the unity of apperception (B 132).

Much earlier in the Transcendental Logic, in a passage some of whose other portions I have already made much use of, Kant says:

> (17) By 'function' I mean the unity of the act [i.e., action (*Handlung*)] of bringing various representations under one common representation. (A 68/B 93)

---

13. This identification has been anticipated in note 1 above.
14. See Chapters 9 and 10.

On the basis of (17) we can infer that the *action* mentioned in (16) must be

(18) the *unity* of bringing the manifold of given representations (be they intuitions or concepts) under the common representation of one apperception, that is, under the "I think."

That action can be said to be the logical function of *judgment*, since proposition 9 asserts that it is through a judgment that the manifold of given representations is brought under one apperception.

If we then use "the logical function of judgment" in the sense just developed, we can say that

(19) the logical function of judgment is that through which given representations are brought to the objective unity of apperception.

From here, we can reconstruct all of (16) by citing (8) as the grounds for asserting:

(20) It is through a certain action of the understanding that the manifold of given representations (be they intuitions or concepts) is brought under one apperception.

Since (19) serves to identify the action mentioned in (20), Kant can assert (16). That is, we can take (17)–(20), along with Kant's grounds for them, as belonging to what he must mean when he asserts (16). In this manner we have provided the promised *analysis* of (16), which is a crucial premise in the Transcendental Deduction.

Kant proceeds to speak of "the manifold, . . . so far as it is given in a single empirical intuition." He seems to reason that since (16) identifies the action of the understanding that is under discussion with the logical function of judgment, such action with respect to "the manifold, . . . so far as it is given in a *single* empirical intuition," will be "*one* of the logical functions of judgment" (my emphasis). His reasoning seems unexceptionable. Such action involved in *one* intuition will always be a particular action of some specific type, where the type is none other than a logical function of judgment. Finally, this reasoning provides the remaining feature of this stage of the argument in § 20, namely,

>(21) All the manifold, therefore, so far as it is given in a single empir-
>ical intuition, is *determined* in respect of one of [*in Ansehung
>einer*] the logical functions of judgment, and is thereby brought
>into one consciousness. (B 143)

For the specification of a particular combination of a manifold of intuition
in a single empirical intuition constitutes a *determination* of the manifold.

A summary of the argument up to this point, the threshold of its penultimate conclusion, might be useful here.

Stage I: Section 15 begins with (1) and (2).

Stage II: Here, in conjunction with §§ 15 and 16, through (3) and (4),
Kant provides the basis for his talk in § 17 of (5), and thus the
combination of the manifold of intuition in one consciousness,
the uniting of the manifold of a given intuition in a concept,
and, through (5), (6), and (7), all unification of representations
(B 136–38).

Stage III: On the basis of Stage II, his assertion of propositions (8)–(13),
and certain considerations involving his notions of a manifold,
intuition, and unity, Kant talks of the possibility of the unity
of intuition and thus asserts proposition 14.

Stage IV: Kant justifies (15) on the basis of (14).

Stage V: Proposition 16 can be reached from (15) on the basis of an
analysis of (16), an analysis that comprises (17)–(20).

Stage VI: The notion of a *single empirical* intuition is introduced into
the proof as something that is an instance of a *single sensible*
intuition.

Stage VII: Since (15) requires of intuition that its manifold be subject
to the original synthetic unity of apperception, and since (16)
requires that that be done through the logical function of judgment, we can conclude proposition 21. That is, it follows from
(15) and (16) that the manifold given in a single empirical intuition, being necessarily subject to the unity of apperception,
must be determined in respect of one of the logical functions
of judgment.

Having reviewed the argument thus far, we can now advance to its penultimate conclusion:

(22) [T]he *categories* are just these functions of judgment, in so far as they are employed in determination of the manifold of a given intuition. (B143)

Evidently, the second clause of (22) comes directly from the first clause of (21). So the question before us concerns the grounds the text cites in support of Kant's identification of the categories with the functions of judgment, where the context of the identification is one in which the manifold of a given intuition is determined in respect of the logical functions of judgment.

The text in the Kemp Smith translation does cite a certain section of the *Critique* in this regard. Unfortunately, it fails to cite the right section. Not that Kemp Smith himself had to be ignorant of it, since earlier he does catch the change in numbering that is responsible for what I consider to be the later mistake. In my opinion, the passage that evidently supports (22) is included in a portion of the *Critique* that belongs to a section that was designated "§ 13" only in the second edition. This is the passage in which Kant asserts:

(23) They [the categories] are concepts of an object in general, by means of which [i.e., through which (*dadurch*)] the intuition of an object is regarded [*angesehen wird*] as determined in respect of one of [*in Ansehung einer*] the logical functions of judgment. (B 128)

So in the second edition it would have been *correct*, as I understand the argument anyhow, to cite § 13 and thus direct the reader's attention to (23) in support of proposition 22. But when the portion of the *Critique* that includes (23) was designated "§ 14" in the third edition, whoever did the proofreading of the Transcendental Deduction must have overlooked the corresponding change that was required at B 143, namely, the citation in support of proposition 22, which I believe to be proposition 23. Apparently the oversight continued until the appearance of the Valentiner edition in the early part of this century. (The *Akademie* edition of 1904, for its part, apparently on the basis of Vaihinger's judgment, takes the citation to be a reference to § 10.) Despite the fact that the Valentiner edition corrects what I take to be an error at B 143, the Kemp Smith translation repeats it, and the Raymund Schmidt edition[15] only inserts a footnote to the effect that the

---

15. Hamburg: Felix Meiner Verlag, 1930.

reference might be either to § 10 (cf. Vaihinger) or to § 14 (cf. Valentiner). Actually, the footnotes inserted into both the Kemp Smith translation and the Schmidt edition contain enough information for the alert reader to put the pieces together as I have here.

We can now turn to the question of how (21), in conjunction with (23), provides the basis for the identification of the categories with the logical functions of judgment in (22). In contexts in which the manifold of a given intuition is determined in respect of one of the logical functions of judgment, that is, in contexts covered by (21), the categories cannot be other than the logical functions of judgment. For if they were, the intuition in which the manifold is given might be represented through a category without being "regarded as determined in respect of one of the logical functions of judgment" (B 128). Thus, "the concept of body" might be "brought under the category of substance" without "its empirical intuition in experience . . . [being] considered as subject and never as mere predicate" (B 129). Since this would contradict (23), and more particularly would contradict the very passage subsequent to (23) from which these quotes are extracted, the categories must be identified with the logical functions of judgment in contexts covered by (21). We thus get the identification of the categories with the logical functions of judgment that is asserted in (22).

This brings us to the ultimate conclusion of the proof:

(24) [T]he manifold in a given intuition is necessarily subject to the categories. (B 143)

Proposition 24 is simply a consequence of the conjunction of (21) and (22). We can thus close this section of the chapter with the summary argument that a manifold in a given intuition must be a manifold that is brought to the unity of apperception if the unity of the intuition is to be possible, and this can be done only through the categories. With this argument we conclude our positive account of the argument in §§ 19 and 20.

IV

It should be kept in mind that the foregoing has been selective with respect to both the various parts of step one of the Deduction and the various critics of those selected parts. So, to reiterate a limitation mentioned at the start of the chapter, the foregoing has not been intended as a complete analysis of step one. Moreover, it should be noted that the conclusions we have reached here would lose some of their purpose if they were not followed up with an examination of step two of the Deduction. Given the significance that step two has come to assume in the literature on the Deduction, it goes without saying that the study of the Deduction also cannot be considered complete until a positive account of step two is provided. This is done in the next chapter.

PERCEPTION AND THE
CATEGORIES

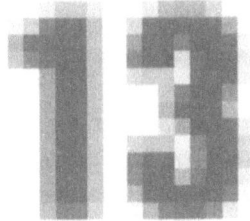

I

Though the first step of the B-Deduction distinguishes objective judgments and intuitions from the subjective vagaries of an individual's perceptions, which are due to the contingency of empirical circumstances and conditions, it stops short of B-relating this abstract, and hence objective, judgment or intuition to our concrete empirical intuitions of *things* (B 146–47).[1] In so doing, it falls short of B-relating those abstractions to our *perceptions*. The point can be made another way. Since the first step explains only how the given *manifold* of an intuition *in general* is brought to the unity of objective consciousness, and thereby explains only how "the unity . . . enters into the intuition" (B 144), and thus fails to include us human beings, who have sensibility, which must be affected by objects if an intuition of ours is to take place (A 19/B 33), the first step cannot explain how *"things in space and time"* also "must be intuited in this [categorial] form" (B 147). In this

---

1. See Chapter 2 and Part Two, "Transcendental Ontology," for the basic role accorded to *things* in the ontology of Kant's theory of a priori knowledge. In this connection it should also be noted that the section that opens the second step of the Deduction, § 22, states its specific concern with knowledge of *things*.

manner the first step leaves to the second the completion of the Deduction of the proposition that appearances must be subject to the categories.

This proposition actually expresses a requirement of *all* the a priori knowledge the explanation of whose possibility is the aim of the Deduction. For even "[m]athematical concepts are not . . . by themselves knowledge, except on the supposition that there are things which allow of being presented [i.e., given] to us" (B 147). Besides mathematics, the objectivity provided by consciousness through the categories is also a requirement of the a priori knowledge of the laws of nature in general (B 159, B 165). This knowledge is arrived at through the principles of the possibility of experience, that is, through "the a priori laws that alone can instruct us in regard to experience in general" (B 165). Consequently, the explanation depends on establishing what are the conditions of the possibility of experience, the same possibility of which these are the principles. Since experience is possible through the connection of the very perceptions with which this chapter begins (see B 161), we have arrived at the objective connection among all of one's perceptions that is to be contrasted with the merely subjective conjunction among them (cf. B 142). Perceptions consist of more than their merely subjective aspect, which makes them vary from "one man . . . to another" (B 140): each must also be free of these vagaries of empirical circumstances and conditions. This takes us to the *possibility* of perception itself, to what Kant calls "the empirical synthesis of apprehension" (B 160).

Thus, that part of Kant's Copernican Revolution according to which the understanding is the lawgiver unto nature is achieved through his single-minded pursuit of an explanation of the objectivity of perception, taken both individually and as a whole.[2] This explanation is to be found in our employment of the categories, as that is explained, first, independently of perception, in step one of the Deduction and, second, through their determination of perception and of the connections among perceptions, and hence of experience, in step two. It is to an account of this second step of the Deduction that we now direct our attention.

II

It is well known that Kant argued for an affirmative answer to the question whether all possible perceptions must be subject to the categories. His an-

---

2. See Chapters 3 and 8 for a discussion of Kant's expression "Copernican Revolution."

swer, of course, has been challenged from many quarters. In the last decade or so, however, two in particular, in criticizing his answer in detail, have perhaps unexpectedly drawn our attention to a particular portion of his answer that so far has been either overlooked or, in my judgment, misinterpreted. In addition, we must examine yet again a much debated footnote (B 160 n) that is crucial to Kant's answer.[3] The criticisms are represented for us by Henry Allison and Patricia Kitcher,[4] who both argue that Kant failed to establish the necessary role of the categories in a certain necessary connection among all possible perceptions, namely, that connection through which experience is possible. In so doing, he failed to establish his Copernican Revolution in philosophy, since his explanation of the necessary lawfulness of nature consists precisely in this necessary connection among all possible perceptions. In other words, in failing to prove that the categories are "valid a priori for all objects of experience" (B 161), he failed to prove that "nature in general . . . is dependent upon" them (B 165).

The portion of Kant's answer that has been overlooked or misinterpreted actually occurs even before perception is introduced into the argument. It consists of the final stages of the so-called first step of the B-Deduction.[5] These are the stages in which Kant distinguishes between the objective and the subjective validity of two types of V-relation that obtain among given representations (B 142).[6] The distinction itself is made on the basis of a prior distinction of his between "inner sense" and "the original synthetic unity of apperception." And he could not have made this distinction unless he had already abstracted from the argument the faculty of representation called "sensibility" (B 144). Since sensibility contains what Kant calls the

---

3. For a review of some of the recent commentary on this note, see Wayne Waxman, *Kant's Model of the Mind: A New Interpretation of Transcendental Idealism* (Oxford: Oxford University Press, 1991), 79ff. Waxman interprets the note as strong evidence for his fundamental thesis that even in the Aesthetic space and time involve the imagination, despite Kant's assertion that he is abstracting the understanding from the discussion of the Aesthetic (A 22/B 36). It is because virtually all previous commentators misinterpret this abstraction, Waxman contends, that they fail to appreciate the involvement of imagination in space and time.

Later in this chapter I make some of the same points as Waxman. But in note 12 below I point out some differences between us.

4. Henry E. Allison, *Kant's Transcendental Idealism: An Interpretation and Defense* (New Haven: Yale University Press, 1983), 167–70. Patricia Kitcher, *Kant's Transcendental Psychology* (New York: Oxford University Press, 1990), 167–69.

5. As already noted, many credit Dieter Henrich, in "The Proof-Structure of Kant's Transcendental Deduction," *Review of Metaphysics* 22 (1969): 640–59, with a convincing interpretation according to which the B-Deduction is a single argument consisting of two steps.

6. See Chapter 11 *et passim* for an explanation of these two types of relation.

"mode" in which the manifold of an empirical intuition is given, that is, the mode in which the subject is affected, the distinction between inner sense and apperception requires abstracting that mode from the manifold of an intuition (B 129, B 144, B 157). Indeed, this is precisely the abstraction he has already made at the start of the B-Deduction (B 129). Consequently, in the concluding stages of step one, he can speak of "the unity which, [by means] of the category, and [through] the understanding, enters into the intuition" (B 144).

As for the much debated footnote referred to above, it is crucial only to Kitcher's criticism of Kant, not to Allison's. The response that shall be made to her is that she misinterprets this note and thus misinterprets Kant.

So the thesis of this chapter is that the shortcomings these critics allege can be found in the second step of the B-Deduction are rather due to their own failure to make the right use of certain propositions Kant has already claimed to have established in the first step of the Deduction as well as certain ones he lays down for the second step alone. Thus, a large part of the main burden of the Deduction is actually carried by the first step, which is apparently what Kant himself thought about the matter.[7] So the validity of the second step cannot be properly appraised until we have got the first step pretty much right and then apply it correctly to the second step. And, of course, we must also correctly interpret key propositions that are unique to the second step.

This thesis stands in contrast to the view I have already noted has been ascendant in most recent commentaries on the Deduction. According to this view, we should look beyond the Deduction,[8] specifically to the Principles of the Understanding, and even more particularly to the Analogies of Experience, to find Kant's best arguments to explain the necessity of the categories with respect to perception or to experience.[9] So the view presented here of the entire Deduction, as already noted in earlier chapters, is that it is much more defensible as an argument that is independent of the Principles than has so far been allowed in the recent literature.

This view is supported by the interpretations presented here of both the

7. *Metaphysical Foundations of Natural Science,* trans. James Ellington (Indianapolis: Bobbs-Merrill, 1970), 13–14 n.

8. See, for example, Robert Pippin, *Kant's Theory of Form* (New Haven: Yale University Press, 1982), 182ff.

9. Besides Allison and Kitcher, see, for example, Paul Guyer, *Kant and the Claims of Knowledge* (Cambridge: Cambridge University Press, 1987), 77ff. See also his "Transcendental Deduction of the Categories," in *The Cambridge Companion to Kant,* ed. Paul Guyer (Cambridge: Cambridge University Press, 1992), 127.

first step of the Deduction and the footnote that is crucial to Kitcher's criticism of Kant. Where she uses that criticism to argue that Kant's best arguments for the categories are to be found in the Analytic of Principles, the present interpretation of the note allows us to view the B-Deduction as a completed argument for the objective validity of the categories.

III

Of the two critics mentioned above, Kitcher will be considered first. She begins her reconstruction of the Deduction by laying down the initial premise that "all concepts of space and time" are necessary for perception. The reconstruction then goes on to the proposition that these concepts in turn must be subject to the categories.[10] Turning critical, however, she asks: *are* these concepts possible in all possible cases of perception? She answers that presumably they would be if (*a*) they "must be available to us in advance of any (other) concepts" and (*b*) some concept or other were necessary for perception. But she concludes that Kant fails to establish either condition, and thus fails to demonstrate the necessary connection among all possible perceptions, which is precisely what is in question.[11]

On Kant's behalf, we can first merely assume the validity of the second condition (*b*) for the sake of examining the validity of the first (*a*). Are there any alternative concepts to those of space and time that would allow for perception? If there are, and if they are empirical (as they are in certain stages of both the subjective and the objective A-Deduction [A 100ff. and A 119ff.]), I would argue that the B-Deduction could not have proceeded even this far, that is, to its second step.

This is where Kitcher's neglect of the first step of the B-Deduction is significant. For, as noted in section I above, its first step depends on the distinction between the objective and the subjective validity of two types of *V*-relation (and thereby two types of *B*-relation) that obtain among given representations. Only one type of *V*-relation follows the "laws of association" (B 142). These are the laws that determine the formation of merely empirical concepts. So, if the alternative concepts to which Kitcher is alluding were empirical, the Deduction would have to rely on these laws of association. But that would keep the Deduction from distinguishing the original unity

10. Kitcher, *Kant's Transcendental Psychology*, 162–63.
11. Ibid. 168.

of apperception from inner sense (§§ 18 and 19, which belong to step one) and thus prevent it from employing that unity in establishing the objective validity of the categories in its first step (at B 143). Indeed, Kant rules out the laws of association, and hence the reproductive imagination, from the B-Deduction altogether (B 152). So empirical concepts cannot provide the alternative (to all concepts of space and time) on which Kitcher thinks some perceptions might conceivably rely.

Might the alternative concepts to those of space and time be a priori? If they were, they would have to be the categories, which would immediately make the second step of the Deduction question-begging. In addition, if they were the categories, the empirical consciousness would be a consciousness of the mere *manifold* of an empirical intuition (B 143), not a consciousness of the *intuition itself* "(as appearance)" (B 160). In other words, it would not be a perception! In effect, we would be back at the conclusion of the *first* step of the B-Deduction (B 143–44).

In clarification of this point, it will be recalled that in the Observation concluding the first step of the Deduction (§ 21), while Kant does speak of "the empirical consciousness of a given manifold in a single intuition," he does not also speak of a consciousness of the intuition itself, and a fortiori he does not speak of an empirical consciousness of it, either. For the latter would make the intuition a perception. The transformation of an empirical intuition into a perception, he tells us, is through the empirical synthesis of apprehension. This proposition is not only stated at the point at which Kant actually accounts for the possibility of perception, in the second step of the Deduction (B 160), but is implied by him as well in his first illustration of a perception (B 162). He there says that "by [i.e., through (*durch*)] apprehension of the manifold of a house I make the empirical intuition of it into a perception" (B 162). The empirical synthesis of apprehension, however, must, he says, "conform" to our "*a priori forms* of outer and inner sensible intuition" (B 160). These, in turn, are none other than the respective modes in which the manifolds of particular empirical intuitions are given, that is, space and time. But Kant abstracts from these modes when considering the manifold of a sensible intuition under the condition of a category—the condition under which the manifold is brought to the unity of apperception. And thus the abstraction is made at B 143–44, when Kant is considering the empirical consciousness of a *manifold* of an empirical intuition, a consciousness that is "subject to a pure self-consciousness *a priori*" through a category. Therefore, the difference between abstraction and nonabstraction from the relevant mode, and hence between the attendant absence and presence of the empirical synthesis of apprehension, is the difference between the empirical consciousness of the mere manifold of an empirical intuition and the empirical consciousness of the intuition itself. Since the categories can be said to "directly" determine the manifold of an empirical intuition just in case they do not determine that manifold through determination of the manifold of the *mode* in which the manifold of the empirical intuition is given, and since the mode is required for the synthesis of apprehension, which, in turn, accounts for the possibility of perception, the categories cannot "directly" determine the manifold of an empirical intuition of which one can be empirically conscious, where it is the intuition itself, and not merely its manifold, of which one is conscious, that is, the manifold of a perception. Consequently, the categories cannot be the *alternative* concepts to those of the modes, that is, to those of space and time, in accounting for the possibility of perception. So, again it is crucial to remember precisely what the first step of the B-Deduction actually accomplishes.

To sum up, since the concepts this particular portion of the second step of the B-Deduction requires for the possibility of perception cannot be empirical or categorial, they must be spatial and temporal—that is, *if* the possibility of some concepts is required for possible perception at all.

And that is precisely the other condition (*b*) whose validity must be examined. Must some concepts be possible if perception is to be possible? Now we must turn our attention from the first step of the B-Deduction to the second, and in particular to the footnote that is crucial to Kitcher's criticism of the Deduction. The note says, *inter alia,* that through determining sensibility the understanding gives unity to the given intuitions of space and time apart from "the concept of the understanding." This determination is then supposed to be compared with the understanding's determination of sensibility that was previously explained in § 24. There the determination is said to proceed "under the title of a *transcendental synthesis of imagination*" (B 151, B 153). It is Kant's account of this synthesis in § 24 that explains the independence of the unity of the intuitions of space and time from "the concept of the understanding" that is mentioned in B 160a. Since sensibility is "the subjective condition [of the imagination] under which alone it [the imagination] can give to the concepts of the understanding corresponding intuition," the imagination "belongs to sensibility" (B 151). Similarly, because it is under the subjective condition of sensibility that the imagination first gives space and time as intuitions, their unity belongs to space and time, "and not to the concept of the understanding" (B 160a). That is Kant's reason for saying in the note that the unity of these intuitions belongs to "space and time, and not to the concept of the understanding," even though the unity presupposes a synthesis belonging to the understanding.[12]

This interpretation of the note indicates a dispute between Kitcher and the view presented here concerning the nature of the synthesis mentioned in B 160a. She speaks of it as providing "determinate spaces and times," and she does so in connection with a passage in which Kant speaks of "a determinate space" (B 137–38).[13] This is a passage in which "the unity of consciousness" provides the determination. But, for the reasons just given, following Kant's instruction to compare the unity of intuition mentioned in the note with that which is referred to in § 24, this latter unity, the original unity of consciousness, cannot be the unity that is under discussion in the note.

To anticipate the more developed elaboration of this point offered in section IV below, which contains the positive account of Kant's theory of the dependence of perception on the categories, something further might just as well be said about it here. Whereas Kitcher holds that the determinateness provided by the transcendental unity of apperception (and therefore through the categories) that Kant speaks of at B 137–38, in the first step of the Deduction, is present in the formal intuition, the contention here is that it is actually absent from that intuition. When Kant tells us in the note that the synthesis through which the formal intuition is given "precedes any concept," he seems to intend that it precedes not just the categories but the transcendental unity of apperception as well, since at this point he obviously must think that the first step of the Deduction has demonstrated that that unity depends on the categories if the manifold of a sensible intuition is to

12. Allison, too, has a preintellectual, or preconceptual, interpretation of the unity of space and time mentioned in B 160a. He attributes this unity to "intuited content," which suggests a connection with his interpretation of Kant's theory of perception as *empirically* subjective (*Kant's Transcendental Idealism*, 165). See my critical discussion of this latter interpretation below.

I would point out here that despite what Waxman (see note 3 above), in my opinion, correctly says about the involvement of imagination in the *given unitary intuitions* of space and time, the *forms* of these intuitions are still independent of the imagination. I would also assert that the independence of imagination from the understanding with respect to space and time, which Waxman acknowledges (*Kant's Model of the Mind*, 109 n. 9), implies for Kant an independence of imagination in this context from the synthesis and spontaneity of the understanding (B 151–52), which Waxman seems to neglect, if not ignore. Finally, where Waxman, like Kitcher, finds an identity between the synthetic unity of the intuitions of space and time in the note at B 160 and the synthetic unity of the productive imagination in § 24, B 150ff., I see rather a difference between the two synthetic unities. The one in § 24 involves the categories and the transcendental unity of apperception, whereas the one in the note to B 160 does not.

13. Kitcher, *Kant's Transcendental Psychology*, 158.

be brought to that unity. Consequently, where Kitcher takes the unity of the intuition in the note to be *determinate,* according to that unity, the view proposed here takes it to be merely *determinable,* in the sense that it *precedes* but may yet receive the determinateness Kitcher claims to find in it, according to that unity. On the present view, that determinateness is rather attributed to the intuitions only in the *body* of the text, where Kant speaks of the "determination" of the unity of the manifold of the intuitions of space and of time (B 160). So it can be said that Kitcher has failed to understand the *determinable, but not (yet) determined* nature of the given intuitions of space and time in the note. This misunderstanding would then explain how so much of her discussion of Kant's view of our "perceiving [determinate] times and spaces" is, from the present point of view, misguided.[14]

14. Ibid., 157. My interpretation also provides a response to Pippin's objection that since Kant must rely on the schematism (I would sooner say "the a priori synthesis of imagination") to account for the unity of intuition that precedes all concepts, his account is incoherent. For the schematism is, in effect, a bridge between two faculties, sensibility and the understanding, that must be kept so distinct from one another that no such bridge between them is possible, if Kant's theory of knowledge is to have any chance of success. Pippin, *Kant's Theory of Form,* 226–28.

According to my interpretation, however, sensibility and the understanding not only can remain distinct from one another, they must do so, since the former is determinable and the latter determining. For the present discussion I would also add that Kant understands the transcendental synthesis of imagination to be "an action [i.e., effect (*Wirkung*)] of the understanding on sensibility" (B 152). Since a cause and an effect must be distinct from one another, so must a cause and that which the cause acts on, or affects, be distinct. Consequently, sensibility and understanding must be distinct from one another, given Kant's understanding of the transcendental synthesis of imagination.

Hoke Robinson throws light on this determination relation between the understanding and sensibility, which I believe must be taken as an affecting relation, in his paper "The Transcendental Deduction from A to B: Combination in the Threefold Synthesis and the Representation of a Whole," in *Spindel Conference 1986: The B-Deduction* (*Southern Journal of Philosophy* 25, supplement), ed. Hoke Robinson (Memphis: Department of Philosophy, Memphis State University, 1987), 47, 49–50. I should mention here that I do not share Robinson's reading of the object of empirical intuition as "an intentional object" (a reading he shares with Aquila, discussed at length above and immediately below as well), if that is meant to imply that the object itself does not represent any further, distinct (external) object (a thing) *whose affect on sensibility results in the matter of the intuition, that is, sensation.*

My interpretation can also serve as the basis for a two-part—positive and negative— response to a particular concern of Aquila's regarding what Kant says in B 160a about the unity of the intuitions of space and of time. See his *Matter in Mind* (Bloomington: Indiana University Press, 1989). First, he interprets Kant's statement that the unity of the intuitions (unfortunately, he considers the formal and empirical [material] intuitions together, whereas the note seems clearly concerned with the formal alone) "precedes any concept" as the condition that makes it possible "actually to conceptualize" the intuitions (114). This explains, he suggests, Kant's remark that under this condition "concepts of space and time first become possible." Since I, too, view this unity of the intuitions through this synthesis as that through

On the basis of the reading preferred here, one would argue that the possibility of perception does indeed entail the possibility of "all concepts of space and time." As Kitcher herself acknowledges,[15] Kant says that "space and time are first *given* as intuitions" through the synthesis of the manifold of the forms of intuition (B 160a). Since concepts are possible, that is, B-relate to given objects, through given intuitions (A 19/B 33, A 68–69/B 93–94), the latter provide the objects in B-relation to which the former are possible. On the other hand, as Kitcher also acknowledges,[16] since all possible perceptions involve the forms of intuition of space and time, and since, as I have just noted, the synthesis of the manifold of these forms gives us the intuitions of space and time, all possible perceptions involve these intuitions if the manifold of these forms is subject to this synthesis. Consequently, all possible perceptions are subject to the synthesis of the manifold of these forms of intuition if the manifold is subject to it. But we have just seen that all concepts of space and time are possible through the same synthesis. Therefore, the possibility of perception entails the possibility of these concepts if the manifold of these forms is subject to this synthesis. And for Kant the manifold *is* subject to this synthesis, since, according to his explanation in the note itself, the understanding "determines the sensibility" (B 160a).

The conclusion of the discussion of Kitcher, therefore, is that Kant does provide grounds for the proposition that the possibility of the concepts of space and time is a requirement of all possible perceptions.

If Kitcher employs a sufficiently weak (broad) sense of perception and its objects that at least some of them escape the reach of our concepts of space

---

which "concepts of space and time first become possible," my proposal, to this extent at least, is in agreement with Aquila's.

But I part company with him when he goes on to say that "in the present passage" Kant holds "that intellectual functions are *also* needed in order for space and time . . . actually to be *given* as 'objects' " (114). I see no dependence on intellectual functions here at all. (Actually, the dependence is the other way around; that is, the possibility of the concepts of space and time consists in the synthesis of the manifold given by the forms of space and time; this is the same synthesis that gives the intuitions themselves as objects, and hence as representations that have a unity.) The possibility of the concepts of space and time is not the possibility of intellectual functions at all. Those functions presumably are the logical functions of judgment, and on my reading of the note, as my disagreement with Kitcher indicates, they are absent altogether from this synthesis. They are rather required in the *determination* of the unity of space and of time, but not in the unity itself, which, as I say, is merely determinable, but not yet determined.

15. *Kant's Transcendental Psychology*, 160.
16. Ibid., 157.

and time, Allison claims to talk about experience and its objects in a sense that goes beyond what he thinks Kant has established as the reach of the categories. According to Allison, Kant succeeds in demonstrating that the categories apply to objects in a sense that at once goes beyond their being objects of mere judgment—"a judgmental or logical sense of object"—and falls short of their being objects of "empirical knowledge . . . objects in the 'weighty' sense."[17] This intermediate sense ties the objects to, *seriatim*, (*a*) "empirical intuition,"[18] (*b*) "the intuited content" of an intuition,[19] and (*c*) "perception,"[20] where perception is a "mode of empirical consciousness," "and its object[,] an appearance[,]" where "appearances are modifications of inner sense; they are 'in us' in the empirical sense."[21] In sum, "the notion of 'appearance' is treated as equivalent to 'perception' or as the object of a perception,"[22] the object "[apprehended] in empirical consciousness."[23] This, then, is the sense in which Allison characterizes the object as "subjective."[24]

Against this subjectivity of object, this intermediate sense of object, Allison contrasts an objectivity of object, object in the "weighty" sense, under which would qualify again *seriatim*, (*a'*) "an object of possible experience," (*b'*) "the correlate . . . of a 'judgment of experience,' " (*c'*) an object in "a 'real' sense of object, that is . . . an object in the sense of an actual entity or state of affairs,"[25] (*d'*) "spatiotemporal entities and states of affairs,"[26] (*e'*) "what can be said to exist independently of the occurrence of representative states,"[27] (*f'*) "whatever objects may present themselves to our senses,"[28] (*g'*) "objects [that] are actually given in human experience," (*h'*) "the transcendental concept of the thing as it appears," (*i'*) "things and events," (*j'*) "objects [actually experienced,] as distinct from our representation of

17. Allison, *Kant's Transcendental Idealism*, 159.
18. Ibid., 158, 164.
19. Ibid., 165.
20. Ibid., 166.
21. Ibid., 167.
22. Ibid.
23. Ibid., 169.
24. Ibid., 168.
25. Ibid., 27, 118, 135.
26. Ibid., 136, in reference to Gerald Prauss, *Erscheinung bei Kant* (Berlin: De Gruyter, 1971).
27. Ibid., in reference to P. F. Strawson, *The Bounds of Sense: An Essay on Kant's "Critique of Pure Reason"* (London: Methuen, 1966).
28. Ibid., 158, a use of Kant's *ipsissima verba* (B 159).

them," and, finally, (*k'*) " 'weighty' objects that are distinct from our perceptions of them."[29]

In addition to these two (or more) senses of object—subjective and objective, Allison claims that there is a corresponding distinction between the respective "orders" in which they occur—a subjective and an objective order. The former occurs "in empirical consciousness"[30] or "in inner sense"; it is the order of "apprehension."[31] Although he does not specifically say where the latter occurs, it seems to be in space and time.

On the basis of this contrast between the subjective and the objective objects-cum-order, Allison contends that the argument enjoys only limited success: a demonstration that the categories apply merely to the subjective.[32] (At that, the success depends on Allison's reconstruction.) He categorically concludes: "Under no circumstances . . . can it . . . be claimed that [the argument] succeeds in showing that the categories make experience possible."[33]

But is there this subjective, intermediate sense of object-cum-order in Kant's theory? The paragraphs above consist of two series of characterizations, (*a*)–(*c*) and (*a'*)–(*k'*), which obviously have led Allison to believe that he has found such a sense in Kant's theory, even though he has not actually done so. Careful consideration will show that Allison's distinction between the subjective and the objective is empty, if not inconsistent; that is, it is empty if the list of subjective features (*a*)–(*c*) is first made consistent.

Tying subjective objects to empirical intuition, intuited content of an intuition, perception, inner sense, empirical consciousness, and the categories is consistent with their being "in us" only in the *transcendental,* not the *empirical,* sense of their being "in us." But the empirical is the sense in which Allison uses the expression. Returning now to the first step of the B-Deduction and the question of the correct interpretation of certain of its key passages, we find at least part of the empirical sense in which Allison uses the expression: "Whether I can become *empirically* conscious of the manifold as simultaneous or as successive depends on circumstances or empirical conditions. Therefore, the empirical unity of consciousness, through association of representations, itself concerns an appearance, and is wholly contingent" (B 139–40). As Allison indicates, this passage from the first step of the B-

29. Ibid., 159, 167, 168, 169, 172.
30. Ibid., 167–68.
31. Ibid., 170.
32. Ibid., 168.
33. Ibid., 170.

Deduction fits a sense of "subjective" that can be applied to the Analogies of Experience, which he also relies on to some extent.[34] But the appearance mentioned in this passage belongs precisely to the objects-cum-order that are *not, apropos* the B-Deduction, "apprehended in empirical consciousness," where that expression signifies the essential condition of the possibility of perception and its specific objects; nor are they subject to the categories. However, if Allison omits these just-mentioned features to characterize his "subjective" objects, he must give up the entire point of the contrast between the subjective and the objective that is in question, since he would then have to give up the claim that Kant has succeeded in the Transcendental Deduction of the categories with respect to subjective objects-cum-order but not with respect to objective objects-cum-order. In a word, the set of features *(a)–(c)* that Allison attributes to these subjective objects-cum-order is consistent only if they are "in us" in the *transcendental* sense.

Once they are taken in that sense, however, they cover the same set of objects-cum-order that exemplify the list of objective features, *(a')–(k')*. Empirical intuitions as appearances are not only modifications of inner sense that occur as perceptions in empirical consciousness and that are brought as a manifold of representations to the necessary unity of apperception through the categories. Being appearances in the transcendental conception of things as they appear, they are also objects that present themselves to our senses, actual spatiotemporal entities or states of affairs that can be said to exist independently of the occurrence of representative states, in the sense that they are distinct from our representations that "have always been [merely] conjoined [*beisammen*] in [the individual's] perception, however often that perception be repeated" (B 142). This exactly fits what I said above in contesting Allison's claim that he was talking about appearances as being "in us" in the empirical sense. It is not perception that is being characterized as subjective here; it is rather the *conjunction* of representations in the individual's perception. The contrast is with the *combination* (*Verbindung*) of the same representations *"in the object,"* not with perception itself. (It also fits with Kant's conception of the independence of appearances from only those representations that make our representations or knowledge *empirical,* that is, *sensations,* provided the sensations are not contained in any knowledge. "[O]f themselves," sensations "do not . . . yield knowledge of any object" [B 44], since they are "effect[s] of an object upon the faculty of representation, [sensibility], so far as we are affected by it" [A 19–20/B 33–34]; that is, they "relate solely to the subject as the modification of its state" [A 320/B 376]).

All the features listed above, except for those deleted, of course, belong to appearances as constituting a single set of objects-cum-order. According to transcendental idealism, actual spatiotemporal entities that exist independently of the conjunction of representations in the perception of the individual subject are modifications of inner sense that occur in empirical consciousness as perceptions, and it is through the connection (*Verknüpfung*) of perceptions that experience is possible. Kant's transcendental idealism includes this much phenomenalism. Finally, since Allison argues for the proposition that Kant succeeds in demonstrating that the categories apply to objects in the intermediate, or subjective, sense of object, and since the necessary difference between the subjective and the objective that is alleged by him cannot be found, then, once the inconsistent, truly subjective features are abstracted from Allison's list, it must be concluded that he has failed to establish his emphatic verdict: that "[u]nder no circumstances . . . can it . . . be claimed that it [the argument] succeeds in showing that the categories make experience possible." Rather, given his belief that the Deduction works for the subjective objects-cum-order, he should have excised the inconsistent features and reached exactly the opposite conclusion.

It should be mentioned that the *realism* to which Allison is referring with the "weighty" sense of object he attributes to Kant's theory is, on the present view, really there. As the matter is viewed here,[35] the transcendental conception of the constituent of that reality, namely, the *thing simpliciter,* is distinct from Allison's transcendental conception of the thing *as it appears.* So long as Allison is determined to take the distinct thing as *appearance,* or as empirical object, he will face the difficulties discussed above. Kant's external realism of *things* must be thought distinctly from the conditions of possible experience.

IV

In the opening section of this chapter, I claimed that a satisfactory defense of the second step of the Deduction could be made on the basis of an adequate appreciation of the first step and its correct application to the second step

35. See Chapter 2.

as well as a correct interpretation of certain propositions in the second step. It is now time we turned our attention to that defense.

In the discussion of Allison, an argument has already been advanced for the abstraction of factors that vary according to the state of the subject if they are considered independently of their role in our knowledge of objects. And as also noted, in the concluding stages of step one Kant speaks of these factors as depending on "circumstances or empirical conditions" that lead to "the empirical unity of consciousness, through association of representations, [which] itself concerns an appearance, and is wholly contingent" (B 139–40). Shortly thereafter, he speaks of a hypothetical statement ("If I support a body, I feel an impression of weight") as "merely stat[ing] that the two representations [of body and of weight] have always been conjoined in my perception." This statement depends on the "state of the subject," whereas the statement Kant wants to make "is that [the representations] are combined *in the object*, no matter what the state of the subject may be" (B 142). And he does so on the basis of his explanation of how a judgment and the objective unity of apperception are related to one another as mutually supporting conditions (B 141–42).[36] To isolate this objective unity of consciousness and to establish that the categories are conditions for "the manifold of representations (be they intuitions or concepts) [to be] brought under [it]" (B 143), Kant must have abstracted sensibility from the argument (B 144). And since sensibility includes the "mode" in which the subject is affected (B 129), including therefore the mode in which the manifold of an empirical intuition is given (B 144), this mode is abstracted as well. This leaves us with the manifold of a sensible intuition *in general* as the manifold that is necessarily subject to the categories, if the manifold of representations is to be brought "under one apperception."

When our attention turns to perception in § 26, we find that the mode in which the manifold of an empirical intuition is given plays the crucial role in establishing the objective validity of the categories. But it only makes its appearance in the later stages of the second step. First, the possibility of perception as "empirical consciousness of . . . [an] empirical intuition (as appearance)" is constituted by the so-called synthesis of apprehension (B 160). This is an empirical synthesis that "brings combination into the manifold of intuition" from "the same spontaneity" as that which brings combination "under the title of understanding" (B 160b). It is to be distinguished from the synthesis of "the *reproductive* imagination . . . [which] is entirely

36. See Chapter 12.

subject to empirical laws" (B 152). This distinction exactly fits my earlier remarks about abstracting from the argument the variable, empirical factors responsible for the mere *conjunction* of representations in an individual subject's perception.

Since perception is empirical consciousness of an empirical intuition as appearance, the synthesis of the manifold of the intuition is a synthesis of the manifold of appearance, and since the form of appearance is "that which so determines [its] manifold that it allows of its being ordered in certain V-relations" (A 20/B 34), the synthesis must "conform" to this form. According to the Aesthetic, the form is either space or time. But these are also represented as "*intuitions* which contain a manifold" (B 160). The reasoning in the conclusion of step one of the Deduction tells us that the manifold of "All Sensible Intuitions" is determined according to the categories. It includes the proposition that the possibility of the unity of a given sensible intuition consists in its manifold's being "necessarily subject to the original synthetic unity of apperception" (B 143), and this depends on the manifold's being necessarily subject to the categories.

This is to be compared with the dispute with Kitcher over the correct interpretation of B 160a. There it was claimed that the unity of the "formal" intuition of space or of time is due to a synthesis of the understanding that is *independent* of the categories and of the original synthetic unity of apperception. Yet here, reference is made to the same categories and unity of apperception in accounting for the possibility of the unity of intuition.

The solution to the apparent discrepancy in the account presented here is that the unity that is independent of the categories and of the unity of apperception precedes the possibility of the *determined* unity of the manifold, the unity that "enters into" the intuition (B 144). As a determinable unity, it is not yet possible with respect to the unity of the understanding itself. This latter possibility is constituted by "the unity of consciousness . . . alone" (B 137). This is the unity that is mentioned at the start of the Deduction as belonging to combination (B 131), and is identified as "the *transcendental* unity of self-consciousness [apperception]" (B 132; see also B 134 n).

Returning to the *note* to B 160 and to the merely determinable unity of space and time that "precedes any concept," we are told by the note to attribute this unity to sensibility, independent of both the categories and the transcendental unity of apperception. What the *body* of the text at B 160 tells us, however, is that it is concerned with something further, the "determination" of this unity. The inference seems to be that since § 20 tells us that the manifold is "brought into one consciousness" through the determination of the manifold of a given sensible intuition according to the categories, the determination of the unity of space and of time consists in bringing their respective manifolds to the unity that belongs to the understanding. This unity is the transcendental unity of apperception (B 134 n). So the determination of the unity of the manifold of space and of time implies that the unity of the synthesis of this manifold is the unity of "original consciousness [the transcendental unity of apperception] in accordance with the categories" (B 161), not the determinable unity that belongs to sensibility. As such, it is also the unity belonging specifically to combination, as first introduced at B 130–31.

Continuing with the Deduction, we remark that space and time contain not only an a priori manifold, they also contain "everything that is to be represented as determined" in them (B 161). This includes the manifold given in an empirical intuition. Thus, space and time are now represented as the respective *modes* in which such a manifold is given. These are the very modes Kant has already spoken of as the basis of the second step of the Deduction (B 144). It is in space or in time that the manifold of a given empirical intuition is to be represented as determined according to the categories. (Earlier in the Deduction Kant makes the same point with respect to the "special mode" in which the manifold of empirical self-intuition is given and determined [B 157, 158, 158 n]).

Starting with its premises that the synthesis of apprehension constitutes the possibility of perception and that this synthesis, and hence perception, necessarily conforms to the forms of space and time, the argument has now reached the point where Kant can claim to have shown that perception is subject to a further condition than that the manifold of space or of time is subject to the categories. This is the condition that perception must also be subject to the *combination* of all the objects of perception—appearances— that are "to be represented as determined in space or in time" (B 161). To sum up, perception not only must be subject to the forms of space or of time, which leads to the requirement that the manifolds of the intuitions of space and of time themselves must be subject to the determined unity of their synthesis, but, as a consequence of this requirement, perception must also be subject to the same combination to which all of the objects of perception (appearances) must also be subject insofar as these objects are "to be represented as determined in space or in time."

Though the reasoning so far has been long and complicated, I have not yet shown how Kant fulfills the purpose of the Deduction, which is to demonstrate how its first step, in which the categories are shown to prescribe unity "to the manifold of an intuition in general," applies to "all objects of our senses" (B 145), "to whatever objects may present themselves to our senses . . . *in respect of the laws of their combination*" (B 159, my emphasis), to "all objects of experience," where experience is taken to consist in "connected perceptions" (B 161), or, finally, to "nature," where "nature" is understood to be "the sum of all appearances" (B 163). So far, the reconstruction of the argument presented in this chapter has only shown how the first step applies to all possible perceptions and their objects insofar as their objects are "to be represented as determined in space or in time." The question with which the chapter began and which I have just reiterated remains, however: how does the first step apply to all possible perceptions and their objects, where now the application will provide for the a priori laws of the *combination among the objects of perception*—the laws that make experience possible? It is the question of the possibility of those a priori laws with respect to all objects of perception—with respect to nature, as Kant understands it.

The distinction between an object's being represented as determined in space or in time and its being represented as determined in nature can be further explained as follows: With respect to the first, only the unity of the synthesis of space (space in general) and time (time in general), and consequently a combination of everything to be represented as determined in one or the other, lie at the basis of a perception (e.g., of a house or of the freezing of water). So, what is subject to the unity is the manifold of space and of time, and what is subject to the combination in question is the manifold of every appearance represented as determined in space or in time. Here, every particular appearance is represented through a combination of its manifold, according to a combination of the manifold of space or of time.

But every appearance in turn belongs to a manifold of appearances—nature, which is also subject to an a priori combination (through the categories) that brings it to the unity of apperception. This requires, however, that the appearances belonging to the manifold be taken as *representations*, since Kant speaks only of representations as being subject to combination in one objective consciousness (apperception) (B 131–32). Moreover, since appearances are explicitly cast as *representations*, they are thereby thought distinctly from the objects they represent. I submit that the concept of these objects is provided precisely by Kant's concept of a *thing*.

So, the concept of a thing reenters the discussion precisely at the point at which Kant is attempting to explain the a priori combination of all appearances, or the manifold of nature. That is why, I further submit, that he says at B 164 that "appearances are only representations of things." If the combination were not a priori, Kant would have no argument that a *combination* is required for the manifold of appearances to be brought to the unity of objective consciousness. For an empirical synthesis of *association*—through reproductive imagination (B 152)—would be sufficient to bring the manifold to a derivative *empirical* unity of a *subjective* consciousness (B 139ff.). That is, association does not require any object that is distinct from the representations that are "conjoined" in perception (B 142). Only the *necessary* synthetic unity of representations entails that the appearances themselves be taken as (mere) representations of distinct objects, that is, things.

V

The answer to the fundamental question concerning the possibility of the a priori laws that make experience possible has two parts. The *first* consists in reaching the simple conclusion that "the categories . . . are . . . valid *a priori* for all objects of experience" (B 161). Since experience consists in the connection (*Verknüpfung*) of perceptions, the first part of the answer to our question consists in a reconstruction of Kant's account of that connection. From the proposition that all possible perception in space or in time is subject to the categories, how does he validly infer that "all possible perceptions," or "all appearances in space and time," are connected through the categories?

Here Allison has partially, but nonetheless correctly, I believe, identified Kant's premise: the understanding produces a transcendental "synthesis of intuitions," which is the transcendental synthesis of imagination (B 152). I would then add that if the intuitions are *accompanied by empirical consciousness through the empirical synthesis of apprehension* (B 160), it is a synthesis of "all possible perceptions" (B 164). So, both the transcendental synthesis of imagination and the empirical synthesis of apprehension (also of the imagination [B 160b]), and consequently the categories, account for the possibility of experience.

I believe that Allison goes off-track, however, with respect to the *second* part of my answer to the question at hand. There is no such distinction of objective experience-cum-order from subjective perceptions-cum-order as he supposes. The second part of my answer, indeed, explains why he, and, of course, those like him in this respect, make what is a mistaken objection to the Deduction.

The mistake is fundamental; indeed, it goes to the heart of the two major themes of this book: Kant's primary objective in the positive epistemology of the *Critique,* and its implications for his ontology and consequently for his transcendental idealism as well. The Deduction, after all, consists of more than the reasoning that leads us to the conclusion that the categories make experience possible. This is the reasoning that we have just concluded and that has led to the *first* of the two parts of my answer to the question at hand. I am arguing, however, that the Deduction also consists in the explanation of the possibility of this very possibility, namely, the possibility that the categories are valid for all objects of experience. To explain the possibility of *this* possibility is to tell us what constitutes the B-relation of the categories to objects of experience, or appearances. This explanation alone is what, according to my reading of Kant's notion of *transcendental,* actually makes the argument *transcendental.* The explanation of what makes experience itself possible, in the sense of what it takes to B-relate experience to its objects, is not transcendental: the only explanation that is transcendental is an explanation of what B-relates the possibility itself, that is, the possibility of experience, to objects (appearances). To repeat, it is not transcendental for Kant to argue that experience is impossible without the involvement of the categories. Rather, his argument for the categories is transcendental only when he argues that they themselves are impossible apart from whatever conditions are necessary for them ultimately to be B-related to appearances or, more specifically, considering the desiderata of the Deduction, to objects of the senses.

To spell out in greater detail this *second* part of my answer to the question at hand, we can begin with Kant's transcendental idealism. It is here that any commentator on the *Critique* must acknowledge the phenomenalism of Kant's transcendental idealism. For unless appearances were "only representations of things" (B 164), they would not be subject to the "I think" through which they are brought to the transcendental unity of apperception (via the categories), since, as already noted, only as a unity of a manifold of *representations* is that unity "[t]he supreme principle of the possibility of all intuition . . . in its [B-]relation to understanding" (B 136). Allison's apparent perception of a gap between subjective perception and objective experience simply reflects his apparent dismissal of Kant's evident phenomenalism in this matter. The phenomenalism of his transcendental idealism is thus one factor of the second of the two parts of my answer to the question before us. The very possibility of the possibility of experience consists, among other things, in the elements of transcendental idealism. Transcendental knowledge of what might be considered this "higher-level" possibility, if knowledge it be, must therefore include transcendental idealism.

It is to this idealism that Kant attends after he illustrates his theory of the possibility of perception with the examples of perceiving a house and perceiving water freezing. From the middle of B 163 to the end of the Deduction, at B 168, he relies on his transcendental idealism for the precise purpose of keeping any gap between subjective perception and objective experience from ever opening. To paraphrase Kant, philosophers themselves create this gap only because they take appearances as things in themselves.

Besides this factor of Kant's idealism, my answer to the question at hand contains the other factors mentioned above. Above all, these deal with the central theses of this book, namely, first, that Kant's theory of knowledge pertains above all to the possibility of a priori knowledge and not to that of empirical knowledge and, second, that the ontology of this theory consists of *things* (again, *vide* Kant's explicit treatment of appearances as being "only representations of *things*" [B 164, my emphasis]). Of course, as I have argued from the beginning, these two factors and that of Kant's idealism are all connected to each other: it is only because Kant's primary interest is in the possibility of a priori knowledge that the ontology of his theory consists of things and not their mere appearances, even though it is to these same appearances alone (i.e., the things as they appear in space and time), and not to the ontology of the theory (i.e., things *simpliciter*), that the a priori knowledge can be B-related.[37] So we must now examine the connection among all three factors as they occur in the concluding stage of step *two* of the B-Deduction, if we are to complete the second of the two parts of my answer to the question at hand: to repeat, how does the first step of the Deduction apply to all objects of the senses in such a way that these objects are determined by the a priori laws of nature in general?

No doubt, at B 161 Kant claims to have established the objective validity of the categories as a consequence of the proposition that they are conditions of the possibility of experience. And the latter was established on the grounds, first, that they are conditions of the possibility of perception (because the respective manifolds of space and time, to which the synthesis of apprehension must conform, are subject to the categories) and, second, that they are conditions of "[a]ll synthesis" and therefore are conditions of the

37. See Chapter 2, section III, for explanation of this point.

connection of perceptions through which "experience is knowledge" (B 161). The question before us, then, is, how should we interpret Kant's claim that the categories are conditions of the possibility of experience, now understood as consisting in connected perceptions? Is he attempting to demonstrate that experience itself is B-related to objects through the categories, and hence is impossible without them, or is he instead demonstrating that the categories themselves, hence the possibility of experience, and thus our a priori knowledge, are B-related to objects? In other words, we must return once more to the question whether Kant is attempting to demonstrate the necessary role of the categories in making experience possible with respect to appearances or is instead attempting to demonstrate the necessary role of some further condition in making the categories themselves (as conditions belonging to the possibility of experience) possible with respect to the same appearances.[38]

It has been my contention throughout, of course, that the right answer cannot be the first alternative, the one that is standard for Anglophone commentary on the *Critique*. In further support of this contention, I now note first that Kant himself says much the same thing in his "Brief Outline of this Deduction" (B 168–69). There he says that he has just provided an "exposition" (*Darstellung*) of the categories, "and therewith of all theoretical *a priori* knowledge." In the Aesthetic, he explains that by "transcendental exposition" (*Erörterung*) he means "the explanation of a concept as a principle from which the possibility of other *a priori* synthetic knowledge can be understood" (B 40, cf. B 44). And, I submit, this sense of *Erörterung* is also involved in the *Darstellung* of the "Brief Outline" of the B-Deduction, for that is a *Darstellung* of the categories "as principles of the possibility of experience" and of "all theoretical *a priori* knowledge." So Kant's own explanation of his term "transcendental *Erörterung*" at B 40 as well as his Outline of the Transcendental Deduction at B 168–69 as a *Darstellung* of the categories supports my negative claim regarding Kant's primary interest in his theory of knowledge, namely, that it is not experience itself that he wants to demonstrate as being possible with respect to appearances insofar as it stands under the condition of the categories.

---

38. Such a condition might be, in one direction, namely, that toward intellectualization and abstraction, the logical functions of judgment, the combination of a manifold in general, or, ultimately, the transcendental unity of apperception. Or it might be, in the opposite direction, that toward "sensualization" and concreteness, the synthesis of imagination, both a priori and empirical, "space and time, the original forms of sensibility" (B 169), or, ultimately, in this same direction, things in space and time, that is, appearances.

These same textual references also support my positive claim that it is rather the possibility of a priori knowledge, including the categories, that he wants to explain in his transcendental exposition, *Erörterung or Darstellung*. For not only does he state that explicitly at B 40, B 44, and B 168, but the very sense of the "Brief Outline of this Deduction" at B 168–69 demands it. As an exposition of the principles (or conditions) of the possibility of experience, the Deduction is explaining this possibility's own *B*-relation to objects, not the *B*-relation to objects of the item, experience, that it determines. In a word, the exposition in question in the Transcendental Deduction is supposed to demonstrate the conditions under which the categories themselves are *B*-related to appearances, instead of demonstrating that the categories are conditions under which *experience* is *B*-related to appearances. That is why I characterized the sought-for explanation in Chapter 1 as an explanation of the possibility of the possibility of experience.

However, there is something even more important than these explanations of Kant's uses of *Erörterung* and *Darstellung* that can support my thesis that in the Transcendental Deduction, as well as in the *Critique* as a whole, Kant is primarily interested in establishing the possibility of a priori, not empirical, knowledge. This more important consideration is the simple fact that Kant does not end the B-Deduction with the argument that "since experience is knowledge by means of [*durch*] connected perceptions, the categories are conditions of the possibility of experience, and are therefore valid for all objects of experience" (B 161). He rather goes on to his account of "*a priori* knowledge . . . of objects of possible experience" (B 166). It is this account of a priori knowledge, I maintain, that is Kant's ultimate objective in the Transcendental Deduction.

The connection among the factors under consideration is the same one that has been advanced since the beginning of these investigations. If, *contra* my interpretation, Kant were in the first instance interested in the categories to the extent that they belong to the content of experience and thus contribute to the *B*-relation of experience to objects, there would be no need to distinguish things, which we can intuit or of which we can have knowledge, from things in space and time, or appearances (in space and time). For a theory of empirical knowledge, or experience, does not require that the knowledge itself have the properties of universality and necessity, which constitute the criteria of a priori knowledge. And since the knowledge itself is particular and contingent, which would include the (empirical) knowledge of what Kant calls the "special laws" of nature (B 165), the existence of the objects that can be said to be intuited and known and therefore considered to constitute the ontology of the *theory* of the (possible) knowledge need not be kept distinct from the conditions of the (possible) knowledge. Moreover, since the knowledge itself is not a priori, the particular contingent existence of its objects need not be distinct from it either. Indeed, the constituents of the ontology of the theory and the objects of the possible knowledge the theory is supposed to explain can be *identical*, which is just what they *cannot* be with respect to the theory of a priori knowledge. This, it will be recalled, was argued for in Chapter 1.

Of course, when it comes to the question of the *B*-relation of the a priori conditions belonging to the possibility of the knowledge to the objects of the knowledge or of its possibility, the existence of the objects of the theory must indeed be kept distinct from these conditions of the knowledge if the conditions are to remain a priori. But that is precisely the conclusion I have argued leads to Kant's positing things in his theory as objects that are distinct from their appearances, and hence distinct from the only objects (i.e., these same appearances) to which the a priori conditions can be *B*-related.

It is in this manner, therefore, that we can understand the connection among these three now obviously related factors that constitute the second part of my answer to the question: how the first step of the B-Deduction applies to all possible perceptions and their objects, where the application will provide the connection among perceptions that constitutes experience. The upshot of this connection among all possible perceptions is the a priori lawlike combination among all appearances that can come to our perception, and consequently such a combination among "whatever objects may present themselves to our senses" (B 159).

THE TRANSCENDENTAL CHARACTER OF THE SECOND ANALOGY

I

What the last chapter tried to establish is how Kant demonstrates the possibility of our a priori knowledge of the laws of nature in general. Just as the appearances to which such knowledge is B-related are not apportioned according to the particular categories that determine or represent them, so the a priori judgments in which the particular categories are V-related either to a concept, such as that of occurrences of alterations, or to successive representations are not themselves (that is, the a priori judgments in question) B-related to the perceptions or the appearances that are represented through the categories. The demonstration of this B-relation, or possibility, is the task of the Analytic of Principles.

The Principle of the Second Analogy, namely, that of "Succession in Time, in accordance with the Law of Causality" (B 232), has been selected from the many principles of the Analytic for the purpose of showing how Kant goes about demonstrating this possibility of an a priori judgment in which a particular category is V-related to a given concept (e.g., that of an occurrence of an alteration) or to a given manifold of successive representations. Involving as it does the category of causality, the Analogy reminds us that Kant said his generalization from the analysis Hume made of this concept led him to see a general problem in our employment of all of the categories. Not that I mean that the Analogy constitutes Kant's so-called answer to Hume; I do not, since I find that "answer" rather in the Transcendental Deduction of all the categories, including, of course, that of causality. My reference to Hume is only meant to draw attention to Kant's statement that that category in particular had special significance for him in regard to his interest in metaphysics.

For us, the significance instead lies elsewhere. For in this Analogy virtually all of the strands of my interpretation of Kant's transcendental epistemology converge: his transcendental idealism, in which appearances are given a decidedly phenomenalistic, if not subjectivist, tinge in their being assimilated to perceptions; his "external realism,"[1] which allows us our phenomenalistic interpretation of Kant's appearances without burdening us with an attribution to Kant of an ontology that ultimately consists of mere representations (the Second Analogy does not seem to allow such a Berkeleian interpretation [B 233ff., A 206/B 251ff.]); and last, something we might call, for want of a better term, his "Copernicanism."[2] By this I mean to include his thesis that were it not for our employment of the categories (in regard to appearances), nature would not be subject to law. For it is none other than our employment of the category of causality, containing in its own particular way time as its schema, that brings objectivity either to the concept of an occurrence of an alteration or to a given manifold of successive representations, and it does this through its representing the objects, or appearances, to which the concept or the manifold is B-related. In this manner are all the main strands of the book brought together in the solution of a particular problem in the theory of the possibility of a priori knowledge in general.

II

The principle Kant wants to prove in the Second Analogy is that we can apply the concept of cause and effect, that is, the concept of causality, specifically to *all occurrences, or happenings, of alterations,* or *all occurrences*

1. See Chapter 2.
2. See Chapters 3, 8, and 13.

of changes in the determinations of substances.[3] The proof itself turns on the condition under which this possibility of application obtains. Kant calls this condition the *schema* of the concept. Generally, it is an "*a priori* formal condition . . . of sensibility" that must be "contain[ed]" in a concept if the concept is to be applied to specific appearances (A 140/B 179). This condition is none other than time itself as it is contained in the concept. For us, in this chapter, the schema is therefore time as it is contained in the concept of causality. This particular schema is specified by Kant as "the real upon which, whenever posited, something else always follows." He goes on to say that "[i]t consists, therefore, in the succession of the manifold in so far as that succession is subject to a rule" (A 144/B 183). To sum up, the schema of causality is the specific condition under which the concept of causality can be applied to certain specific appearances, namely, alterations of substances.

Now, recent British-American scholarship on the Second Analogy gener-

---

3. I have chosen the second-edition (B) statement of the principle in question rather than the first-edition (A) statement. Where the first concerns the occurrence of a *state* of a substance, or a thing, a state that "begins to be" (A 189), the second concerns "a successive being and not-being of the determinations of substance," that is, an *alteration* (B 232). One obvious difference between them is that the first suggests a procedure ("formula" [A 202/B 247]) that considers the state that "begins to be" apart from its immediately preceding, opposite state, whereas the second considers the state that "begins to be" as a constituent of an alteration (of a substance) that consists of the opposite state as well.

One advantage of the B-statement, I believe, is that it makes it easier for Kant to apply the principle of the Second Analogy to causes that are simultaneous with their effects. Kant observes that such simultaneity is true for "[t]he great majority of efficient natural causes" (A 203/B 248). One of Kant's examples in this regard is that of a heated stove that heats a room. Another example consists in a leaden ball's impressing a hollow in "a stuffed cushion" as it "lies on the cushion" (A 202–3/B 248).

The A-statement suggests that causes are to be found in the opposite states of a substance that precede the effects in question. Therefore, when Kant comes to acknowledging that natural efficient causes are usually simultaneous with their effects and hence usually not to be found in the earlier, opposite states of a substance but in another substance altogether, we cannot proceed as we did when we looked for the causes of later states of substances in the immediately preceding opposite states of the substances. The procedure can be changed, but not without some "difficulty" (A 202/B 247ff.). The statement of the principle in the B edition, on the other hand, makes it easier to move from thinking of the cause as contained in an earlier state of a substance to thinking of it as simultaneous with its effect and as belonging to another substance altogether. It provides for this easy transition by allowing the cause to be independent of the earlier state. It does so by separating the thought of the earlier (e.g., flat) state (of the cushion) from that of "the causality of the cause" (A 203/B 248) (the leaden ball) and combining it rather with the thought of the effect (the hollow state of the cushion), that is, with the later state, the one whose occurrence is to be explained. Thought of the later state now belongs to that of an "alteration," or "change," from the earlier state to the later one.

ally agrees that crucial to Kant's use of the schema of causality in the proof of the Second Analogy principle is the premise that the representations comprised by a "successive apprehension" be subject to the concept of causality if the succession is to be objective. Alternatively, it is the premise that this apprehension itself (A 192/B 237), or its succession (A 194/B 239), be subject to that concept if the succession is to be objective. Since the schema requires that the succession be subject to a rule, and since that requirement is a condition for the succession to be objective, the schema itself constitutes such a condition. As such, it can be considered criterial, if not definitive, with respect to determining the objectivity of a succession.[4]

Something about this agreement in British-American scholarship on the Second Analogy seems so far not to have been recognized, however. It has to do with the tendency to follow Norman Kemp Smith and use the single English word "relation" to translate what I have distinguished throughout as two quite distinct terms in Kant's theory—*Verhältnis* and *Beziehung*.[5] We can briefly anticipate Kant's use of *V*- and *B*- relations in the Second Analogy with the hypothesis that *V*-relations of cause and effect in time obtain among representations only if the latter (alterations of substances or events) are *B*-related to distinct states of substances and this *B*-relation obtains only through the schematized category of cause and effect.

In addition to the agreement concerning the crucial premise in the proof of the principle of the Analogy mentioned above, there exists among British-American commentators on the Second Analogy an agreement to which I,

---

4. As I understand this statement of the Principle, it involves what Aquila describes as the "strongest" thesis that might be attributed to Kant's attempt to prove the Principle in the Second Analogy. See Richard E. Aquila, "Necessity and Irreversibility in the Second Analogy," *History of Philosophy Quarterly* 2 (1985): 203. Like Aquila, I want to defend the "strongest" claim concerning the necessity of a causal relation between an object and an event itself (*not* an object or an event *in* themselves). That is, I am not limiting the thesis to the connection of "mere" perceptions in experience, in contradistinction to the objects perceived. This contests, for example, Strawson's claim that Kant has failed to extend the reach of irreversibility beyond the succession of perceptions to the objects of the perceptions. Strawson pronounces Kant's claim to have extended it to these objects a "*non sequitur* of numbing grossness" (*The Bounds of Sense: An Essay on Kant's "Critique of Pure Reason"* [London: Methuen, 1966], 137). Indeed, I go on to interpret Kant's idealism such that the objects, or appearances, in question *are,* as Kant almost always says they are, the perceptions themselves. I argue below, in the body of the chapter, that the subjective-objective distinction rather pertains to the absence or presence of a necessary rule that can subsume the perceptions. Nevertheless, my position cannot be typed according to Van Cleve's typology as either subjectivist, phenomenalist, or realist, since it seems to partake of features of all three. See James Van Cleve, "Four Recent Interpretations of Kant's Second Analogy," *Kant-Studien* 64 (1973): 71–87.

5. See Chapter 4 *et passim*.

in accordance with the main thesis of my investigations into the *Critique*, must take exception. This is the proposition that the question addressed by the Second Analogy is a question about the possibility of *experience*. Most commentators agree that part of the defensible objective of Kant's proof is to establish that time-determination among objects (and their representations) is a condition of possible experience.[6] More generally, they agree that any defensible notion of "transcendental" that might be attached to the concept of epistemology on Kant's behalf would pertain to the a priori considerations that allow us to determine that something is a condition of possible *experience*. Accordingly, I will henceforth call this the *empiricist* view of Kant's defensible objective in the Analogy. This view, however, is sufficiently liberal to allow that the conditions of possible experience may themselves be a priori, as would therefore be any knowledge we might have of them. What is to be distinguished from such knowledge is knowledge of further conditions that make it possible for us to have knowledge of the conditions in question. That is, knowledge of possible experience is not identical with knowledge of its own possibility. On the other hand, a view that holds that Kant's defensible notion of "transcendental" actually characterizes this higher level of knowledge would not be empiricist, as I am using the term. This alternative view, the one I adopt, might rather be described as *apriorist*. But the empiricist view is clearly the view customary today among commentators not only on the Second Analogy but on the *Critique* as a whole, as I have been arguing from the very start of these investigations.

Another view prevalent in recent scholarship on the *Critique*, a view I have commented on in regard to the Transcendental Deduction of the categories,[7] holds that although Kant there considers himself to have shown that the categories apply to appearances (B 150–51) and are conditions of possible experience, and hence are objectively valid (B 161), his judgments on this matter are premature, and hence mistaken. He should rather have waited for his completion of his proofs of the Principles before making such claims. For only in these later proofs do we get any defensible arguments for the particular categories themselves. The only arguments for them in particular that the Transcendental Deduction actually relies on are to be

---

6. Two leading commentators who adopt this tack are Arthur Melnick (*Kant's Analogies of Experience* [Chicago: University of Chicago Press, 1973]) and Paul Guyer (*Kant and the Claims of Knowledge* [Cambridge: Cambridge University Press, 1987], chap. 10).

7. See Chapter 10.

found in the Metaphysical Deduction and at the conclusion of the first step of the second-edition Transcendental Deduction.

Since we have already dispensed with this latter view,[8] we are free to take another look at the purpose of the proofs of the Principles, and, in particular, at the proof of the Principle of Succession in Time in the Second Analogy, since we are no longer bound to see them as completing those arguments for the specific categories that were left incomplete at the end of the Transcendental Deduction. But if that purpose is not to complete the proof that the category of cause and effect applies to appearances and is a condition of possible experience, and to do so by establishing that time-determination among objects (and their representations) is a condition of possible experience, what, then, is it?

This question immediately takes us to the heart of the distinction between the empiricist and the apriorist views of this objective. For the latter, it is to show a priori that the application of the particular concept of causality specifically to all occurrences of alterations *itself* is B-related to appearances. Such an a priori specification of the application of the category to a specific kind of appearance, namely, an occurrence of an alteration, is made in the form of a synthetic a priori judgment, which is enunciated in the Analogy as the Principle of Succession in Time. The *proof* of the Principle in the Analogy, however, obviously tries to give us more than the mere enunciation of the Principle itself. For the apriorist, it tries to demonstrate the B-relation of *the Principle* to objects, that is, its real possibility, or its objective validity. This amounts to demonstrating the B-relation of the a priori judgment to appearances. For the empiricist, however, the Analogy rather tries to demonstrate the B-relation of *experience* to objects. The empiricist view thus construes the proof as arguing that it is through the time-determination of objects that *experience* is possible. And it includes in this argument the proposition that this time-determination itself depends on the employment of the concept of causality. In this manner, according to the empiricist, the Second Analogy helps complete the demonstration of the objective validity of the categories that was begun in the Metaphysical Deduction and then continued in the Transcendental Deduction.

Finally, the distinction between these two views of the purpose of the Analogy can be highlighted, albeit from the apriorist's point of view, in the empiricist's wholly unsatisfactory answer to a question posed by the apriorist. The latter asks: how can we, a priori, specify occurrences of alterations

---

8. See Chapter 10.

as the objects to which we can apply the concept of causality? To reply by saying that time-determination of objects, through the concept of causality, is a condition of possible experience is no answer at all. For the apriorist is raising the question of the B-relation of the empiricist's answer itself—the answer to the empiricist's question about the possibility of experience—to experience and its objects. The apriorist view is not concerned with the B-relation of experience to objects; it is rather concerned with the B-relation of our synthetic a priori judgments to experience and its objects.

If the apriorist is right, that Kant wants to show how (and/or that) we can apply the concept of causality a priori to appearances of a specific kind, namely, occurrences of alterations, then the task of the Analogy is to show how we can arrive at this specification through a mode of knowledge that is purely a priori. It is to specify occurrences of alterations as the objects (appearances) to which we can apply the concept. The specification consists in the determination of the sort of appearances that can empirically instantiate the concept in question. Whereas the Transcendental Deduction tries to establish that the concept of causality, without its schema, yet nonetheless through a priori imagination,[9] applies to appearances, the Second Analogy goes on to address the further question of the *possibility* of that application of the concept, only now containing its schema. And since that possibility consists in the B-relation of the application or of the judgment to objects (appearances), the proof of the Principle of Succession in Time can only provide for that possibility by distinguishing the objects from all other objects (appearances). Since the possibility of the application consists in its B-relation to objects, the distinction of the objects in question from all others must also be made through the concept itself, again containing its schema. In other words, the very concept of causality, with its schema, that constitutes the B-relation of its application to objects also distinguishes these same objects from all other appearances. In this manner, Kant arrives at a specification of the objects in question through a mode of knowledge that is purely a priori.

9. Though the Transcendental Deduction says that the understanding determines inner sense, it also says that it does so "through the manifold of representations" (B 150), not through the form of inner sense, time. It says pretty much the same thing at B 153. So in these passages the Transcendental Deduction does not speak of time determination. (Incidentally, this point tends to vitiate Allison's account of the penultimate stages of the Transcendental Deduction. See his *Kant's Transcendental Idealism: An Interpretation and Defense* [New Haven: Yale University Press, 1983], 160–62.) Nor does the Deduction speak of time determination when it comes to perception, in § 26. It is the *unity* of (the manifold of the intuition of) time that is determined there (B 160).

Now let us return to the *first* point of agreement among commentators on the Second Analogy mentioned at the beginning of this section. It is a point that is agreed to, not only by the empiricist commentators, from whom I am distinguishing the apriorist, but by the apriorist as well. The point is that the crucial premise in Kant's proof of the Principle of Succession in Time is the proposition that the "successive apprehension" of representations must be subject to the concept of causality, which contains its schema, if the succession is to be objective. Now, since the objectivity of the succession is none other than its B-relation to objects, and since I have just argued that that B-relation distinguishes the objects that need to be distinguished, this distinction among objects, if the application of the concept is to be possible, therefore also consists in distinguishing the apprehension whose succession of representations is objective from "every other apprehension," whose succession of representations is only subjective (A 193/B 238). And since the concept of cause and effect is a particular "mode of combination" of the manifold, which contains its schema (A 191/B 236), it is to be expected that Kant would speak of "the mode of combination" as that which distinguishes the object "from every other apprehension" (A 191/B 236; see also A 197/B 242–43).

To sum up, the apriorist view takes it as already having been proved in the Transcendental Deduction that the concept of causality, without its schema, both applies to appearances and is a condition of possible experience, and hence is objectively valid. In addition, it takes the proof in the Second Analogy to be that of the possibility, not of empirical causal judgments themselves, but rather of the synthetic *a priori* judgment in which the concept of an occurrence of an alteration is subject to the concept of causality, where the latter now contains its schema. In addition, the apriorist interprets the Analogy as showing the role of the concept of causality, still containing its schema, in providing for the possibility of its own application to appearances. These conditions thus belong to the content of the concept.[10] That possibility consists in its B-relation to these appearances, namely, occurrences of alterations. And finally, according to the apriorist view, the concept of causality, again still containing its schema, distinguishes occurrences of alterations from all other appearances by subsuming an otherwise merely subjective succession of representations, thereby rendering the succession objective. As such, the succession is "the objective succession

10. See Chapter 4, section I, on the connection between Kant's notions of content and possibility.

of appearances," that is, a succession of objects (A 193/B 238). In this manner the time-determination of objects in experience is, for the apriorist, crucial to the proof in the Second Analogy.

III

The distinction between the empiricist and the apriorist views of the proof only raises the question of what difference it makes in interpretation of the proof. What advantage does the apriorist have over the empiricist in this regard? The answer consists in first explaining how the proof depends on Kant's transcendental idealism—more precisely, how it involves his distinction between appearances and things in themselves. As much as one might think that it goes without saying that his idealism is necessary to the proof, given what he himself says about the matter (A 190/B 235), at least one prominent commentator has nonetheless rejected the idea that his idealism plays much of a role at all in the proof.[11] If this rejection is ill founded, it casts into doubt, of course, whatever part of one's interpretation of the proof depends on it. My answer to the question of the advantage of the apriorist view then continues by claiming that the apriorist view alone allows an interpretation of Kant's idealism that satisfies the transcendentally idealistic requirements of the proof. I conclude my answer to the question, and the chapter as well, with an examination of how the apriorist view actually leads to solutions, more promising than those that have so far been provided from the empiricist view, to some problems that have arisen in the literature and stand in the way of the success of the proof.

If we turn our attention first to Kant's own claim that the proof depends on his idealism, we find his statement that it is "from the succession of representations" that we can determine "how their [i.e., appearances'] manifold may be connected [i.e., may be combined (*verbindun sei*)] in the object." He then goes on to say that we could not make this determination if appearances were taken as things in themselves (A 190/B 235). So our question is, why could we not determine that the manifold of an appearance is combined in the object if the appearance were taken as a thing in itself?

11. See Guyer, *Kant and the Claims of Knowledge*, 262, 450. Guyer mentions Allison as an ally in this regard, but Allison explicitly disavows such alliance in his *Kant's Transcendental Idealism*, 227. Guyer suggests that despite Allison's disavowal, we look at the procedure he actually employs. Van Cleve, for his own part, in "Four Recent Interpretations of Kant's Second Analogy," sees strands of realism as well as of idealism at work in the proof.

In response, we note that Kant goes on to explain that the representations from whose succession one can determine the combination of the manifold in the object are those through which "we are affected by" "things in themselves." So, things in themselves here are the things that affect us, qualified as "in themselves" in the sense, suggested by the text itself, that what is at issue is *how* the things are, and, moreover, how they are "in themselves" is how they are "apart from the representations through which they affect us" (A 190/B 235). (Henceforth, I will simply refer to the things that affect us, viewed in this way, as "being independent of these representations.") This implies that the object in which we are to determine, "from the succession of representations, how [its] manifold may be combined in [it]," is not the thing in itself. Rather, just as the combination of the manifold of the object is to be determined from the succession of these representations, so the concept of the object is "derived" from these same representations (A 191/B 236). Obviously, the object is the appearance. And since the concept of the appearance is "derived" from these representations, it cannot be as appearance that the thing in question affects us, since the latter is here viewed as being independent of these representations.[12]

Kant goes on to specify the "rule of apprehension" necessary to the combination as the "mode" of the combination (A 191/B 236). Since its necessity entails that it is a pure concept, and since it is a mode of *combination,* Kant must be referring to a *category* here. And since it is the succession of the representations that is to be made objective, then, since the schema of causality is that of succession that is subject to a rule, the mode can be none other than causality.

According to this use of transcendental idealism, the objects that affect us are independent of the representations through which we are affected by them. They are thus viewed as things in themselves. This makes them distinct from appearances, which are the objects in which the manifold is com-

---

12. This conclusion obviously eliminates as inadequate all those interpretations that view the proof as using, perhaps implicitly, two essential conditions of Van Cleve's notion of "perceptual isomorphism": (1) "The perception of an objective item is an effect of the existence of that item," (2) "There is no relevant difference in the modes of causal dependency of 'a' on A and 'b' on B" ("Four Recent Interpretations of Kant's Second Analogy," 81), where the capital letters "stand for states and parts of things" and the lowercase letters "stand for representations (perceptions, observings) which are respectively *of* A and B" (75). (The notion is part of Van Cleve's account of Strawson's interpretation of the Second Analogy.)

For example, it eliminates Lewis White Beck's interpretation in "Six Short Pieces on the Second Analogy of Experience," in *Essays on Kant and Hume* (New Haven: Yale University Press, 1978), 148.

bined, and which are thereby determined, according to the category involved in the combination (or determination). That is, appearances are not independent of these same representations. They are instead a "sum" (*Inbegriff*) of the representations (combined through a category). As such, they themselves are representations. This, for Kant, explains how we can "determine from the succession of the representations how their [the objects'] manifold may be combined in the object." Such a determination *from the succession of representations* obviously would be impossible if the objects were independent of the representations.[13]

The apriorist has no problem interpreting Kant's recourse to idealism here. The knowledge it is supposed to B-relate to objects—a priori knowledge—is itself independent of these same representations. So these same representations give the apriorist view the distinction it needs to make sense of a B-relation of knowledge to objects through synthesis. This, of course, is the B-relation the view is intent to explain. So the very purpose of the apriorist view depends on this distinction.

Just the opposite is true of the empiricist view. Since these same representations are constituents of all experience, and since they are also involved in the objects that are the "sums" combined through a category, they cannot give the empiricist view the distinction it needs to make sense of a B-relation through synthesis of an experience to objects—the B-relation the empiricist is intent to explain. So the very purpose of the empiricist view is not yet explained. This presents the empiricist view with a dilemma. Either it gives up trying to explain such a B-relation through synthesis, opting rather for a relation through identity, or the objects cease to be "sums" of these representations, and hence are no longer themselves representations. They would then be independent of these representations; that is, they would be things in themselves. In that case, however, we could have no a priori knowledge of them. For a priori knowledge, if B-related to objects, must be B-related to these representations, or to the objects of these representations (appearances). Of course, we could have *experience* of these objects, since they can be known *empirically* through these representations. The use of a category in an experience would then have to be explained as providing the B-relation of the experience to objects that are independent of these representations. Thus, the category would provide for our thought of the objects as

13. This constitutes an effective rebuttal of Strawson's charge that Kant committed a "*non sequitur* of numbing grossness," since the charge depends on taking the objects of perception not to consist "merely" in a combination of the same representations that belong to the succession of apprehension whose objectivity is being determined.

things in themselves, which is just the opposite of the role of the category with respect to the possibility of a priori knowledge.

Each view thus has its own reliance on the category, containing its schema, of course. The empiricist who wants a B-relation through synthesis, not through identity, of an experience to objects, relies on it to view the objects as they are independently of the representations through which we are affected by them. It *separates* the objects from the mind and its states. It is a *realistic* reliance on the category. The apriorist, on the other hand, relies on the category to view the objects *as they are represented through those same representations,* which is an *idealistic* reliance on the category. For the apriorist, the category so B-relates the representations to the objects that the respective manifolds are combined in the objects. But then the objects cannot be those that affect us through these representations (the things in themselves).

It might be objected that the empiricist is intent to explain the same B-relation of knowledge to objects as concerns the apriorist. This is the B-relation of representations of apprehension to appearances. The empiricist thus relies on the category in the same way that the apriorist relies on it: to distinguish the "sum" of all representations through which we are affected by an object from the mere synthesis of apprehension of the same representations. It is the distinction of an a priori synthesis according to a category, containing its schema, from an empirical synthesis of apprehension.

The problem with this objection is that though the empiricist might rely on the synthesis of the schematized category to account for the B-relation of an *apprehension* of succession to objects, it could not in that case do the same for the B-relation of an *experience* to objects. For the schematized category would then cease to distinguish experience from apprehension, which would contradict the whole purpose of the Second Analogy. To put the point another way, since apprehension and experience are not identical with each other, if the schematized category provides the objectivity of one, it cannot do the same for the other. After all, it is through the schematized category that an otherwise merely subjective succession of apprehension is an objective succession of experience.

IV

One question that has arisen concerning the success of Kant's proof of the Principle of Succession in Time has its origins at least as far back as Schopenhauer.[14] Kant has understandably been read (e.g., at A 199–200/B 244–45) as having connected the thought of the preceding state of some thing with the thought of the cause of that which follows, that is, the succeeding state. But this is no better than committing the fallacy of *post hoc, ergo propter hoc*. As Schopenhauer remarks, night and day are not commonly taken to be successive causes of one another.[15]

But Kant nowhere even suggests that mere passage of time between two appearances implies that the earlier state is connected with the cause of the later state. On the contrary, a major premise of the entire Analogy is rather the proposition that a succession of apprehension may be wholly independent of causal considerations altogether—as it is in the case of one's looking at different parts of a house (A 190/B 235). That is, the succession may be merely *subjective*. What Kant does say is that if the passage of time between opposite appearances is objective, the occurrence of the later state must be B-related to its preceding state through the concept of causality; that is, if the succession is to be objective, it must be subsumed under the concept of causality through the schema of the concept. Kant would say that, far from defending the fallacy of *post hoc, ergo propter hoc,* he is actually diagnosing it as the mistake of taking the mere passage of time between appearances as a passage in which the appearances are determined in time—specifically, where their order or position in time is so determined. That determination is a constraint imposed on the succession of appearances through its subsumption under the concept of causality.

But Schopenhauer is correct to the extent that for Kant an objective succession of appearances does imply causality, provided the appearances are opposite states of the same thing. Once we factor in Kant's discussion of natural efficient causes that are simultaneous with their effects, the succession of day and night in either the Western or the Eastern Hemisphere does entail an object that is represented as the cause that produces the occurrence of the later state of the hemisphere in question.

Kant's basic idea here is that the objectivity of a succession of apprehension of a manifold of representations is constituted through a rule to which

14. Arthur Schopenhauer, *The Fourfold Root of the Principle of Sufficient Reason*, trans. E. F. J. Payne (LaSalle, Ill.: Open Court, 1974), § 23, p. 127; also cited in Allison, *Kant's Transcendental Idealism*, 230, and in Guyer, *Kant and the Claims of Knowledge*, 240.

15. The discussion of simultaneity of a natural efficient cause and its effect, in note 3 above, deals only with the independence of a cause from the preceding state of a thing. Schopenhauer's objection, on the other hand, concerns the apparent converse dependence, in Kant's work, of the preceding state on the cause of the event or the succeeding state.

the apprehension is subjected. The subsumption of the apprehension under the concept of causality through the schema of the concept constitutes the B-relation of the apprehension to an apprehension of the preceding state, as described above. These are the terms in which Kant speaks of an appearance as a "sum" of the representations that are apprehended. And in these terms Kant can effectively deal with the fallacy of *post hoc, ergo propter hoc.*

It is essential to this would-be response of Kant's to Schopenhauer that the state of the substance to which the apprehension is B-related through the concept of causality be viewed as an appearance, not as a thing in itself. But the previous section (III) of this chapter shows the empiricist cannot do that and at the same time rely on the concept to distinguish the appearance from the mere apprehension; that is, the empiricist cannot provide for the B-relation in question through synthesis instead of identity. Consequently, the empiricist view cannot avail itself of this aprioristic reply to Schopenhauer's objection.

A second problem the literature has found in Kant's proof is that the Principle that is actually proved is *analytic,* whereas Kant wanted to prove a principle that is *synthetic.* The problem is rooted in the premise, referred to at the start, that British-American scholarship agrees is "crucial" to Kant's proof. The problem thus goes to the heart of the proof. When I first mentioned this premise, I noted that it has the effect of making irreversibility of representations criterial with respect to determining the objectivity of a succession of representations. We can now further note that the premise makes this irreversibility criterial with respect to, if not actually part of the analysis of, the perception of an event or an alteration containing an event.

We can see how the premise renders the Principle analytic. If we understand the occurrences of alterations mentioned in the Principle logically to involve our perception of them, then, since irreversibility is taken to be criterial, if not definitive, with respect to our determining the perception, it is also criterial, if not definitive, with respect to our determining the occurrences. Since irreversibility is what is provided through the schema of causality, causality itself becomes criterial, if not definitive, with respect to the occurrences. But statements of criterial or definitional (V-)relations among representations are analytic. So Kant's proof of the Principle makes it analytic.

Our very understanding or concept of occurrences of alterations of substances should help dispel the confusion over this issue. If our very understanding or concept of the occurrences involves our perceptions of them, then it also involves the *B*-relation of the concept to the perceptions (appearances), since it is through that relation that the thought of the perceptions can be brought into the thought of the occurrences.[16] (Henceforth I shall abbreviate my "the objects to which the concept is *B*-related" as "the perceptions.") In this instance, we would therefore already be taking the concept of the occurrences as referring (*B*-relating) to the perceptions. In the proof, however, Kant's explanation of this *B*-relation consists in the concept's being subject to the concept of causality, containing its schema, and thus containing the notion of irreversibility. Therefore, it would be *analytic* for the concept of the occurrences to be *B*-related to the perceptions if the concept of causality, containing its schema, were predicated of the former concept. But that does not imply that the predication, or judgment, itself would be analytic. On the contrary, it would remain *synthetic;* that is, the concept of the occurrences would remain distinct from the schematized concept of causality, and thus would remain distinct from the notion of irreversibility.[17] Indeed, it would have to remain so if the schematized concept were to provide for the *B*-relation in question. So, the a priori judgment Kant wants to prove would be analytic only if we were to stay with our understanding or concept of the occurrences that started the confusion in the first place; otherwise, it would be synthetic, as Kant intended it to be.

Finally, we should not forget in all this the main negative thesis of this chapter, not to mention the entire book, namely, that in the Analogy Kant is not interested in establishing that the concept of causality, containing its schema, applies to occurrences of alterations because he is interested in establishing the conditions of the possibility of experience. Nor is he interested in demonstrating that the same concept, now not containing its schema (though nonetheless determining inner sense and affecting sensibility as transcendental imagination), has application (*Anwendung*) to appearances or objects of the senses in general, since he thinks he has already done that, I maintain, in the Transcendental Deduction (B 150–51). His interest in the Transcendental Aesthetic and in the Transcendental Logic is rather the demonstration of the possibility of a priori knowledge, and his specific

16. Since these appearances are given objects of perceptions, and hence of the senses (appearances), the objects are empirically real. This property of theirs is logically independent of both the concept of causality, containing its schema, and that of the occurrences. In other words, though the concept of causality, containing its schema, provides for the *B*-relation of the concept of the occurrences to the perceptions, it does not provide the perceptions themselves. They contain the empirical reality of the given objects of the senses, which are logically independent of both concepts in question.

17. This is the point that agrees with Van Cleve's correction of Lovejoy's interpretation.

concern in the subsection of the Transcendental Logic entitled the "Second Analogy" is the demonstration of the possibility of the synthetic a priori judgment that all occurrences of alterations are subject to the concept of cause and effect. This consists in showing that the concept of the occurrences is B-related to appearances through the V-relation the concept of causality, now containing its schema, has to the concept of the occurrences; that is, he takes himself to be demonstrating the objective validity of the former concept through its being subject to the latter concept (in a [synthetic a priori] judgment).[18] In so doing, Kant identifies, in a wholly a priori manner, the specific appearances to which the concept of causality applies, and thereby fulfills the purpose of the Analogy.

A third problem, and the last one we will consider, concerns causality's role in the irreversibility of two states of a thing, such that an earlier state must be followed by a later one. Van Cleve cites the counterexample of a whole egg followed by the egg scrambled.[19] Though the order is irreversible, the whole egg obviously might have hatched. No necessary rule of causality connecting the two states seems to be implied by the mere irreversibility of the occurrences of the states. This problem differs from Schopenhauer's. His point was that merely being earlier is not sufficient ground for taking the earlier state as the cause of the later one. The problem here is that mere irreversibility of two states does not seem to imply any causal rule connecting them.[20]

18. Of course, throughout the demonstration, appearances are taken to be given through intuitions of the senses. Otherwise there would be nothing belonging to empirical reality to which the concept of occurrences of alterations could be B-related through the *synthetic V*-relation of the concept of causality, containing its schema, to it.

19. Van Cleve, "Four Recent Interpretations of Kant's Second Analogy," 74.

20. Allison (*Kant's Transcendental Idealism*, 230–32) makes the same negative point as Van Cleve, but cites Gerd Buchdahl (*Metaphysics and the Philosophy of Science* [Cambridge, Mass.: MIT Press, 1969], 650) instead of Van Cleve in support of his position. His and Buchdahl's view is that there are "contingent happenings," including the downstream motion of Kant's ship, which belong to objective successions even though there may be no causal "covering law" to explain them. For Allison, the principle of causality is rather a "transcendental condition" that requires of any experience of objective succession that the occurrence of a state that comes into being follow "some antecedent condition" (*Kant's Transcendental Idealism*, 231).

But this seems too weak to fit Kant's strong claim that "that which precedes an event [contains] the condition of a rule according to which this event invariably and necessarily follows" (A 193/B 238–39. See also A 198–99/B 243–44 and A 201/B 246–47). And it also seems too weak to accommodate Kant's statement of the schema of causality: "the real upon which, whenever posited, something else always follows" (A 144/B 183).

Nevertheless, it seems Allison is right that the causal rule required for a succession to be

Kant's discussion of simultaneity between cause and effect tells us that he would not even think of the whole egg as the cause of its being scrambled.[21] What he would say, however, is that whether the whole egg were followed either by the egg's being scrambled or by its being hatched, or by the occurrence of yet another state, the irreversibility of the order of (the occurrences of) the states would still imply that the alteration was caused. In fact, as we have noted, Kant makes this argument with respect to perceptions of the states, where perception of the succeeding state, whether it is the egg's being scrambled, hatched, or otherwise changed, is considered by Kant as a perception of an event—the coming to be of a state—following a time in which the state was not in being. The cause in question is the cause of that event. It is Kant's position that the order between the event and the cause is determined, even if they are simultaneous with one another (A 203/B 248). So the critics would still find a problem in Kant's proof.

At this point we must ask ourselves, how could Kant's position be otherwise, given the idealistic framework in which he sets up the proof? He begins with a succession of apprehension of the manifold of appearance (A 189/B 234) and notes that, so far, the succession is undetermined, and thus is not yet constituted as objective. The appearances are subject merely to the empirical synthesis of apprehension, or imagination. The object might be a house whose parts one is perceiving successively (A 190/B 235). He then notes that any manifold of appearances that is apprehended and combined in an object (appearance), and thus distinguished "from every other apprehension," is done so through a "necessary rule of apprehension" (A 191/B 234). So the rule or the category containing it constitutes the B-relation of the apprehension to an object. It makes the apprehension objective. Since the schema tells us that if it is "the succession of the manifold" that is to be subject to the rule (so that the succession itself is made objective), the rule in question is that of causality (A 144/B 183). Consequently, the succession of apprehension must be subject to that rule if it is to be an objective succession.

The argument thus begins with a premise to the effect that an apprehension in general must be subject to a necessary rule to be B-related to an

---

objective is not an "empirical law" that connects appearances insofar as they satisfy certain empirical concepts of objects (*Kant's Transcendental Idealism*, 231). I am in agreement with Allison in taking the rule of causality Kant has in mind to belong to the category of causality, containing its schema, and therefore to be pure. This also seems to be the position adopted by Steven M. Bayne, "Objects of Representations and Kant's Second Analogy," *Journal of the History of Philosophy* 32 (1994): 381–410.

21. See note 3 above.

object (appearance). It then relies on the schema of the concept of causality to reach the conclusion that if it is the objectivity of succession in time that is in question, that same concept of causality contains the rule that provides the objectivity. So, in the end we find that the proof actually depends on a premise that is more universal than the one cited at the beginning of the chapter as "crucial" to the proof. That premise was limited to causality and the objectivity of succession. But in our apriorist reply to Van Cleve's contention that irreversibility of opposite states of a thing does not imply a causal rule for the succession, we have employed a proposition cited later in the chapter as essential to the transcendental idealism that is present in the proof. This is the proposition that an apprehension in general must be subject to a necessary rule to be objective. It is this latter proposition that I have claimed throughout to be essential to the proof. It is the proposition that confers on the proof its transcendental character.[22]

I have mentioned the analytic nature of Kant's complex thesis that a successive apprehension of appearances is an objective succession of states of a given thing through its being subject to the concept of causality (containing its schema), which represents the thing (as appearance). But this no more vitiates the synthetic nature of the V-relation of the concept to the apprehension than did the analytic character of Kant's thesis concerning the Principle of Succession in Time, which I discussed earlier, vitiate the synthetic nature of that principle. The solution to keeping this V-relation synthetic has the same form as the solution I relied on previously. Though the complex thesis is analytic, the V-relation of the concept of causality, containing its schema, to a successive apprehension of appearances remains synthetic. The apprehension can be thought quite apart from the concept of causality, containing its schema. The introduction of the complexity in the form of the B-relation of the apprehension to an object, and the claim that the concept of causality, containing its schema, constitutes that B-relation, however, make the entire thesis analytic. But that is acceptable, since it only means that the parts of Kant's theory are conceptually related to each other, as they should be.

This conceptual relation among its parts should be reflected in a conceptual relation among the parts of any adequate interpretation of the theory. This is a desideratum that I will now try to fulfill as I now turn to the conclusion of this entire investigation into the theory of the possibility of a priori knowledge that is contained in the *Critique*.

22. Though I consider Allison's view of the proof empiricist and not apriorist, the point of this last paragraph agrees with the point Allison makes as he "anticipate[s]" his own account of "the essential argument" of the proof. See his *Kant's Transcendental Idealism*, 222.

PART 4

REVIEW

TRANSCENDENTAL
EPISTEMOLOGY

I

It is easy for us, mindful of the strictures of positivistic and postpositivistic analytic philosophy, to slip into thinking that independently of his interest in our a priori knowledge of objects, Kant intends to prove that, and how, the possibility of empirical knowledge depends on the concepts of space and time, the categories, and the a priori knowledge that comes from them. For he certainly does attempt to prove their objective validity by showing them to be necessary conditions of the possibility of experience. And with these proofs most commentators in our analytic tradition, before Guyer and Friedman, have largely contented themselves.

In the preceding chapters, however, I have tried to direct our attention to the *converse* dependence, namely, that which the concepts of space and time, the categories, and the a priori knowledge that comes from them have on empirical knowledge, or experience, and ultimately on the *empirical intuitions* that are contained in it. If we allow Kant his own stated objective in the *Critique,* I have argued, it is rather only in the service of demonstrating this *converse* dependence that he tries to establish the first one, namely, the dependence of possible experience on these concepts and the a priori knowledge that comes from them.

What may confound us in determining what I consider the correct ranking of the two dependencies is our failure to appreciate what I think are the quite distinct ways in which the concepts and a priori knowledge in question and experience depend on each other in regard to their respective possibilities. Here I find especially helpful what I consider the triadic structure of the model of representation that I attribute to Kant and that I have accordingly employed, sometimes quite explicitly, throughout the preceding chapters.

As already noted in Chapter 4, the tradition I am contesting takes experience for Kant to be the *subject*, S, that is *B*-related to *objects* (appearances), O, through the concepts in question, R, that thus are *V*-related to possible experience and also represent the objects of possible experience (appearances), where this *B*-relation can obtain, and can be shown to obtain, *independently* of the *B*-relation *a priori knowledge, S,* has to possible experience, O, through the very same concepts and a priori knowledge. In addition, I have been arguing that for Kant it is necessary that he try to prove that, and how, *these concepts themselves* and the a priori knowledge that comes from them are the *subjects, S,* that are *B*-related to possible experience, the *object,* O—ultimately to its empirical intuitions—if he is to prove that, and how, they are necessary for the possibility of experience itself. Again, the difference between myself and the tradition that has been delineated so far in terms of the triadic structure of Kant's model of representation is that according to the tradition, experience stands in the *subject* position in the structure, S, *independently* of its place in the *object* position, O, vis-à-vis the possibility of a priori knowledge (as *it* stands in the subject position); whereas I have been arguing that experience is the *subject,* S, of the concepts in question *only insofar* as it is also the *object,* O, to which the distinct *subject, S,* a priori knowledge, is *B*-related.

Accordingly, I would first rank experience as a necessary condition (as *object*) of the possibility of a priori knowledge, whereas the tradition would first rank the concepts and a priori knowledge in question as necessary conditions (as *representations*) of the possibility of experience. The notion of a necessary condition of a possibility thus applies to items that occupy two different positions in the triadic model of representation: representation of object and object of representation. The *possibility* of a subject of representation is (partly) constituted by the representation that is *V*-related to the subject. In that respect, the *representation* is a necessary condition of the possibility of the subject, that is, of the subject's *B*-relation to an object. However, the same possibility also depends on the *object* with respect to which the subject is possible, and this object is none other than the object of the same representation (insofar as the representation is V-related to the subject). In this respect, the *object* is a necessary condition of the possibility of the subject. So, both the representation of the object and the object of the representation are necessary conditions of the possibility of the subject of the representation, but of course they are necessary in the different respects that have here, and throughout the previous chapters as well, been distinguished from each other.

To sum up, the tradition I am contesting takes the concepts of space and time, the categories, and the a priori knowledge that comes from them to be necessary conditions (as representations) of the possibility of experience (as the subject of the representations) insofar as the concepts are V-related to the experience, which, in turn, is B-related to appearances (as objects), which, again in turn, are themselves represented through the concepts and the a priori knowledge. I agree with all of this. However, in contradistinction to the tradition, I back up and claim that Kant employs his model of representation with respect to the possibility of experience only as a necessary condition (now as the *object* of the representations) of the possibility of the concepts of space, time, the categories, and the possibility of the *a priori knowledge* that comes from them (as the subjects of representation) that are thus B-related to the same possible experience—ultimately to its empirical intuitions—through the *means* of representation and of knowledge that consist of outer and inner sense and the transcendental unity of apperception, respectively. I therefore contest the tradition's view that Kant's epistemology of empirical knowledge is independent of his transcendental epistemology. As I see it, Kant has no transcendental theory of experience that is thus separable from his transcendental theory of a priori knowledge.

My interpretation of Kant's epistemology thus directs us to the centrality of the possibility of a priori knowledge, which I contend the tradition either ignores or rejects. I claim that this possibility is the true and essential object of Kant's theory.

II

Transcendental epistemology, in contradistinction to empiricist epistemology, thus consists of an investigation into the a priori conditions under which a priori knowledge of objects is B-related to possible experience, and ultimately to the empirical intuitions contained in it. These conditions can be divided in two ways: between *modes* and *means* and between mere *representations* and *cognitions* (items of knowledge). Cognitions are the same as representations, except for satisfying the further condition that they are subject to a *mode* of knowledge.

Among the modes of knowledge, space and time are the intuitive ones, and concepts in a possible judgment and the categories of a sensible intuition in general are the conceptual ones. The modes have their respective means of representation and of knowledge. Space and time correspond to the means of representation entitled outer and inner sense, respectively (A 22–23/B 37), and concepts in a judgment and the categories correspond to the means of analytic unity and the synthetic unity of the manifold in intuition in general, respectively (A 79/B 105).[1] By means of the former, the logical form of a judgment (i.e. the transcendental unity of apperception [B 141]) is produced in the concepts, and by means of the latter, transcendental content (i.e. the logical functions of judgment)[2] is introduced into the categories. Since the modes of knowledge are considered the "forms" of their corresponding means, we are invited to consider the means as that by which these "forms" get their "content," or their B-relation to objects.[3] Indeed, Kant speaks precisely this way with respect to the categories and how they get their "transcendental content" by means of "the synthetic unity of the manifold in intuition in general" (A 79/B 105).

All this fits with my remarks about Kant's model of representation. All of the above-mentioned modes of knowledge can be considered *representations* that provide for the B-relation of a *subject*-cognition to *objects* through their respective V-relations to the cognition. Since that B-relation, or possibility, belongs to the content of the cognition, it can be said that the cognition gets this content through the representation insofar as the representation is V-related to the cognition.[4] The question of how the representation in turn gets *its* content is answered in terms of the *means* of the representation. Thus, space gives to an intuition of ours the content it gets by means of outer sense; time gives to an intuition of the mind the content it gets by means of inner sense; concepts give to a judgment the transcenden-

---

1. See Chapter 10. Let us not forget the very first sentence of the body of the *Critique* itself: "In whatever *mode* and through whatever *means* a cognition may [B-]relate to objects, intuition is that through which it is in immediate [B-]relation to them, and to which all thought as a *means* is directed (A 19/B 33, my translation and my emphasis).

2. See Chapter 9 for an explanation and defense of the idea that Kant's logical functions of judgment have content.

3. See Chapter 4, section I.

4. Again, see Chapter 4, section I.

tal unity of apperception by means of analytic unity; and the categories give to a sensible intuition in general the transcendental content (the logical functions of judgment) it gets by means of the synthetic unity of the manifold in intuition in general.

III

Endowed with the modes and means of representation and of knowledge, most of which were just recapitulated, as well as with the faculty of consciousness,[5] we have a certain a priori knowledge of all the things that affect us, but only insofar as they affect us. This is none other than the a priori knowledge that was adumbrated at the very beginning of this book, specifically in the second paragraph of Chapter 1. The things we thus know are none other than the things we intuit empirically or through the senses.[6] So we have this a priori knowledge of these things, but *only* insofar as they are, or are taken as, objects of empirical intuition or of the senses. That is, though this knowledge is independent of experience, it must nonetheless be B-related to experience, since it contains judgments that are synthetic and its possibility is a real possibility and both entail a B-relation to experience.

The *"only"* that is employed immediately above signifies that this knowledge does not extend to the same things insofar as we consider what they are whether we intuit them or not.[7] Without this caveat, all the objects we could thus know would be given only through a synthesis of the understanding, that is, through the effect of the understanding on inner sense through a manifold given to the understanding. In that case, the objects that exist in space and time as well as space and time themselves would be given through such a synthesis. In other words, they would not be given to us through *the senses*—the manifolds of their intuition would only be given to the understanding for possible synthesis. (The distinction between space and time and the objects that exist in them would then be based on the difference between a priori synthesis of an a priori manifold given by the *forms* space and time [B 160a], on the one hand, and an empirical synthesis of an empirical manifold [B 160], on the other.)

Under these circumstances, however, since the objects that exist in space

5. See Chapter 12.
6. See Chapter 2 for an analysis of Kant's concept of a *thing*.
7. For the extended discussion of this point, see Chapter 2, section II, and Chapters 7 and 8.

and time would not be distinct from this empirical synthesis of apprehension, the demonstration of the real possibility of a priori knowledge would consist in showing its *B*-relation to this empirical *synthesis* instead of its *B*-relation to empirical *intuition*.[8] In other words, the dependence between the synthesis and the intuition would be just the reverse of what Kant envisages it as being. He thinks of the synthesis as a synthesis of a manifold *in an intuition*. The constructivist alternative we are considering, however, thinks of the intuition itself through the synthesis of a manifold. But what manifold is this? Unfortunately, the alternative does not give us a way to think of it. For his part, Kant thinks of it as the manifold in an empirical intuition. But this thought is not available (without circularity) to the alternative view, since it thinks of any such intuition through this synthesis. That is, the intuition is constituted through the synthesis.

The ontology of this constructivist alternative is rejected on at least two Kantian grounds. Both concern the possibility that an object of empirical intuition is given. First, in transcendental epistemology, for such objects to be given, we must be affected by objects.[9] However, according to the alternative, synthesis alone, and hence only the effect of the understanding on inner sense, accounts for an object's being given. The second reason for the rejection of this constructivist ontology is an objection we have already noted: namely, its reliance on synthesis in its account of an intuition's being given leaves us without any concept of the identity of the manifold in the intuition, whether the latter is given or thought.

This analysis takes us some distance toward explaining Kant's otherwise seemingly paradoxical thesis that despite the fact that we can have a priori knowledge of objects, they can nonetheless be known only in experience. In saying that objects can be known only in experience, Kant is not denying that they are known in a priori knowledge. He is rather saying both (*a*) that they are *not* known as they are, whether they are in experience or not, that is, as they are in themselves, and (*b*) that they are known a priori only if they are known in experience as well. To know them a priori is to know them in experience, but specifically in respect of their formal a priori *V*-relations, or determinations—those of space, time, and the categories—and the a priori knowledge that comes from them, all of which are constitutive of possible experience. Hence, in this sense, to know them a priori is to know them independently of experience.

8. This point is covered in Chapter 13, section III.
9. See Chapter 2, section IV.

The analysis just concluded further helps us dispel the air of paradox in question by directing our attention to the given empirical intuition and its object, the appearance, rather than to the synthesis of the manifold of such an intuition. It does so by identifying the intuition and its object, rather than the synthesis of a given empirical manifold, as that to which a priori knowledge must be B-related if the latter's possibility is to be real, and not merely logical. This gives us the central tenet of transcendental idealism, namely, that the object can be known only in empirical intuition or as appearance, not as it is in itself. But, as we have seen, that does not keep the a priori knowledge of the object from being a priori, since that knowledge is still supplied from the faculty of knowledge itself, is not learned from experience, and is possible, or B-related to the object (appearance), a priori.[10] In this manner Kant solves the problem of a priori knowledge with which we began our investigations in Chapter 1.

IV

Transcendental epistemology rests on two grand distinctions, each one bridged by B-relations that one part of the distinction has to the other. The first distinction is that between space and time, on the one hand, and objects, on the other. The other distinction is that between the self, such as our own thinking its self-consciousness, and any manifold given in sensible intuition in general. The B-relations in which one part of the distinction stands, or refers, to the other in turn depend on V-relations in which a representation is related to that part of the distinction that stands in the relevant B-relation (of reference) to its counterpart. Bridging the first distinction accounts for Kant's transcendental idealism, and bridging the second provides him with transcendental arguments, whether they consist in a transcendental exposition of the concept of space or of time (*Erörterung*) or a transcendental deduction of the categories (*Darstellung*).[11] Though the two distinctions, the relevant B-relations and their respective V-relations, and the two aspects of transcendental theory—its ontology and its arguments—are all distinct from each other when taken individually, certain interrelations of their combinations can be expressed in statements that are analytic in the theory. Two such statements, for example, were examined in

10. See Chapter 7, section ii.
11. See Chapter 13, section v.

the previous chapter, in my analysis of the Second Analogy. Finally, the combination of all such statements constitutes a transcendental episte-mology.

The two grand distinctions are alike in a certain respect. They allow something to be *thought* apart from something else that is *given* to it. Thus, space and time can be thought distinctly from given objects, whether the objects are distinct things or their appearances in space and time, and self-consciousness can be thought distinctly from any sensible manifold given to it. So they both can be said to allow for the distinctness of what is thus *thought* from what is *given*. If we then raise the question whether something *is* given to what is thought, that which allows for an affirmative answer must itself be distinct from what is thought if the question is not to be begged. In other words, that which allows a nontrivial, or informative, an-swer must be distinct from what is thought. Specifically, if there is to be a nontrivial answer to the question whether anything is given to us in space or in time, the objects that allow that something *is* thus given must be dis-tinct from space and from time.[12] Similarly, the manifold that can be given to a self-consciousness such as ours, which allows that a manifold *is* given to the self-consciousness, must be distinct from the self-consciousness. It therefore must be sensible.[13]

One of these two grand distinctions has us thinking space and time (one part of the distinction) without any objects (the other part of the distinction) that are given to us as existing in them. If there are such objects, as I have just reiterated, they must be able to be thought distinctly from our thinking space and time.[14] Kant's concept of a thing as an object of transcendental affirmation provides for such a distinct thought. It would be circular to argue that the concepts of space and time are objectively valid on the grounds that space and time are occupied by objects, that is, that there are occupants of space and time. There must be something about such an occu-pant, independent of its being an occupant, that can be used to argue that there *is* an occupant. That is, the argument requires that any objects men-tioned in support of the objective validity of space and time must be thought distinctly from the proposition that they occupy space and time—they must be thought distinctly from the space and time that are claimed to be thereby occupied by them. Again, the concept of *thing* provides for such a distinct

---

12. This point is covered in Chapter 1, section v, and Chapter 2, section iii.
13. See Chapter 11, section iv, and Chapter 12, section i.
14. See Chapter 1, section v.

concept. Accordingly, it provides for the ontology of transcendental epistemology, if it is also distinct from the categories, or at least a certain use of
them.[15] But transcendental affirmation does not constitute a transcendental
use of the categories. Such a use is impossible, since no manifold of intuition
can be given to the transcendental understanding—just as there is no transcendental intuition altogether.[16] We must remember that though they are a
priori, space and time are not transcendental representations (see A 56/B
81).

The other distinction, as already indicated, takes self-consciousness to be
separate from any manifold sensible intuition in general. If such a manifold
is given to self-consciousness, it must be able to be thought distinctly from
the thought of the self-consciousness. Such a distinct thought is provided by
the concept of the manifold of a sensible intuition in general. This concept
is explicitly introduced at the beginning of the B-Deduction (B 129). Our
type of self-consciousness would be confused with that belonging to a pri-
mordial being (B 72) if instead Kant were to argue that a self-consciousness
such as ours *could* provide for self-identity on the (mistaken) grounds that
such a manifold could be given by the self-consciousness itself (B 135, 138–
39, B 157–59). Kant's actual argument explicitly requires that any such
manifold mentioned in support of the synthesis presupposed by such an
identity (B 133) be thought distinctly from the proposition that the manifold
is given to the self-consciousness. The concept of a manifold of a sensible
intuition in general provides for such a distinct thought. Accordingly, it provides a manifold of intuition to the categories, since they are conditions
under which the manifold is brought to the synthetic unity of a self-consciousness such as ours (B 143).

The distinction of space and time from the objects that exist in them is
bridged by the B-relation that space and time, and hence the a priori knowledge that comes from them, have to objects as they exist in space and time,
that is, to appearances. And the distinction of the self-consciousness from
any manifold that is given to it is bridged by the B-relation that manifold
has to the unity of the self-consciousness. As I have argued, the first B-
relation is provided by the transcendental V-relations outer and inner sense
have to space and time, and hence to the a priori knowledge that comes
from them, respectively. Things are thus known a priori only as appearances, and it is only as objects of such knowledge that it makes sense to
speak of them as appearances.

15. Again, see Chapter 1, section v, and Chapter 2, section i.
16. Again, see Chapter 2, section i.

The *B*-relation of a manifold of a sensible intuition in general to the synthetic unity of self-consciousness, on the other hand, is provided by the a priori relations the categories have to that manifold. The synthetic unity of self-consciousness is thus represented through the categories. The argument for the conceptual connection among these three nodes of the triad belonging to the model of representation I have attributed to Kant—the subsumption of (*a*) a given manifold of sensible intuition in general by (*b*) the categories that represent (*c*) the synthetic unity of self-consciousness, to which the manifold (*a*) is thereby *B*-related through the a priori relation of the categories to the manifold, that is, through the subsumption—constitutes step one of the B-Deduction of the categories. In Chapter 12 we found these three nodes of the triad at the beginning of the B-Deduction: "the concept of combination includes, besides the concept of the manifold [(a) above] and of its synthesis [(b) above], also the concept of the unity of the manifold [(c) above]" (B 130).

The second step of the B-Deduction brings the two grand distinctions together into a unified theory of our a priori knowledge of objects.[17] By itself, each distinction obviously misses what only the other can provide. Without the concept of an object (*Objekt* [B 137]) provided by the unity of consciousness, and without a manifold of a sensible intuition that is distinct from that unity, there could be no objective (*objektive*) validity demonstrated in the transcendental expositions of the concepts of space and of time, and hence no objective validity of any a priori knowledge that is *B*-related to objects represented through space or time. Without the concepts of space and time, and without the distinct things that can exist in space and time, there could be no objects of the senses (appearances), and hence no objects of experience, in which alone given objects can be known. And without a *B*-relation to such knowledge, that is, to possible experience, a priori knowledge would again be without its objective validity. So, it is only together that the components of the two grand distinctions—space and time and things, on the one hand, and the manifold of a sensible intuition in general and self-consciousness (and hence, the categories), on the other—can complete the great argument of the *Critique,* namely, the Transcendental Deduction of the categories. Though the entire theory of the possibility of a priori knowledge constitutes a unity, certain of whose combinations of distinct elements are conceptually, or analytically, interrelated to one another, nevertheless, since the elements remain distinct from one another,

17. See Chapter 13.

their combinations must themselves be synthetic. Indeed, they must be so if the theory is to explain the possibility of synthetic a priori knowledge. This last point was highlighted, finally, in my discussion of the specification of the appearances to which the concept of an alteration is B-related through the concept of causality.[18] In the end, we have a theory whose combinations are both conceptually, or analytically, unified in it and yet themselves synthetic.

V

Perhaps the most fundamental criticism of Kant's theory of knowledge leveled by analytically minded, empiricist commentators who follow Strawson is that the theory is incoherent. It is alleged that the theory employs certain concepts in a manner that violates strictures the theory itself lays down as general principles governing the legitimate employment of concepts. Transcendental idealism itself, including the interpretation of it offered in this book, thus falls into derision, as its concept of a thing in itself violates what many in this tradition take to be a principle of the *Critique,* that the significance of concepts depends on, if not consists in, their B-relation to possible experience and to its objects, appearances. Of course, things in themselves have no such B-relation. Without his idealism, Kant has no argument in support of his claims regarding the possibility of our a priori knowledge. That is, Kant loses a fundamental ground of his transcendental arguments.

There are other serious charges of incoherence as well. The theory tells us that the categories have only empirical application. Yet it unabashedly contradicts itself when it proceeds to apply the category of causality to things in themselves, which, needless to say, is not an empirical application of the concept. It is applied to those objects in that part of the theory that speaks of our being affected by things in themselves, an action on us that results in the existence of appearances. This same charge would be leveled against the theory even as it is interpreted in Chapter 2. There it is things, not things in themselves, whose affecting us makes it possible that our empirical intuitions (of them) take place. And similar criticisms have been made against Kant's alleged employment of virtually all the other categories as well.

The wish to exhibit good manners seems to have played a role in British-

18. See Chapter 14.

American commentary on the *Critique* since Strawson appeared on the scene. One way of accommodating these empiricist strictures of analytic philosophy is to take the bite out of Kant's transcendental idealism. This has resulted in a variety of so-called anodyne interpretations of the doctrine, the most prominent of which is Allison's view that it is only a methodological, not an ontological, stricture for Kant. Another way is to separate the supportable strands of Kant's theory from those that are either groundless or indefensible. Strawson, Bennett, and Guyer follow this path.

But the road followed in the chapters put forward here takes us in another direction altogether. It exempts the theory from its own strictures on theory. The question of the objective validity of the theory cannot be raised within the theory itself. Though a priori, its transcendental character exempts it from the question of such validity it raises, and resolves, with respect to the subjects of a priori knowledge it is talking about. To many, this approach to Kant's theory may seem no better than a bypass around a fundamental question the theory is not at all reluctant to raise with respect to the theories it is holding up to inspection. What right does it have to exempt itself from the same scrutiny it imposes on others—the same standards it holds others to? Can its disavowals to any claims extending beyond our modes of knowledge (A 11–12/B 25, A 56/B 80–81) absolve it of its responsibility to give an account of its own objective validity? Perhaps more pointedly, are not such disavowals grounds for the very anodyne interpretation my approach itself has explicitly rejected?

To answer the second question first, the approach I have adopted does not constitute an anodyne interpretation of Kant's theory, however one may view the question of its obligation to provide an account of its own possibility. That sort of interpretation keeps the theory from making such an ontological commitment to things that it allows of legitimate thought of how they are apart from sensibility. But the approach I have followed has us finding the ontological commitments of Kant's theory in the concept of a thing that allows precisely such a thought in regard to them. Moreover, it attempts to explain how things can be considered or can exist apart from sensibility. So, it is not an anodyne interpretation.

But what of its supposed responsibility at least to assure, if not explicitly account for, its own objective validity? How can it justifiably assume an Archimedean standpoint on other a priori theories for which it claims the status of knowledge? The question itself seems to indicate a deep divergence of point of view. If no ontological commitment can be made without containing the grounds that support it, then the very question of demonstrating the possibility of any theory is illusory. For such a demonstration only returns us to the very concepts that are in question. This point was the guiding principle of my arguments in section IV above. Things cannot be the successful candidates that serve as occupants of space and time, and hence serve in the demonstration of the objective validity of the concepts of space and time, if they cannot be thought independently of the concepts of space and time. And I made a similar argument regarding the distinction between the manifold of a sensible intuition in general and self-consciousness of the type we humans possess. So, if we adopt a point of view from which the request for such a demonstration of objective validity makes sense, we have no choice but to leave the question of the objective validity of the theory in which the demonstration is carried out to some further theory. That is why we must leave the issue with an awareness that there is another point of view that deeply disagrees with mine. But is that not how things always stand in philosophy?

INDEX